A Recipe for Disaster

A Recipe for Disaster

Four Ways Churches and Parents Prepare Individuals to Lose Their Faith and How They Can Instill a Faith That Endures

John Marriott

WIPF & STOCK · Eugene, Oregon

A RECIPE FOR DISASTER
Four Ways Churches and Parents Prepare Individuals to Lose Their Faith and How They Can Instill a Faith That Endures

Wipf & Stock
An Imprint of Wipf and Stock Publishers
199 W. 8th Ave., Suite 3
Eugene, OR 97401

www.wipfandstock.com

PAPERBACK ISBN: 978-1-5326-4069-8
HARDCOVER ISBN: 978-1-5326-4070-4
EBOOK ISBN: 978-1-5326-4071-1

Manufactured in the U.S.A.

To the mentors of my youth, who prepared me well:

Tim Allyn

Steve Tulloch

Wes DiPietro

A chord of three strands is not easily broken.

ECCLESIASTES 4:12

Contents

Acknowledgments

THERE ARE A NUMBER of individuals who have played a role in this project that I would like to acknowledge and thank. My wife Nancy has endured months of me being mentally and physically absent as I focused more time and energy on writing this book than I should have. She has patiently and lovingly supported me in the process and without her it would not have happened. I love her dearly and consider her God's greatest blessing in my life. My friend and advisor Todd Hall played a major role in the production of the manuscript. His advice and support were invaluable throughout the writing process. Carrie Kaiser's hard work on proofreading the manuscript and offering helpful suggestions have made this a better book than it otherwise would have been. I am also grateful for the help of Bryan Windle, who advised me on several historical and archeological facts, and my good friend and former colleague Derek Brover, who read portions of the manuscript and offered helpful suggestions. I need to thank Beth McIntee who, along with David and Shirley Lawrence, provided me with an education on baking and shared their stories with me. Also, I would like to acknowledge my good friend David Yule, who was willing to reflect on, and share with me, his thoughts on the relationship between God and suffering. Additionally, the support of my close friend Craig Dellandrea was indispensible in bringing this project to publication. Finally, I want to thank Rachel, Craig, Derek, and James, along with their counterparts, David, Alan, Richard, and Devyn for sharing their stories with me. Without them this book would not exist.

Introduction

Writing about the loss of faith is a tricky business. Trying to provide a general account of a very individual and personal phenomenon such as the loss of faith is fraught with difficulties. On the one hand, a number of commonalities in deconversion narratives can be identified, and recognizing those can be helpful for the church. On the other hand, in an attempt to identify contributing factors of deconversion, the complex stories of individuals can get reduced to their lowest common denominator. When that happens, individuals may feel like they have been misrepresented and that the analysis I offer is off base. I want to acknowledge, upfront, that the stories of the former Christians I include at the beginning of each chapter are multifaceted and resist being reduced to one issue that brought about their deconversion. The experiences of Dave, Alan, Richard, and Devyn are particularly good examples of ways the church inadequately prepares believers for a life of faith, but it is too much to claim that the church caused their loss of faith. In fact, it is impossible to ever say why anyone loses or comes to faith because so many factors are at work. In every case of deconversion, what brought about the loss of faith is complex and irreducible. At the same time, the process is not completely inscrutable.

When you ask former believers why they lost their faith, without exception they'll tell you it's because they could no longer believe that Christianity is true. What we believe is often not a matter of choice any more than what we like the taste of is a matter of choice. Beliefs, in some sense, have us as much as we have them. I can't believe the world is flat no matter how hard I try or how much I might want to. There will always be that little voice inside telling me that I am not only wrong but also dishonest with myself. The same is true for deconverts.

Which raises the question, why can't they believe Christianity is true? The answer to that question is complex and different for every person.

Finding the cause for why an individual loses their faith is a fool's endeavor. And that's because there are so many factors that go into producing a loss of faith, there is no way that one could discover them all or piece them together to discover what the tipping point was. As a friend of mine once said, the reasons why people lose their faith are interwoven, and, like ingredients in a cake batter, they are impossible to separate. He is exactly correct. In terms of identifying causes to explain events, philosophers tend to speak of two kinds: those that are necessary and those that are sufficient. Necessary causes are those that must be present for a specific event to occur but are not in and of themselves sufficient to bring the event about. Sufficient causes are those that are comprised of all the necessary causes needed to produce an event. An example may help make this clear. To make fire, there are three necessary elements: sufficient oxygen, fuel, and heat. None of the three are sufficient on their own to create fire. However, if those three elements are present and combined properly, they are jointly sufficient and fire will occur. Undoubtedly, the causal factors that go into producing deconversions are much more complex and difficult to discern than those that create fire. Given that humans are social, emotional, spiritual, and biological creatures with brains that are composed of over 100 billion cells interconnected by trillions of synapses, it's easy to see—why it's not easy to see—what "caused" an individual to lose their faith.

In this book I am not claiming that former believers lost their faith because of how they were prepared, socialized, spiritually formed, or discipled by their parents or churches. I have no doubt that if you were to ask the former believers highlighted in the following chapters if their religious socialization played a role in their loss of faith, they might guess that maybe it did, but ultimately the question is irrelevant to them. The reason why is because regardless of what their Christian experience was like, in their minds they rejected the faith because they came to see it as false. For them, how they were discipled, whether their parents were legalists, or their church rabid fundamentalists has nothing to do with the fact that (in their minds) Christianity is objectively untrue. In one sense they are correct; if they lost their faith because they became convinced Christianity is false, then what does it matter how they were socialized into the Christian faith? Well, it all depends.

Although I am not arguing that individuals lose their faith because of their religious socialization, I am claiming that the way believers are socialized can often set them up for a crisis of faith that can lead to deconversion. While the methods of preparation I outline in what follows are not necessary to cause a person to lose their faith, they undoubtedly make it more difficult to maintain. They may even serve as the catalyst for the process to begin. They are stumbling blocks that can cause a believer to trip and fall. They are seeds that can grow into a plant that eventually is choked out by weeds or dried up by the sun.

To illustrate how poor preparation impacts deconversion, I have chosen to highlight the stories of four former believers whose deconversion stories give indications of where their Christian community may have let them down. I use their stories because they are good examples of themes that repeatedly show up in the deconversion literature. Whether Dave lost his faith because he suffered from the Tyranny of the Necessary is open for debate, but it seems pretty clear from his story that he did suffer from it. Alan may not have lost his faith because of Spiritual Culture Shock, but he was clearly infected with it. Richard may have lost his faith even if his theology wasn't Half-Baked, but that it was, is clear from what he says he expected from God and how he read the Bible. And Devyn may have abandoned her faith even if she hadn't been hit with Friendly Fire, and instead been treated with grace and love by her church community, but there is no denying that she was deeply wounded by Christians and never recovered. All of the major issues that stand out in their deconversion narratives can be traced back to their religious socialization. That should be of great interest to Christian parents and church leaders who have a vested interest in raising up the next generation of believers in Jesus Christ.

Looking at deconversion from a different angle may be helpful. Consider conversion for a moment. Why do people become Christians? Ultimately, because at some level they were either convinced that Christianity is the true account of reality, or are at least they were willing to risk that it is. But aren't people more likely to seriously consider the truth claims of a belief system if they find it reasonable and attractive and presented in a winsome, loving manner by someone who faithfully represents the message by how they live? It seems to me the answer to that question is an uncontroversial, "yes." Does the winsome, loving manner by which the message is presented make it any more true than if it is presented by an obnoxious, legalistic Christian? No, it doesn't. But as the old adage goes, you can catch more flies with honey than with vinegar. So too with the loss of faith, poor preparation, like vinegar, can leave a bad taste in the mouths of believers and play a role in why and how they come to the conclusion Christianity is untrue.

Christian parents and leaders need to do everything we can to nourish and develop a healthy faith in our children and those we are responsible to lead. By avoiding the four ways the church inadequately "prepares" believers outlined in the following chapters, we can avoid our part in the

Recipe for Disaster. By following the advice outlined in the final chapters, we can have a Recipe for Success.

Chapter 1 tells the stories of two individuals, each of whom identified as committed Christians, only to eventually lose their faith and become atheists. What could have caused two seemingly devoted believers to deconvert? Unfortunately, there is no clear answer to that question. As I previously mentioned, identifying a single cause for why deconversion occurs is impossible. However, just because a causal factor for deconversion can't be found, we are not left without hope in understanding and preventing deconversions. I maintain that a general theory of deconversion can be developed, and, if my theory is correct, it can not only help understand why large numbers of professing Christians are abandoning their faith, it can also help us prevent it from happening. I argue that we need to think of deconversion in terms of the product of a recipe. Recipes are comprised of three parts: ingredients, preparation, and cooking environment. In terms of deconversion, the ingredients are the personality traits and personal values of professing Christians. The preparation is the religious socialization or discipling they received from either their church, home, or a combination of the two. The environment where the cooking takes place correlates with our post-Christian and increasingly secular culture. Given the right ingredients, the wrong methods of preparation, and the formative pressures of our post-Christian culture, many individuals who identify as Christians will lose their faith.

Chapter 2 looks at the biblical data on falling away from the faith. The New Testament has much to say about apostasy. Jesus himself warned of it, Judas committed it, and the epistles frequently speak of it. From Matthew to Revelation, the writers of sacred Scripture are deeply concerned about individuals not maintaining their faith profession. The question that such warnings raise is whether a believer can lose their salvation. For the sake of transparency, a word about my position on that question is warranted. I understand the Bible to teach that a Christian is one who has believed essential propositional content about Jesus and his work on the cross. Furthermore, Christians not only believe correct information about Jesus but also place their trust in him to be who the Bible says he is, Savior and Lord. Throughout the book, I use the terms deconverts, former believers, former Christians, and apostates interchangeably. When referring to deconverts as former believers or former Christians, I am speaking sociologically, not theologically. I apply those terms to individuals who made a profession of faith in Christ at one point in their lives and identified with a church community. These are individuals who identified as Christians and claimed to have taken their faith seriously. I am not passing judgment on whether such persons were regenerated, justified, and genuine members of the body of Christ. Therefore, I am not entering into the debate over whether such people were once saved but have lost their salvation. However, it may be helpful to indicate my position on the matter. I tend to believe that an individual who has been born-again will persevere in faith to the end, kept by the power of God. Theologically speaking, it is difficult for me to see how a person who is "in Christ" can somehow ever be separated from the love of God. Conversely, there are so many warnings in the New Testament about the danger of falling away that I am unwilling to be dogmatic on the issue. It seems illogical to warn against something that is, in fact, impossible. If deconversion is not a real possibility, one wonders why then—as I show in chapter 2—it gets so much attention. One thing I am quite convinced of is that the language of "losing salvation" is a misnomer. If an individual can become unregenerate and no longer be a member of the Body of Christ, it is not because they have lost their salvation but because they have apostatized. By which I mean they have intentionally renounced their faith.

Chapter 3 introduces Greg, a young man who came to know Christ but eventually lost his faith. Greg's story is unique because it illustrates the four ways that churches or parents inadequately prepare believers and set them up for a crisis of faith. Greg's experience shows how important the preparation aspect of the Recipe for Disaster truly is. Because he could not endure the well-intentioned, but ultimately harmful, religious socialization at the hands of his church, he lost his faith.

Chapters 4 through 8 focus on the four specific ways that believers can be set up for a crisis of faith: over-preparation, under-preparation, ill-preparation, and painful preparation. In this section of the book, a chapter is dedicated to each inadequate method of preparation. Here, I unpack and illustrate the nature, characteristics, and impact of the four methods. By becoming aware of what I call the Tyranny of the Necessary, Spiritual Culture Shock, Half Baked, and Friendly Fire, parents and churches can avoid the pitfalls that are so often correlated with the loss of faith.

After looking at the various ways believers can be inadequately prepared, I offer four counter methods of preparation. Chapters 9 and 10 are intended to help parents and church leaders think well about how they are socializing believers into the faith. Each chapter speaks to two of the inadequate methods of preparation. In chapter 9, in response to the Tyranny of the Necessary and Spiritual Culture Shock, I offer what I call the Tranquility of the Sufficient and Appropriately Acclimated. Correspondingly, in chapter 10, being Well Done is suggested as the antidote to being Half-Baked, and the Wounds of a Friend are presented as a healthy alternative to Friendly Fire.

My desire for this book is that it will help churches and parents to better prepare those they are responsible to disciple, and, in doing so, reduce the number of individuals losing their faith. As our culture continues to move in a more secular direction it will become increasingly difficult for some to maintain their Christian profession. By avoiding the mistakes made by churches and parents that repeatedly show up in the stories of former believers and thus constitute A Recipe for Disaster, we can reduce the likelihood of deconversion. By implementing the suggestions offered in the final chapters, we will be following a Recipe for Success, one that increases the likelihood of instilling a flourishing, lifelong faith.

Chapter 1

A Tale of Two Christians

A man is like a novel: until the very last page
you don't know how it will end.

Yevgeny Zamyatin

Leap of Faith

On a warm evening in Gothenburg, Sweden, in August of 1995, Jonathan Edwards sprinted down the triple jump runway and leapt into history. That evening, he shattered the world record in the triple jump, not once but twice, and in the process broke the 60-foot barrier with a jump of 18.29 meters. It was unbelievable, a superhuman performance. Edwards immediately became the toast of the athletics world. The International Amateur Athletics Federation, the governing body of track and field, named him Track and Field Male Athlete of the Year, and the BBC honored him as Sports Personality of the Year. But the British press took note of something else about Edwards that they found almost as fascinating as his athletic accomplishments—the level of commitment he had to his Christian faith.

Growing up the son of an Anglican vicar and a very devout mother, Edwards adopted the faith of his parents at an early age. At six years old, he gave his life to Christ. Edwards's mother, Jill, recalled, "With all the children, we read the Bible to them at night and prayed until they were old enough to read it for themselves. One evening, Jonathan asked a question and I said to him, 'You need to have asked Jesus to come into your life for that to be true.' Jonathan said, 'Oh, I've done that. I did that the other day.'"[1] So began

1. Folley, *A Time to Jump*, 34.

Jonathan Edwards's journey of faith, a faith that would be the guiding force for every area of his life, including athletics.

Being raised in a devoutly Christian home meant that Jonathan was subject to his parents' religious convictions. One of the convictions that his parents firmly adhered to was their belief that Sunday was a day of rest. As such, they were staunchly against playing games, watching television, or even cooking food on what they considered "the Sabbath." Of course, that also meant any sporting event that happened to be on Sunday, Jonathan could not take part in.

Just as Edwards had embraced his parents' Christian faith as a child, he naturally accepted their belief about the sacredness of Sunday as well. As he matured into adulthood, his religious commitment deepened and formed the core of his identity. Although he did change some of the beliefs he inherited from his parents, he continued to believe that Sunday was a day of rest. Though it would mean that he would miss out on chances to further his athletic success, Edwards's commitment to his conviction was resolute. So firm was he, that he wouldn't compromise even though it might have cost him the opportunity to compete on the world's largest stage. In 1988, Edwards passed up an opportunity to qualify for the Seoul Olympics because the trials were held on a Sunday. He said at the time:

> I see my Christian life as the most important thing, and I realize that I have to make certain sacrifices . . . I was brought up in a Christian family and happen to believe the Sabbath is holy. I feel this has given me a chance to demonstrate the sincerity of my Christian beliefs and to show other people just how important Christianity is . . . Athletics is not everything to me, but my faith is.[2]

Although he eventually was named to the team by the British Athletic Federation and competed in the Seoul Olympics, three years later he would sacrifice his hope of athletic glory for his beliefs. In 1991, he chose not to compete in the triple jump at the World Championships in Tokyo because it was being contested on Sunday.

After winning the World Championship in Gothenburg and smashing the world record, he became an instant celebrity. But, the British press wasn't quite sure what to do with him, as Edwards was more comfortable in the athletes' village playing his guitar and leading worship choruses for the other Christian athletes than speaking to reporters about his athletic accomplishments. Edwards was the real deal. He "walked the talk" and he "talked the walk." He was the closest thing to Eric Liddell, the beloved Scotsman

2. Folley, *A Time to Jump*, 57–58.

and Olympic track and field champion who refused to run on Sunday, that Great Britain had seen since Eric Liddell himself. In a country relentless in digging up dirt on its celebrities, it was no small thing that the British press seemed as impressed with the character of Edwards's life as they were with his athletic exploits.

Four years later in 2000 in Sydney, he won the crown jewel of track and field glory, the gold medal at the Olympics. He followed that up with another gold medal at the World Championships in 2001 held in Edmonton, Alberta, Canada. But, as the saying goes, all good things must come to an end, and in 2003, Edwards, the greatest triple jumper in history, retired. No one else even comes close. He was Olympic, World, European, and Commonwealth Games champion. He not only was the world record holder, but also had five of the six longest jumps in history.

After retirement from athletics, Edwards transitioned into a second career as a television personality working mainly for the BBC as a sports commentator. However, it was his role as the host of the BBC's "Songs of Praise" program that elevated him to the status of a national Christian personality. Debuting in 1961, "Songs of Praise" is one of the longest running television programs of its kind in the world and is the BBC's flagship religious broadcast. As host, Edwards was one of the most famous Christians in all of Great Britain.

Today, Jonathan Edwards is an atheist. In February of 2007, Edwards announced that he had lost his faith. In an interview with *The Daily Mail* he said, "I just stopped believing in God."[3] Not only had he stopped believing in God, he removed himself from the Christian community. "I don't go to church anymore, not at all,"[4] he revealed. Astonishingly, he claimed, "I don't miss my faith. In many ways I feel more settled and happier in myself without it."[5] Being a Christian had been the core of who Jonathan Edwards was. His faith had been of greater importance to him than fame, athletic success, or wealth. How was it that someone who was willing to miss the Olympics and the World Championships out of his fidelity to Christ could just stop believing in him? But he had. The face of Christianity in Great Britain had deconverted.

What explains why a highly successful, famous athlete like Jonathan Edwards would renounce his belief in Christ, something that was so dear to him for his entire life? Some will suggest that it was his success that contributed to his loss of faith. While it's conceivable that such a thing could happen,

3. Daily Mail, "I've Lost My Faith," line 9.
4. Daily Mail, line 11.
5. Daily Mail, lines 14–15.

in the case of Edwards, it doesn't seem likely. Edwards's success peaked in 1995, and he did not lose his faith until 2007, four years after he retired from athletics. If success is to blame, it had a long gestation period, taking over twelve years before it birthed unbelief in his heart. Perhaps it was the opposite of success, an experience of failure, that caused him to apostatize? But that explanation is even more unlikely. Edwards knew what failure and disappointment were like long before he had success on the track. He had gone through periods of illness that sidelined him from competing, missed out on participating at the World Championships, and went through bouts of bad jumping, and yet none of that caused him to even question his faith, let alone jettison it. If the above explanations don't answer the question of why Jonathan Edwards lost his faith, what does? What could possibly cause one of the most famous Christians in England to become one of the most famous atheists in England?

Daniels in the Skeptics' Den

On the edge of the Sahara Desert in the country of Niger, live the Daza people. The Daza are a nomadic group that has traditionally lived by herding cattle, goats, and camels. While some individuals live in towns, most Daza continue to live as they have for hundreds of years, in tents near pasture for their animals. The Daza are not a large people group, numbering approximately 500,000. All in all, the Daza are easy to overlook. So what was it that caused Ken Daniels to leave the comforts of his home in North Carolina and move to Niger in order to connect with them? It was the fact that none of the Daza had ever heard the gospel. Ken Daniels was committed to changing that by doing whatever it took to bring the good news of God's plan of salvation to them.

Growing up in Ethiopia as the son of missionaries, Ken Daniels knew what a life of committed service to Christ looked like. His father, a Baptist pastor, traveled to Ethiopia in the early 1960s to work as a construction engineer for a major missions organization. It was there that he met Ken's mother, who was also a missionary. She began her missionary career as a nurse riding through the mountains of Ethiopia to treat the needy. She led Ken to faith when he was four years old. Ken recalled:

> One of my earliest memories is of a frightening nighttime thunderstorm when I was four while on furlough in California. I called to my mother, who came and comforted me, assured me Jesus would protect us, and invited me to ask Jesus into my heart. Trustingly, I prayed a prayer to accept Jesus as my

> personal savior. I don't know how much this decision affected my life at such an early age—I couldn't claim a dramatic conversion from a profligate life, though I did understand I was a sinner and needed to accept Jesus's sacrifice to take away my sins so I could be with God.[6]

Despite making a profession at such a young age, over the years, Ken's life began to show signs of what looked like spiritual fruit. When he was only ten years old, he read through the entire New Testament and half of the Old, a feat many adult believers have never managed to accomplish. But, it was an experience during ninth grade that would change his life. After watching the missionary movie *Peace Child*, Daniels was convinced that God was calling him into missionary service to an unreached people group. Further, he believed that God not only wanted him to take the gospel to those who had never heard it, but that he should translate the Bible into their language. And so, in the ninth grade, Ken committed himself to that end.

In his remaining years of high school, he distinguished himself as a serious Christian who demonstrated a zeal for God that was unlike that of any of his fellow students. After graduation, he attended seminary to receive further training and then joined the mission organization Wycliffe Bible Translators. However, before heading to the mission field he was required to take linguistics courses in North Dakota and Texas. With those behind him, he and his wife Sherry left for Belgium where they would learn to speak French, the official language of Niger. After stops in Switzerland and Cameroon for more training, they finally arrived in Niger in 1997.

For fifteen years, Ken Daniels had been committed to his goal of bringing the gospel to an unreached people group. In the process, he earned two college degrees, spent time in two language schools at opposite ends of the country, and served in various ministries in the local churches he attended. Seven years into their marriage, he and Sherry had lived in eighteen different places for at least one month or more in six different countries. They traveled extensively throughout Canada and the United States to raise financial support despite having to do so while pregnant or with toddlers in tow. When they arrived in Niger, they had three children in cloth diapers at the same time, and running water was unavailable during the daytime.

What would motivate someone to endure such a long and arduous journey to a place that offered no financial reward, was devoid of western comforts, and would likely produce so little fruit for his labor? To Ken Daniels the answer was simple:

6. Daniels, *Why I Believed*, 18.

> On the basis of Paul's theology, we believed that those who die without hearing and responding to the gospel will not be saved: "Everyone who calls on the name of the Lord will be saved." How, then, can they call on the one they have not believed in? And how can they believe in the one of whom they have not heard? And how can they hear without someone preaching to them? And how can they preach unless they are sent? As it is written, "How beautiful are the feet of those who bring good news!"[7]

Ken Daniels counted the cost and concluded that the benefit of saving souls outweighed whatever it would cost him. The rigors of study, the sacrificing of western comforts, the sense of alienation that comes with being in a radically new and different culture, and the toll it would take on his wife and children were worth it. In light of eternity, what isn't worth sacrificing in order to bring the good news to those who have never heard it? And so, after years of preparation, planning, and sacrifice, Ken Daniels began his work as a Wycliffe missionary, intent on translating the Bible into the language of the Daza people. However, Daniels never did translate the Bible for the Daza because before the missionary had an opportunity to do so, he had come to the conclusion that the Bible was not the word of God and that the story it told about God was untrue. Ken Daniels, a committed believer from the time he was four, had lost his faith and renounced Christ. He had deconverted. Today he lives back in the United States, is employed as a computer programmer, and identifies as an atheist-leaning agnostic.

How could such a thing happen? Ken Daniels didn't grow up in an unbelieving home that eventually wooed him back to his unbelieving roots. On the contrary, he was thoroughly socialized into the Christian faith by committed parents. He didn't go off to college and lose his faith because of the teaching of an atheist professor. Instead, he went to a Christian college and seminary. He didn't deconvert in a bar in Amsterdam, but on the mission field serving God. Nor is there any hint of sin or moral failing in his life that might prove to be the explanation for why he lost his faith. Yet, that is exactly what happened. How does a committed missionary, a man who was willing to sacrifice so much for the cause of Christ, lose his faith?

Although the stories of Jonathan Edwards and Ken Daniels are shocking, sadly they are not all that uncommon. People who once professed allegiance to Jesus can and do renounce their faith. In fact, Edwards and Daniels are just the tip of the iceberg when it comes to individuals who once identified as committed Christians and now no longer do. Former

7. Daniels, *Why I Believed*, 27.

pastors, missionaries, worship leaders, evangelists, apologists, and others once in full-time Christian ministry today identify as deconverts. This raises two questions: Why does deconversion happen, and what can be done to prevent it?

A Lost Cause?

There are many reasons offered by deconverts and faithful believers for why individuals leave the faith, yet none rise to the level of being an actual cause of deconversion itself. As Phil Zuckerman has pointed out, subjective reasons for the loss of faith of an individual are not necessarily objective causes that account for the phenomenon of deconversion. While the reasons individual apostates give for *their* deconversion are causes for *them*, they are not necessarily objective factors that would cause anyone else to deconvert. Most people who experience problems with the Bible, or disappointment with God do not eventually deconvert. Zuckerman adds, "The best that one can safely conclude when it comes to the subjective reasons . . . is that they may increase the likelihood of a person's eventual rejection of religion."[8] In other words, there is no single issue that can be identified that necessarily leads to deconversion.

Cause for Concern

Where then does this leave us? If there are no identifiable, objective causes of deconversion, it seems all we are left with are innumerable personal reasons that may increase the likelihood of one particular individual deconverting. The task of addressing each and every possible reason that any given individual may encounter that will prove lethal to his faith becomes impossible. For every individual there can be equally as many unique reasons capable of sinking their faith. If this is the case, it leaves little hope of discovering a theory that can meaningfully respond to the problem of deconversion in general. That's tragic, because failing to do so will only result in an increase in deconversions, which are already occurring at record rates. Studies show that people who once identified as followers of Jesus are deconverting from their faith, leaving the church, and no longer identifying as Christians in record numbers and at record rates. The data indicates the fact that we are on the verge of a deconversion epidemic.

8. Zuckerman, *Faith No More*, 165.

In 2001, the Southern Baptist Convention reported they are losing between 70 and 88 percent of their youth after their freshman year in college. Of SBC teenagers involved in church youth groups, 70 percent stopped attending church within two years of their high school graduation.[9] The following year, the Southern Baptist Council on Family Life also reported that 88 percent of children in evangelical [Baptist] homes leave church by the age of eighteen.[10]

The Barna Group announced in 2006 that 61 percent of young adults who were involved in church during their teen years were now spiritually disengaged.[11] Supporting Barna's findings, a 2007 Assemblies of God study reported that between 50 percent and 67 percent of Assemblies of God young people who attend a non-Christian public or private university will have left the faith four years after entering college.[12] A similar study from LifeWay Research that came out the same year claimed that 70 percent of students lose their faith in college, and of those only 35 percent eventually return.[13]

In May 2009, Robert Putnam and David Campbell presented research from their book *American Grace: How Religion Divides and Unites Us* to the Pew Forum study on "Religion and Public Life," in which they claimed that young Americans are leaving religion at five to six times the historic rate. They also noted that the percentage of young Americans who identify as having no religion is between 30 and 40 percent, up from between 5 and 10 percent only a generation ago.[14] That same year, the Fuller Youth Institute's study "The College Transition Project" discovered that current data seems "to suggest that about 40 to 50 percent of students in youth groups struggle to retain their faith after graduation."[15]

The 2010 UCLA study "Spirituality in Higher Education" found that only 29 percent of college students regularly attended church after their junior year, down from 52 percent the year before they entered college.[16] A second UCLA study, "The College Student Survey," asked students to indicate their present religious commitment. Researchers then compared the responses of freshmen who checked the "born again" category with the

9. Pinckney, "We Are Losing Our Children," lines 4–5.

10. Walker, "Family Life Council Says It's Time to Bring Family Back to Life," line 4.

11. The Barna Group, "Most Twentysomethings Put Christianity on the Shelf."

12. Kingsriter, "Is the Lower Cost Worth the High Price?"

13. Lifeway Research, "Reasons 18- to 22-Year-Olds Drop Out of Church."

14. Dyck, *Generation Ex-Christian*, 40.

15. Fuller Youth Institute, "The Sticky College Campuses," lines 13–14.

16. Astin and Astin, "Spirituality in Higher Education."

answers they gave four years later when they were seniors. What they found was shocking. On some campuses as high as 59 percent of students no longer described themselves as "born again."[17]

Given what we know regarding the loss of faith among American young people, it will come as no surprise that America's Class of 2018 cares less about their religious identity than any previous college freshman class in the last forty years. A third study by UCLA found that students across the U.S. are disassociating themselves from religion in record numbers. "The American Freshman" study reveals that nearly 28 percent of the 2014 incoming college freshman do not identify with any religious faith. That is a sharp increase from 1971, when only 16 percent of freshman said they did not identify with a specific religion.[18]

Those are scary statistics, and they tell us something that we ignore to our peril. Unless the church is willing to take a hard look at why so many young, college-aged people are losing their faith and leaving the church, it will lose an entire generation. Without a general theory that successfully accounts for deconversion, we will be left unequipped to respond.

Cooking Up a Storm

A Recipe for Disaster maintains that there is a general theory that sheds light on the loss of faith. I maintain the best way to understand deconversion is not to seek specific reasons for deconversion, but rather to think of it as the product of a combination of factors that together often lead to deconversion. The subjective, personal reasons often cited by former believers for their loss of faith may be necessary, but they are by no means sufficient to account for their deconversion. These reasons are only one factor in a complex mixture that often results in apostasy, but others are needed too. A helpful way to think about it is to consider the process of deconversion as similar to that of baking a cake. Baking a cake requires three things: a combination of specific ingredients, the manner in which the ingredients are prepared, and the environment in which the prepared ingredients are baked. The same is true for deconversions. Like a cake, deconversions are the result of the appropriate ingredients, a method of preparation, and an environment where the prepared ingredients are baked. In everyday terms, we refer to this combination of ingredients, preparation, and environment as a recipe. In the case of deconversion, it is *A Recipe for Disaster.*

17. UCLA Graduate School of Education and Information Systems, "The College Student Survey."

18. Eagan, et al., "The American Freshman."

Ingredients

Ingredients supply the raw material for a recipe. Without them there is no final product. Substitute a different ingredient and you will get a different outcome because many ingredients have a special function in the baking process. For example, baking powder—the combination of baking soda and acid—is responsible for making the batter or dough rise. Leave out the baking powder and you will have a very flat cake. *A Recipe for Disaster* also has important ingredients as can be seen in the stories of Edwards and Daniels.

On the surface, Edwards's and Daniels's journeys to apostasy appear quite different. One was a wealthy, famous athlete living out his faith under the scrutiny of the white-hot spotlight of the British press; the other, a relatively poor linguist, known only to family and friends, laboring in obscurity in the middle of Africa. But, appearances are deceiving. Their individual journeys out of the faith have much more in common than what we can see on the surface. When one looks deeper, it becomes clear that both deconversions include the same five ingredients, which are all provided by the individual deconverts themselves.

Ingredient 1: Deconverts Tend to Have Above Average Intelligence.

First, both Edwards and Daniels are quite intelligent. Had Jonathan Edwards not succeeded at athletics, he may have had a future as a scientist. Growing up in England, he attended private school, where he was at the top of his class in most subjects. He earned top grades in math, physics, chemistry, Latin, French, and German and was rewarded with admission to the University of Durham, where he studied physics. After graduation, he worked in the cytogenetics laboratory at the Royal Victoria Infirmary in Newcastle, analyzing chromosomes. He also was a keen Bible student who intended to attend seminary after his athletics career ended. Likewise, Ken Daniels is very bright. He graduated from Le Tourneau University with a dual degree in computer science and engineering. He then attended graduate school studying theology and after that, two language schools to learn to read the Bible in the original languages. Mastering enough Hebrew and Greek to translate the Bible into a language that one has to first learn isn't a job for a sub-par intellect! Today he works as a software developer.

That Edwards and Daniels are bright isn't surprising. Studies show that atheists in general and deconverts in particular tend to be quite intelligent.[19]

19. Intelligent here means: possessing the ability to reason, plan, solve problems,

Psychologists at the University of Rochester conducted a meta-analysis of sixty-three studies on the relationship between religion and intelligence dating back to 1928. They discovered that fifty-three of those studies found that the more intelligent a person is, the less likely he is to be religious. Only ten of the studies found that highly intelligent individuals are more likely to also be religious. The explanation offered by the researchers for the negative relationship between intelligence and religiosity was that intelligent people believe that "religious beliefs are irrational, not anchored in science, not testable and, therefore, unappealing."[20] Testimonies of deconverts overwhelmingly confirm that explanation. Over and over again, assertions that Christianity is "unscientific" and "contradicted by sound reason" appear in deconversion narratives as catalysts for the loss of faith.

In 1921, Lewis Terman, a psychologist at Stanford University, began a study to examine the development and characteristics of highly intelligent children throughout the course of their lives. To do so, he created a cohort of 1500 students with IQs above 135 at the age of ten.[21] Data was collected on the students throughout their entire lives. Information on matters of college education, income, career, marital status, number of children, and several other categories was amassed over the course of ninety years. In the process, the study achieved the status of being the longest running longitudinal study in the world. As of 2011, participants were still being studied, although the number had dwindled down to only a few remaining individuals. Terman's study has provided other researchers a wealth of data on a multitude of categories related to highly intelligent individuals. Two researchers, Robin Sears at Columbia University and Michael McCullough at the University of Miami, took it upon themselves to review the data as it related to the level of religiosity exhibited by the highly intelligent participants of Terman's study.[22] [23] They each concluded that the members of the cohort turned out to be significantly less religious than the general public despite the fact that over 60 percent of the students reported being raised in "very strict" or "considerably" religious environments.[24] Raised religiously, the highly intelligent children dropped their religious beliefs at some point in later life at a much higher rate than those of average intelligence.

and think abstractly.

20. Bates, "Atheists Have Higher IQs," lines 19–20.

21. Terman and Oden, *Genetic Studies of Genius*.

22. Holahan and Sears, *The Gifted Group*.

23. McCullough and Brion, "The Varieties of Religious Development," 78–89.

24. Terman and Oden, *Genetic Studies of Genius*, 116.

The Hunter College Elementary School for the intellectually gifted, in New York, conducted a similar study.[25] Graduates of the school between thirty and fifty years of age with IQs over 140 were surveyed about their religious commitments. The study uncovered that only 16 percent of the intellectually gifted graduates had maintained any religious faith by the time they had reached middle age. They, like the gifted individuals in Terman's study, had very little use for religion in their lives. Other studies could be cited, but the above are sufficient to make the point that the more intelligent one is, the less likely he is to be a person of faith.

The findings that high intelligence and atheism are related also seem to be true of the relationship between high intelligence and deconversion. Between 1994 and 1995, 4,000 incoming freshmen at two Canadian universities were surveyed concerning their religious beliefs. The purpose of the study was to find those students who identified as either former believers or former atheists and discover what factors played major roles in their religious transitions. One of the more remarkable findings of the study was that deconverts from religion—but not converts *to* religion—typically ranked as above-average students. Moreover, the reasons offered by deconverts to account for their loss of faith were almost always intellectual problems with religious teachings, while converts to religion nearly always cited emotional, rather than intellectual, reasons for adopting religious faith. Of those who deconverted, 65 percent were straight-A students who spoke of being in the top of their classes, being placed in gifted classes, and getting high grades with little work. Thirty percent of deconverts were above average, garnering, B's and B+'s. Only 6 percent were C, or average, students.[26]

Like the unbelievers in the above studies, deconverts are no slouches when it comes to being smart. They may not have been geniuses like those in the Terman study, but they were above average in their intelligence. Although it may not be true for all deconverts, in general, atheists—including those who were once believers but have renounced their faith—are above average in intelligence.

Ingredient 2: Possessing the Personality Trait of Being Open to New Experiences.

One of the central areas of psychology over the past century has been the development of personality theory. Personality theories are models that seek to shed light on the psychological structure of individuals. Although there

25. Sobotnik et al., *Genius Revisited*, 6.

26. Altemeyer and Hunsberger, *Amazing Conversions*, 121–22.

are numerous theories, the idea that there are five personality traits that are largely assumed to be inherited and remain stable over time is shared by many personality psychologists. These traits play a major role in determining who we are as individuals. Interestingly, it turns out deconverts, when tested, consistently score high in one of the five traits. That trait is *openness to experience*. Those who score high in *openness to experience* tend to be individuals who are intellectually curious, possess aesthetic sensitivity, and often hold non-conformist attitudes. Whereas those open to new experiences enjoy novelty, variety, and unpredictability, those who score low regarding *openness to experience* favor routines, predictability, and structure. Such individuals find comfort in the traditional beliefs of their community and are unlikely to question or change them.

Research shows that deconverts are willing to seek out experiences and ask questions about the world and their faith even though it may lead to actively questioning their beliefs.[27] Not only are they willing to seek experiences and ask questions, they're willing to seek answers from sources that are not disposed to confirming their faith. Individuals open to new experiences want to "hear both sides," as it were. Those who remain faithful believers, on the other hand, are inclined only to seek answers from sources that will confirm what they already believe. They seek out pastors, religious authorities, and parents but do not look to sources outside of the safe confines of their faith tradition.[28]

Openness to experience is a major contributing factor in deconversion. There is ample evidence that being open to new experiences negatively affects belief in God. For example, a study by Harvard researchers found that those who score high in *openness to experience* are less likely to believe in God.[29] And a survey conducted by the Center for Inquiry concluded that being open to experience is the single most important factor that distinguished those who considered themselves religious from those who did not.[30] Heinz Streib of the University of Bielefeld in Germany, the world's foremost authority on religious deconversion, claims that his research shows that openness to experience, more than any other psychological trait, is the most significant factor in predicting deconversion.[31]

27. Altemeyer and Hunsberger, *Amazing Conversions*, 18–19.

28. Altemeyer and Hunsberger, *Amazing Conversions*, 18–19.

29. Shenhav et al., "Divine Intuition: Cognitive Style Influences Belief in God," 423–28.

30. Galen, "Profiles of the Godless," 41–45.

31. Streib et al., *Deconversion*, 92.

Not surprisingly, there is a strong negative correlation between *openness to experience* and *religious fundamentalism*. It makes sense that those scoring high on the Openness to Experience scale would likely be unsatisfied with fundamentalist and conservative religions that maintain their teachings are absolute truth and thus unchanging. They would also naturally bristle at the claim by fundamentalists that there is no value in dialoguing with other religious traditions since they are opposed to the truth of the Bible.[32] Their openness to experience would also lead them to re-examine their social, political, and religious values. Additionally, their intellectual curiosity is likely to cause them to investigate the limits of the traditions they were socialized into, in ways that those lacking the trait do not.

What this implies is that even though at one time former believers might have embraced fundamentalist or conservative versions of Christianity, they don't seem to be fundamentalists by nature. Though they may embrace the faith for long periods of time— usually beginning at childhood—eventually who they really are breaks through in a rejection of fundamentalism and the authoritarianism that accompanies it.[33] Because those open to new experiences are willing to question beliefs and exhibit intellectual curiosity, it should come as no surprise that such individuals also place a high value on rational inquiry. Disinclined to accept the Bible as their unquestioned authority, they look to their own reasoning ability as the criterion by which they evaluate truth claims. For some this can deepen their faith, but for others it leads to their undoing.

Though Jonathan Edwards and Ken Daniels have not taken personality tests, I suspect if they did they would score high in Openness to Experience. We see evidence of this in their deconversion stories. This comes through in Edwards's life clearly when he retells the story of what first caused him to question his faith. While filming a documentary on the life of the apostle Paul, he was intrigued by the suggestion from liberal scholars that Paul's Damascus Road experience was best explained as an epileptic seizure rather than an authentic religious experience. That suggestion planted the seeds of doubt in Edwards. For the first time, he began to ponder not only the question of Paul's encounter with Jesus, but all of the questions that for years he had been too preoccupied with sports to think about and had just taken for granted on the authority of the Bible.

> It was as if my twenty-plus-year career in athletics, I had been suspended in time. I was so preoccupied with training and competing that I didn't have the time or emotional inclination

32. Streib et al., *Deconversion*, 79.

33. Streib et al., *Deconversion*, 79.

> to question my beliefs. Sport is simple, with a simple goal and simple lifestyle. I was quite happy in a world populated by my family and close friends, people who shared my belief system. Leaving that world to get involved with television and other projects gave me the freedom to question everything.[34]

For years, Edwards's intellectual life was in neutral due to his focused concentration on triple jumping. But, once that phase of his life was over, he suddenly found himself open to "question everything." Could it be that his preoccupation with athletics suppressed an aspect of his personality that came to the surface once he had the time? It appears likely. Edwards acknowledges as much when he speaks of the inner turmoil he experienced resulting from his retirement. When Edwards retired, he went through somewhat of an identity crisis.

> But when I retired, something happened that took me by complete surprise. I quickly realised that athletics was more important to my identity than I believed possible. I was the best in the world at what I did and suddenly that was not true anymore. With one facet of my identity stripped away, I began to question the others and, from there, there was no stopping. The foundations of my world were slowly crumbling.[35]

The result of his identity crisis was a wholesale quest to discover who he was and what he really believed. Had he not been open to new experiences, it is likely that he would have continued to neglect such questions, remaining content in his faith. As he searched for answers to his questions, he left the borders of his Christian community, not simply seeking to have his beliefs confirmed by consulting Christian apologists, but he subjected his belief to what he calls "analysis." In the end, he concluded, "When you think about it rationally, it does seem incredibly improbable that there is a God."[36]

Ken Daniels's journey is very similar to that of Edwards. He too experienced a crisis event that caused him to reconsider and critically analyze the Bible.

> My own journey away from Christianity began within as I reflected on the contradictory elements in the Bible, and on the conflict between fundamentalist Christianity and my observations of the real world. It was only after my doubts began that I undertook to read materials written from a skeptical

34. Syed, "I've Never Been Happier," lines 72–78.
35. Syed, "I've Never Been Happier," lines 60–65.
36. Syed, "I've Never Been Happier," lines 85–87.

> perspective, and I quickly became struck by the magnitude of the evidence corroborating my initial doubts. Doubt cannot be imposed from the outside; it must begin from within.[37]

Daniels, like Edwards, was open to subjecting his faith to critical inquiry. His intellectual curiosity led him to question what he believed were contradictory elements in the Bible along with re-evaluating how his faith related to the real world. He was unwilling to ignore what he believed were problems with the Bible and his Christian experience. Others, less inclined to being open to experience, would likely have shied away from pursuing solutions. Instead they would have likely chosen to trust that there was an answer that supported their faith, if they even noticed such problems in the first place. It is important to note that he locates the catalyst for his journey in his own inquisitive nature when he points out, "Doubt cannot be imposed from the outside; it must begin from within." And, like Edwards, he too subjected solutions to his problems to rational analysis. Instead of looking to Christian authorities alone, he sought insight from a "skeptical perspective" that presented distinctly anti-Christian answers. In deciding the truth, Daniels, like Edwards, was no longer content to submit his reason to a religious authority, such as the Bible, but looked to his own autonomous reason as the best criterion by which to evaluate truth claims.

To summarize, deconverts are characterized by being open to experience. Being so inclined leads them to investigate the claims of their own religious tradition. In seeking answers to the questions they have about their religious tradition, they actively look to those within and without. Not willing to locate authority in external sources such as religious leaders or the Bible, they locate it internally, subjecting the claims of the Bible to the bar of their own reason.

Ingredient 3: A Low Tolerance for Fundamentalist and Right-Wing Authoritarian Attitudes.

Third, as previously mentioned, studies show there exists a strong negative correlation between *openness to experience* and being attracted to *religious fundamentalism* and *right-wing authoritarianism*.[38] The Religious Fundamentalism scale measures a distinct style of adhering to religious beliefs that include: 1) there is one set of teachings that is inerrant and reveals the essential unchangeable truth about humanity and God; 2) that this essential

37. Daniels, *Why I Believed*, 13.

38. Altemeyer and Hunsberger, *Amazing Conversions;* Streib et al., *Deconversion.*

truth is fundamentally opposed by forces of evil the righteous must oppose; and 3) that those who believe and follow this truth have a special relationship with God.[39] The Religious Fundamentalism scale measures religious openness. Deconverts tend to strongly disagree with the above fundamentalist statements much more than faithful in-tradition believers do.[40] Deconverts are open to questioning and challenging the narrowness of the above three claims. Conversely, faithful in-tradition believers affirm the unique nature of their faith tradition and maintain that it is both necessary and completely sufficient for securing eternal happiness. Closely related to the Religious Fundamentalism scale is the Right-Wing Authoritarianism scale. The Right-Wing Authoritarianism scale measures three factors: 1) authoritarian submission, defined as a high degree of submission to authorities perceived as legitimate leaders in society; 2) authoritarian aggression, defined as a general aggressiveness directed at others, especially when positively sanctioned by established authorities; and 3) conventionalism, defined as a high degree of adherence to social conventions and cultural traditions.[41] In relation to the Right-Wing Authoritarianism scale, Altemeyer and Hunsberger discovered that former believers had an average score of only 93.7, much lower than the sample mean of 123.8. Most of these scored in the bottom quarter of the overall authoritarianism scores scale. Faithful believers, on the other hand, averaged 173.3, well above the sample mean. Furthermore, half of faithful believers scored as high on the scale.[42] What these numbers tell us is that former believers are the kind of individuals who are much less inclined to be members of institutions that they perceive as "right-wing authoritarian" in nature. Faithful in-tradition members of conservative Christian churches, however, tend to exhibit an affinity for right-wing authoritarian institutions. Such individuals have been described as "authoritarian followers." Altemeyer and Hunsberger define authoritarian followers as those who "tend to be the truest believers in their religions, the most faithful church-attenders, the most frequent prayers, the most dutiful Scripture readers."[43] It should be easy to see why those scoring high concerning *openness to experience* will almost certainly have little affinity for religious traditions that they perceive as doctrinally narrow or requiring submission to strong leadership.

39. Streib et al., *Deconversion,* 61.
40. Streib et al., *Deconversion,* 76.
41. Streib et al., *Deconversion,* 61.
42. Altemeyer and Hunsberger, 209.
43. Altemeyer and Hunsberger, 236.

It is unclear whether Edwards and Daniels possess the psychological traits of low tolerance for *religious fundamentalism* and *right-wing authoritarianism*. Their pre-deconversion Christian experience seemed to display a certain amount of tolerance for both. Edwards and Daniels each came out of conservative Christian traditions tainted with fundamentalism and right-wing authoritarianism. They appeared to have felt at home in these traditions, at least for most of their time in them. After abandoning their faith, however, each has made comments that indicate they reject not only their former beliefs but their former way of thinking. Edwards has said about his Christian experience, "I think I was probably quite narrow-minded and fundamental in my views and a bit of a scary person."[44] He went on to tell Sky News. "I believed that what I believed was the truth. Some of those extremes I feel slightly embarrassed about now."[45] Daniels, too, expresses criticism with his former way of looking at the world. He criticizes his church for not encouraging him to read more broadly and think critically about his beliefs: "In all my years of faithful church attendance, Bible studies, Christian college, missions training, and seminary, I do not recall one sermon, not one injunction encouraging me to examine my faith critically."[46] He also is quite clear about his displeasure for fundamentalism, now that he no longer identifies as a Christian.[47] In contrast to his days as a fundamentalist, he now considers himself a freethinker and has openly criticized a number of fundamentalists and their positions on his blog.[48] The question is: Does Edwards's and Daniels's intolerance of fundamentalism reveal an aspect of who they were, even as Christians, that lay dormant until they deconverted? Or, is their change of attitude toward their former fundamentalist, authoritarian tradition a result of their loss of faith? Regardless of whether Edwards and Daniels score low on the two measurements, studies show that a prominent personality trait of former believers is that they do consistently score low in their appreciation of *religious fundamentalism* and *right-wing authoritarianism*.

44. Brooke and Turvill, "I've Lost My Faith but I Am Happy," 21–22.

45. Brooke and Turvill, "I've Lost My Faith but I Am Happy," 23–24.

46. Daniels, *Why I Believed*, 66.

47. Daniels, *Why I Believed*, 65–98.

48. www.kwdaniels.com

Ingredient 4: An Inability to Process and Reconcile Difficulties with Their Faith.

In his classic work *Stages of Faith*, James Fowler identified six developmental stages that individuals advance through as their faith matures. According to Fowler, faith is the fundamental means by which individuals relate to and engage with the world. Fowler defines faith as the "universal quality of human meaning making."[49] In other words, faith describes the underlying meaning making process that all people employ. Faith, then, is the means by which an individual makes sense of the world. As such, all people possess faith and express it by indwelling a story that attempts to make sense of the world. How that faith develops and matures is the focus of Fowler's project.

Stage 1 generally occurs around preschool. At this stage, ideas about God are largely absorbed from the adults in a youngster's life. Due to their young age, individuals at this stage cannot think abstractly nor can they distinguish between reality and fantasy. Their faith is the result of being socialized into the rituals of their community; it is not a thought through set of ideas. The second stage begins to develop in school age children. Their faith and beliefs about God are more logical than those of persons in stage 1. They are able to make distinctions between fantasy and reality but will take many of the stories and symbols of their faith very literally. As individuals move into adolescence, they usually transition into stage 3. At this stage, an individual's belief system is largely taken for granted. That is, they do not realize that their belief system is one of many possible takes on the world. For them, it is just a description of the way things are. Little reflection or critical analysis occurs at stage 3, and authority rests largely with religious teachers. Fowler maintains that most individuals in traditional churches are at and remain at this stage for their entire lives.

Stage 4 is characterized by a more reflective approach to one's faith. Individuals at stage 4 ask questions about what justifies the teachings and authorities that provide the foundation of their faith. Rather than vesting authority in external sources, the individuals attempt to harmonize and make sense out of discrepancies and apparent contradictions in their faith that they have become aware of. It can be a time of intellectual and emotional upheaval due to unresolved doubt and the insecurity that it generates. It is here that the believer reaches a crisis point. Once he has moved through stage 3 to stage 4, there is no going back to stage 3 and its naiveté, but neither is it possible to remain in the turmoil of stage 4. One must find a way to retain faith and move to the fifth stage or let go of the faith altogether.

49. Fowler, *Stages of Faith*, 31.

For those who manage to progress to stage 5, faith survives but is now marked by an ability to live with the apparent contradictions and ambiguities that stage 4 had raised, without needing a solution to them. Doing so allows an individual to return to a sense of emotional security. However, this time it is with a more authentic personal faith that is more nuanced, able to survive despite the tensions that exist. At stage 5, the believer is capable of living in the grey and not needing the degree of coherence in his faith that was sought at stage 4.

It is clear that Edwards and Daniels managed to progress to stage 4 in the development of their faith. Their stories illustrate that each arrived at the place where they could critically reflect on what they believed. But once at stage 4, they could not overcome the tensions and difficulties that reflecting on their faith commitment produced. Each had serious periods of reflection on what he believed and why, but neither was able to find enough coherence to retain his faith. Neither could they return to the third stage. Since remaining perpetually at the fourth stage is practically unlivable, Edwards and Daniels were ultimately forced to either live perpetually in limbo at stage 4 or renounce their faith. What they could not do was return to the third stage and live according to teachings they no longer found believable. What was it that pushed them towards apostasy and kept them from progressing to stage 5? It has been suggested that a fifth personality trait might be the culprit; a significant number of atheists tend to be more tolerant of ambiguity and uncertainty than religious believers.

Ingredient 5: A High Tolerance of Ambiguity and Uncertainty

A personality trait consistently associated with atheists is that they score higher in tolerance of ambiguity and uncertainty than religious believers.[50] This has led to the belief among researchers that a person who has low tolerance of ambiguity and uncertainty fits better within a dogmatic religious system. The reason being that dogmatic systems of thought provide nice, neat, black and white answers about complex issues and this is attractive to those with low tolerance for ambiguity. Conversely, those who are more tolerant of ambiguity and uncertainty find such systems of thought confining, simplistic, and unworthy of their allegiance. Therefore, individuals who recognize that life is often not lived in the black and white of dogmatic religious certitude, but rather in the grey of uncertainty are less likely to be able to affirm a system of thinking that requires them to deny the complexities

50. Wink et al., "Religiousness, Spiritual Seeking, and Personality."

that they see. Although there are at present no longitudinal studies that demonstrate this, it is likely that deconverts are by nature more tolerant of ambiguity than those who remain religiously steadfast, rather than it being a personality trait they have acquired since their deconversion.[51] If so, it is reasonable to assume that when such individuals attain Fowler's forth stage of faith development and become aware of the ambiguity and uncertainty that exists within their faith, they will feel a tension between themselves and the expectations of their religious community. They cannot return to the dogmatism and naiveté of stage 3, but they may either assume that they have to in order to be a "biblical" Christian or at least be expected to by their community. Given their high tolerance for ambiguity and uncertainty, such individuals can perceive their situation as somewhat akin to being presented with an ultimatum; either ignore the ambiguities and uncertainties they have become aware of in their faith system and return to stage 3 or abandon their faith to save their intellectual integrity. At work in the background of this dilemma is the assumption that to be a real or biblical Christian, there is a large body of beliefs and practices that must be affirmed and affirmed with a great deal of psychological certainty. Unable to do so, given their high degree of tolerance for ambiguity and uncertainty, future deconverts may feel they have no other choice but to abandon a faith they believe they must be certain about.[52]

51. Saroglou et al., "Values and Religiosity."

52. A recent longitudinal study by Hui et al. (2018) tracking 632 Christians over three years suggests three further "ingredients" that appear to be common to deconverts. What sets the study apart from all others is that it provides information on personality traits and personal values held by individuals who identified as Christians *before* they deconverted. This is important because it allowed researchers to determine if the traits and values of deconverts were preexisting or a result of their loss of faith. No other studies have collected data on individuals both while they were Christians and after they left the faith. All previous studies have only collected data on deconverts after the fact. Doing so leaves open the possibility that the values of former believers are a result of losing one's faith, not a factor in contributing to deconversion. After three years, 188 individuals of the 632 in the study had left their faith and no longer identified as being Christians. The individuals who lost their faith scored higher in valuing power (defined as social status, prestige, and dominance over others), self-determination (understood as autonomy), and stimulation (understood as seeking new and novel experiences, excitement, and life changes). These findings are not surprising, since numerous previous studies have associated nonreligious individuals with the above values. What makes the findings of the study so interesting is that these characteristics are not just consistent with those who are nonreligious, they act as predictors of who will lose faith. Individuals who score high in the above values are more prone to lose their faith than those who score low. Researchers concluded, "In terms of values, although they were still professing their Christian faith, the would-be exiters put less emphasis on conformity, tradition, and benevolence (values that have been espoused by many Christians) and more on self-direction, stimulation, hedonism, achievement, and power. All in all,

What then was it that made it so difficult for Edwards and Daniels to manage to get past the difficulties they encountered at the fourth stage of their faith development? It's impossible to say for sure, but I propose that a clue may lie in the way that Edwards and Daniels were "prepared." In other words, a major factor in their deconversion may be how their families and/or their Christian communities socialized them into the faith. I suggest this because it is clear from stories of other deconverts that the manner in which many have been socialized into the faith made it very difficult to push through to stage 5, leaving only deconversion as a live option.

Preparation

A recipe is more than just a list of ingredients. It also includes instructions on how the ingredients necessary to make the dish are to be prepared. Preparation is as important as the ingredients themselves in the outcome of a recipe. Having the correct ingredients is necessary, but not sufficient, for creating any dish. In order to have the dish be a success, the ingredients need to be prepared correctly. If they aren't, the end result can be anything from a dish that is mildly unappealing to deadly. In Japan, one of the most celebrated delicacies is the puffer fish. However, if not prepared correctly, the puffer fish is lethal. If the fish is not prepared correctly, even a tiny drop of the toxin resident in the skin of the fish can leave diners paralyzed. Fully conscious, they will die of asphyxiation as they lose the ability to breathe. Because the potential for disaster is so great, Japanese chefs must go through extensive training and be officially licensed to prepare it. To make sure they have prepared it correctly, they are required to eat a piece of the fish before it is served. But it's not only exotic foods like the puffer

the would-be exiters already had a belief and value profile that mimicked more the nonbelievers than the believers." It is easy to see how individuals who once identified as Christians but who highly value their own autonomy, social status, control, and new and novel experiences would not fit well in a religious system that emphasizes obedience, submission, personal sacrifice, and tradition, which are incompatible with pursuing status and power. I have chosen not to include these values in the list of ingredients in the *Recipe for Disaster* for two reasons. First, all of the participants were Chinese citizens with varying degrees of Christian socialization. Some were new converts, others were Christians for a significant time, but little information was provided regarding their church background. I am focused on North American believers from conservative evangelical and fundamentalist church communities. It is unclear at this point whether the findings of Hui et al. (2018) are transferable to the focus of this book. Second, the study has yet to be corroborated by further research. Until they are, the findings, although quite possibly accurate, are at this point speculative. If such turns out to be the case, it will prove to be an important discovery in the list of ingredients that make up *A Recipe for Disaster*.

fish that require proper preparation, even such mundane foods as rhubarb, kidney beans, and almonds have dire consequences if eaten without being properly prepared.

Reading the narratives of deconverts reveals that not only do they share similar personality traits, but that those ingredients were prepared in such a way that they combined to produce a mixture that tilted the scales toward producing a deconvert rather than a disciple. The character formation, experiences, expectations, and assumptions that were passed on to them laid the groundwork for their eventual departure. If deconverts provided the ingredients in the recipe, then who did the preparing?

Running through the stories of Edwards, Daniels, and other former believers is a common thread, and that is that former believers claim they lost their faith because they became convinced Christianity was false. Edwards and Daniels, for their own reasons, came to the conclusion that the story the Bible tells is untrue. They found it impossible to believe anymore. When this happened, they felt they had no choice but to leave their faith since they could not make themselves believe something they had become convinced was false. In other words, deconverts are highly committed to truth and integrity. They would not simply ignore what they discovered to maintain their religious commitments. What accounts for this deep commitment to truth and integrity in the lives of Edwards, Daniels, and other deconverts?

Ironically, the answer is their spiritual formation. Psychologists Bruce Hunsberger and Bob Altemeyer point out that:

> For all of their lives deconverts were told their religion was the true religion and they had to live according to its teachings. Were they not being implicitly told that truth was even a more basic good than even their religious beliefs, that the beliefs were to be celebrated because they were truth? Furthermore, all the training in avoiding sin and being a good person "on the inside" would have promoted integrity. You have to be good and true, through and through. That's what counts. If this teaching succeeded it would produce a person who deeply valued truth and had deep-down integrity. The religion would therefore create the basis for its own downfall, if it came up short in these departments.[53]

Deconverts not only place a high value on truth and integrity but also have a number of assumptions and expectations about their faith that play a major role in their loss of faith. If you read enough deconversion stories, you'll

53. Hunsberger and Altemeyer, *Amazing Conversions*, 120.

notice the same objections appear over and over again. The thing about objections is that they presuppose certain beliefs and attitudes that give the objections their force. Former believers have a lot of expectations and assumptions about God, the Bible, and Christianity. When those assumptions and expectations are unmet, the result can be a crisis of faith. For Daniels, it occurred when the Bible didn't match up with what he believed it had to be. For Edwards, his crisis came when the existence of God didn't meet his assumptions about what constituted a rational belief. Behind every objection is an assumption or expectation of the way things should be but aren't. Sometimes those assumptions are justified. Other times they are not.

Where did former believers get their assumptions and expectations about God and the Bible? From the same place they received their commitment to truth and virtue, their evangelical training. Conservative evangelicals and fundamentalists hold and consequently pass on assumptions and expectations about the faith that are understood to be nonnegotiable. Some of these assumptions and expectations are explicitly taught while others are caught. Many believers never question these assumptions and expectations. Deconverts, on the other hand, inevitably find at least one critical assumption or expectation of Christianity to be either false or unmet. If they have been taught that the unmet expectation is essential to the Christian faith, it only makes sense that they would conclude that Christianity is false. The question that needs to be asked is whether the assumptions and expectations that many deconverts harbor about Christianity really are essential to it. If they aren't, then, tragically, they were set up for a spiritual crisis by the very faith communities that birthed them.

Cooking

Like an oven that bakes the prepared ingredients of a recipe into a cake, the secular age acts like a pressure cooker, shaping and molding us into adopting its view of reality. Individuals who identify as Christians and are intelligent, open to experience, care about truth, have low tolerance for right-wing authoritarianism and religious fundamentalism, and have unmet expectations and negative experiences are particularly susceptible to the toll the secular age can have on faith. Sometimes the result is a loss of faith.

Heating changes food. Proteins coagulate, starches gelatinize, sugars caramelize, water evaporates, and fats melt. Cooking is chemistry; the process of applying heat to a combination of ingredients forges it into something different. But, not all heat sources produce the same results. There are some contexts that are more conducive to baking a cake than others. No one would be happy with the result that came from putting the prepared ingredients for a cake into a microwave oven for baking. Likewise, no one would enjoy a cup of coffee warmed up in a deep fryer. The environment where the ingredients are cooked makes a difference in the outcome.

We no longer live in the Middle Ages, and for that we should all be glad. The convenience and comfort of modern life, not to mention medical advances, make life in the twenty-first century much easier in many ways than the life in the eighth century. One exception to that is having a robust religious faith. Life in the twenty-first century makes that much more difficult. That's because the socio-cultural context we live in powerfully impacts what we believe. It provides the environment where the prepared ingredients in *A Recipe for Disaster* are baked, resulting in apostasy.

In the Middle Ages, belief in God was nearly universal throughout Europe because it was reinforced by the dominant social institutions of the day. The courts, royalty, universities, and, of course, the church all presupposed the existence of God and the truth of Christianity. When everyone you know assumes the truth of Christianity, believing comes easily. Times, however, have changed. Edwards, Daniels, and the rest of us live in a culture in which believing in God is increasingly difficult because Christianity is no longer afforded the status as the official story underwriting our culture. We no longer live in an age where it is nearly impossible *not* to believe in God. On the contrary, we in the West live in an increasingly post-Christian society. By that, I mean the hegemony of Christianity is waning, particularly among social institutions that are located at the center of cultural production. While the grassroots of American society may be quite religious, the elites at the top of powerful social institutions are not, and it is their influence that makes the difference.

As a result, secularists, not the church, are increasingly in control of and write the "official" definition of reality. The narrative shaping culture is no longer that of the Bible but a cocktail of modern Enlightenment rationalism and scientism. The result is that religious expression and belief are marginalized and excluded from public discourse, the legal system, and the political process. Whereas the West once looked to the Bible as the criterion of truth, progressive secularists view that period in western civilization as intellectually immature, reliant on religious superstition and stories to account for what they otherwise couldn't. Today, we "know" better. The steady progress of science leaves little need to appeal to God as an explanation of natural phenomena. But, even if we did, it certainly wouldn't be the God of the Bible who seems to behave in such a petty and barbaric manner. No enlightened, educated, objective modern could believe, let alone place any authority in, the writings of a Bronze Age nomadic tribe and their God.

Religious belief may have been okay for our unenlightened ancestors, but it should play no role in shaping society today. Science and reason are the tools for shaping society in the Secular Age.

Admittedly, the secular narrative is more felt than articulated. To be fair, few progressive secularists would likely express their beliefs as explicitly as above. That's because, like Christians in the Middle Ages, the secular narrative resides at the foundational presuppositional level of their worldview. It is an "unthought" taken for granted of how things are. Only when it is brought to the surface and analyzed does it become explicit. Regardless of whether it remains at the taken-for-granted level or is explicitly acknowledged, the secular narrative is the primary force setting the intellectual and cultural agenda in the West.

Of the three parts in *A Recipe for Disaster*—the ingredients, the preparation, and the environment where the cooking takes place—the preparation is most important in preventing deconversion, at least as far as parents and church leaders are concerned. Parents and church leaders can do little about the personality and psychological traits of their children and those they minister to. Nor can they do much to alter modern secular culture. In fact, the typical strategy employed by evangelicals and fundamentalists in response to contemporary culture has tended to only contribute to deconversion. The one aspect of the recipe that parents and church leaders do have control over in the spiritual formation of their young people is the assumptions and expectations that they pass on to them. For that reason, the majority of this book will focus on the four main ways parents and church leaders participate in the loss of faith and will offer suggestions on how to avoid them.

Recipe, Not Reasons

Deconversion is the undoing, the reversal, or the making of no effect one's religious conversion. It is a renouncing of one's allegiance to a specific set of beliefs or to a religious community. Some of the most outwardly committed and apparently sincere followers of Christ can and do deconvert from Christianity. Christians understandably desire to know why. Deconverts themselves point to problems with the Bible, conflicts between science and faith, the problem of evil, and disappointment with God along with many more reasons for their deconversion. But none of those reasons alone is enough to do the trick. Likewise, Christians, in an attempt to explain away deconversion, can be quick to level shallow and insulting accusations at former believers. Often former believers are accused of deconverting because they are either in sin (or at least want to be), are not spiritual enough, are too worldly, are becoming too educated, or worst of all, they were never true believers in the first place. But once again, such reasons do not sufficiently explain the deconversion phenomenon. Worse yet, instead of shedding light on the problem of why individuals lose their faith, they act as a hindrance by offering simplistic explanations that largely absolve the church from any liability. The truth is much more complex and turns out to be contrary to what many believers might expect.

The deconversion of Edwards, Daniels and others can best be understood by thinking of them as the product of a recipe. Recipes consist of three elements: ingredients, preparation, and an environment where the prepared ingredients are baked. In a similar way to how a cake is the outcome of a particular set of ingredients and preparation, so too are deconversions. However, in the case of the deconversion recipe, the outcome is never as certain as it is for a recipe for German chocolate cake. Rather, it is better to consider "the deconversion recipe" as analogous to what is often referred to as a "recipe for success." In *Outliers*, Malcolm Gladwell identified the key ingredients in achieving success in any given endeavor.[54] Gladwell found that despite what many presume are the key factors in success—skill and knowledge—in reality other more surprising factors were more important. He maintained that three factors were essential in any recipe for success: good timing, persistence, and cultural background. Of course, Gladwell never promised that his recipe for success was a guarantee of success. Even if you follow Gladwell's recipe for success to the letter, there is no guarantee you will be a professional hockey player, world-class ballerina, or Nobel Prize-winning scientist. But, your likelihood of doing so increases significantly. The same is true for the deconversion recipe; there's not a guarantee that it will produce an apostate. But, follow it and the likelihood of deconversion significantly increases.

Recipe for Success

If we understand the ingredients, preparation, and environment that constitute the deconversion recipe, we can address the growing trend of deconversion from Christianity in a productive manner. To discover what those are, we will look at those individuals whom we would least expect to renounce their faith: pastors, worship leaders, seminary graduates, biblical studies professors, and apologists. We will discover the methods of preparation that such individuals have in common. We will identify the

54. Gladwell, *Outliers*.

recipe for disaster that so often leads to deconversion. In doing so, we will be better prepared to answer the question of why apparently committed believers lose their faith and, perhaps more importantly, what we can do to instill faith that endures.

Chapter 2

The Word on Deconversion

They believed for a while, then they fall away when they face temptation.

JESUS

Godless

IN 1974, AT FIFTEEN years of age, Dan Barker committed himself to a lifetime of Christian ministry. Barker, raised in a fundamentalist charismatic home, adopted the beliefs of his parents and identified as a Christian from an early age. Growing up, Dan and his musically talented family regularly performed in churches in Southern California. His father often preached while he, his mother, and his brothers played their instruments and sang. Looking back on his life, Dan described his work in full-time Christian ministry by saying:

> My commitment lasted nineteen years. It gave my life a feeling of purpose, destiny, and fulfillment. I spent years trekking across Mexico in missionary work—small villages, jungles, deserts, large arenas, radio, television, parks, prisons and street meetings. I spent more years in traveling evangelism across the United States preaching and singing in churches, on street corners, house-to-house witnessing, college campuses and wherever an audience could be found. I was a "doer of the word and not a hearer only." I went to a Christian college, majored in religion/philosophy, became ordained and served in a pastoral capacity in three California churches. I personally led many people to

> Jesus Christ, and encouraged many young people to consider full-time Christian service.[1]

He was a preacher, a missionary, and an evangelist. What a testimony! However, where Dan really excelled was in his musical abilities. A gifted pianist and composer, Dan composed over one hundred Christian songs that have been published or recorded by numerous Christian artists. He and his wife Carol regularly traveled and performed his music in churches across the United States. During that time, they had no regular income and lived on the offerings they received at the churches they ministered at. Dan Barker was by all appearances a true believer, serving Jesus and living by faith.

Today, he is one of America's leading atheists. Currently, Barker is co-president of The Freedom From Religion Foundation, an avowedly atheist organization dedicated to eradicating religion from the public square. He regularly engages in debates with theists and has written several books intended to deconvert Christians from their faith, including the story of his own loss of faith, entitled *Godless*.

How are Christians to make sense of Dan's story and those of the many others like him who have lost their faith after seemingly serving the Lord with distinction? Surely, such stories strike most readers as surprising, if not downright shocking. But should we be so surprised when we hear of people like Dan Barker, or even those we know, who at one time professed to be believers, abandon their faith? Not if we have eyes to see. That's because Scripture addresses the issue of apostasy over and over again. My suspicion is that we rarely notice that fact because we're not looking for it. The kind of things we fail to see because we are not looking for them—even those that are in plain sight—can be surprising. But, when they are pointed out to us, we wonder how we ever missed them.

For example, I once worked for a residential window cleaning company in Southern California. It was a small operation, consisting of just the owner and me. He and I would drive from job to job in his truck, carrying everything we needed in the back. When we got to a job site, I would head into the home and clean the inside of the windows while my boss cleaned the outside. Cleaning windows is an art, and my boss had a technique and order in which he wanted me to clean each window. After I was finished, I would look at the window to make sure that I had not only cleaned it, but also had left no streaks behind. When I first started out cleaning windows, he would check on my work to make sure I had done a good job. I remember how surprised and embarrassed I was when he inspected my windows. I was convinced I had done a great job because to me the windows looked

1. Barker, "I Just Lost Faith," 22–28.

clean. But, it seemed he always found smears and streaks that I hadn't noticed. Why was it that he saw them, and I didn't? The reason, I later came to realize, was that I was looking *through* the window, whereas he was looking *at* it. He was specifically looking for smears and streaks; I was just looking to see if the windows were clean of obvious dirt. When I started looking *at* rather than *through* the windows, I was taken aback by how many streaks and smears I had left behind. Not until I looked specifically for them did I see how many there were.

I think there's a parallel between my surprise at seeing the streaks and smears on my windows and the surprise we often have when we discover someone has abandoned the faith. The similarity lies in what we're *not* looking for. In the case of my early career as a window washer, it was streaks. I wasn't looking for them, so I didn't see them even though they were right there in front of my face. In the case of deconversion, it is the biblical data. We're often surprised at stories like Dan Barker's, because we've never taken the time to look at just what Scripture says about the issue of apostasy. And, after my boss pointed the streaks out to me, I wondered how I had never noticed them. I suspect you, as well, will wonder how it is that you were so surprised in the past when you had heard of someone losing his faith, after I share with you how often the New Testament refers to it. So, what does the New Testament have to say about those who once identified as Christians but no longer do? The answer is that it says quite a bit. In fact, the New Testament repeatedly talks about the issue of deconversion, if only we have eyes to see it. If we take a close look at what the New Testament has to say about the dangers of falling away, we might be surprised at how much attention it gets.

Apostasy in the Gospels

Turning to the gospels and looking at the words of the Lord Jesus, it's clear that he wasn't taken by surprised by those who, like Dan Barker, began to follow him but eventually turned and walked away. In his apocalyptic discourse, Jesus said:

> See that no one leads you astray. For many will come in my name, saying "I am the Christ," and they will lead many astray. And you will hear of wars and rumors of wars. See that you are not alarmed, for this must take place, but the end is not yet. For nation will rise against nation, and kingdom against kingdom, and there will be famines and earthquakes in various places. All these things are but the beginning of the birth pangs. Then they

> will deliver you up to tribulation and put you to death, and you will be hated by all nations for my name's sake. And then many will fall away and betray one another and hate one another. And many false prophets will arise and lead many astray. And because lawlessness will be increased, the love of many will grow cold. But the one who endures to the end will be saved. (Matthew 24:4–13 ESV)

There are three things to note from this passage. First, Jesus is genuinely concerned that false messiahs will lead his disciples astray. He was well aware that there would be others coming after him who claim to be the "real" Christ and that many of those who identified as followers of him *would* be led astray. The word "astray" that Jesus uses is the Greek word *planao*, which describes being deceived, getting off course, and deviating from the correct path. Jesus knew, and so warned his disciples, that false messiahs would deceive some of those who followed him, leading them to get off course and wander away. Second, to be led astray from following Christ presupposes that at one time these people identified as followers of Jesus. In other words, they professed *some* type of faith in Christ, but at some point in the future they would abandon that faith. This tells us that Jesus is under no delusion that everyone who professes to be a follower of his will remain faithful. He is well aware that "many" will turn away from the faith. Not some, or a few, but many. Third, Jesus emphasizes the fact that persevering in the faith is essential to salvation. Jesus, raising the issue of perseverance in the face of hostility, implies that not everyone who starts out as a follower of his will manage to endure the hardships to come. These three points tell us that the warning to the disciples was real. Jesus wanted them to be on their guard against the very real temptation to depart from their loyalty to him, either by being deceived by false messiahs or because of the threat of tribulation.

Jesus again addresses the issue of deconversion in Luke 8:4–15. There, Jesus tells one of his most well-known parables, the story of a farmer who went out to plant seeds in his field. As he did so, he randomly tossed his seeds onto different kinds of soils. Some he threw onto a footpath that had no chance of putting down roots, and birds quickly devoured them. The second kind of soil the seeds fell into was rocky. The seeds that fell into this soil did put down roots but because the soil was rocky the roots were shallow and weak. As a result, they lacked moisture, withered, and died. The third soil the seeds fell into was thorny soil, and the thorns grew up along with the seed and choked it. The fourth soil, however, was good and the seeds that fell into it yielded a great harvest.

When the disciples asked Jesus what the parable meant, he told them that the seeds represent the Word of God and the different soils, the people who hear it. The seeds that fell on the footpath represents those who hear the word, but have it stolen from them by the devil so that they may not believe and be saved. The seeds that fell on the thorny soil symbolize those who hear the word, but as they go on their way, they are choked by the cares of the world and the pleasures of this life. The seeds that fell on the good soil represent those who hear it and hold to it with an honest and good heart, resulting in fruit that is consistent with salvation. But what about the rocky soil, what does it represent? The rocky soil, according to Jesus, is symbolic of those people who "hear the message and receive it with joy. But since they don't have deep roots, they believe for a while, then they fall away when they face temptation." (Luke 8:13 NLT) Did you hear that? Jesus says that there are some people who believe, at least for a while, and then fall away. Now, the difficult question is, what does Jesus mean by believe? Is it a belief that resulted in salvation, but that salvation was ultimately lost when they stopped believing? Or, is it possible they had a belief in Jesus that didn't produce salvation? If so, Jesus is saying that some people who believe in him will fall away, but they are falling away from something other than salvation. Regardless of what one believes about the matter of eternal security, it is clear that Jesus expects that there will be many that once identified as believers who will "fall away."

The phrase "fall away" that is used by Luke in this passage is the Greek word *aphisteme*, which means to desert, forsake, abandon, or defect from. It is a strong choice of words and identifies people who become faithless and depart from their commitment to follow him. Interestingly, it's the exact word that Jesus uses again in Luke 13:27, when he tells the Pharisees that despite the fact that they think they are in good standing with God, they are in for a big surprise. On that great and final day when God settles all accounts, they will not be honored, but rather they will be shamed. God will declare that he does not know them and that they must depart. That word "depart" is the same word used to describe those in the parable of the farmer who received the word with joy and believed for a while but "fell away." They departed, they left, and they no longer identified as believers.

But it's not only those anonymous people in Jesus's parables and prophecies that should get our attention when it comes to deconversion. Jesus's own disciple, one of his closest friends who shared in his ministry and acted as one of his representatives, Judas Iscariot, fell away. What makes Judas so interesting is that he not only had the respected position of being the treasurer for the group, but in all likelihood, when Jesus sent out the disciples to preach, heal, and cast out demons, Judas did all three of those things. There is no indication in the text of Scripture that any of the disciples had any reason to suspect him of being a traitor. At the Last Supper, when Jesus said that one of the disciples would betray him, no one looked at Judas and said, "Well, we know it's you, you couldn't heal anyone, you couldn't cast out demons, and your preaching was terrible!" No, they had no idea. Judas followed Jesus for at least three years, listening to him preach to the crowds. He traveled with Jesus throughout Israel and watched as, on one hand, he engaged the self-righteous Pharisees in debates about the law and, on the other hand, he compassionately ministered to the broken and outcast. Judas witnessed the resurrections of Lazarus and the widow's son, and surely he knew of the raising of Jairus's daughter. He had constant access to Jesus and was privy to private explanations that Jesus offered the disciples for some of his more difficult teachings. Being one of the twelve disciples chosen by Jesus identified him as a member of his inner circle. And yet, as Judas demonstrates, it's sometimes the people we would least expect, those who on the surface look too spiritually impressive to deconvert. But such people can and at times do depart from their profession of faith.

Farewell to God?

Several years ago, I was speaking at a large church in Toronto, Canada. On the wall in the foyer there were pictures of the church's former pastors. As I looked at the pictures, I noticed that side by side on the wall were the two most famous former pastors of that church. One was A. W. Tozer, the prolific writer and speaker, who called a generation of believers to a deep commitment to the Lordship of Christ. Tozer's work challenged the church to take discipleship seriously. He was like a twentieth-century prophet, reminding believers of the holiness of God and of the responsibilities of those who name the name of Christ to obey his word. And, like a prophet, his message was often sharp and convicting. Because of those things, Tozer gained a wide audience, and his influence on the American church through his many books and sermons has been tremendous. Next to Tozer on the wall was another former pastor by the name of Charles Templeton. Templeton actually founded that church in Toronto and served as their pastor for a number of years. Templeton was also immensely successful as an itinerant evangelist, traveling extensively throughout Canada, the United States, and Europe preaching the gospel in churches and sports stadiums. So popular was he that the venues he preached in rarely were large enough for the crowds that attended.[2] In Canton, Ohio, he preached to more than 90,000

2. Templeton, *An Anecdotal Memoir,* 82.

people over two weeks of meetings. He recounted one campaign on the east coast of Canada as follows:

> Each year, I spent four months holding missions in Canada. On the closing night in Charlottetown, which then had a population of fourteen thousand, there were some six thousand either in the hockey arena or listening to loudspeakers in the streets. In the Sydney arena there were as many outside as within. In two weeks, 10,000 attended; the population was 30,000. The meeting in Fredericton was held in winter weather. The congregation huddled in coats and hats and scarves; one night I preached wearing a topcoat. Portable furnaces were rigged to push heat through vents cut in the arena walls. Regardless of the inconvenience, every seat was filled each night and the ice area was crammed with people huddled on improvised seating. In each city, all-time attendance records were set for any event, secular or religious.[3]

Along with Billy Graham and Torrey Johnson, Templeton founded the international organization Youth for Christ, which seeks to reach young people everywhere with the gospel and to raise up lifelong followers of Jesus. Every week, thousands of young people across the United States and Canada would gather for meetings that included singing and gospel preaching.

So successful was Templeton at stadium evangelism that he was recruited to preach alongside Billy Graham, who has preached to more people than anyone in history. For over fifty years, he has traveled the world preaching at stadiums filled with people who wanted to hear the gospel. In 1946, Templeton and Graham went on an evangelistic tour together preaching throughout Western Europe, England, Scotland, Ireland, and Sweden. They even roomed together. Billy Graham became so fond of Charles Templeton that he said of him, he was "one of the few men I have loved in my life."[4]

Judging by appearance alone, Templeton had accomplished more to spread the gospel in the ten years since his conversion than most people do in a lifetime. He started and pastored a church, he founded a major youth ministry that to this day operates around the world, and he preached with the greatest evangelist the church has ever known! And yet, the last book he wrote several years before his death was entitled: *Farewell to God: My Reasons for Rejecting the Christian Faith*. Charles Templeton had deconverted, left the faith, and renounced Christ. Prior to his death he claimed, "Is it not foolish to close one's eyes to the reality that much of the Christian faith is

3. Templeton, *An Anecdotal Memoir,* 84.

4 59 Frady, *Billy Graham,* 186.

simply impossible to accept as fact?"[5] He added, "Should one continue to base one's life on a system of belief that for all its occasional wisdom and frequent beauty—is demonstrably untrue?"[6] He left no doubt about his loss of faith when he said, "I believe that there is no supreme being with human attributes—no God in the biblical sense—but that all life is the result of timeless evolutionary forces . . . over millions of years."[7] He went on to say, "I believe that, in common with all living creatures, we die and cease to exist as an entity."[8] He also had harsh words for Christianity: "I oppose the Christian Church because, for all the good it sometimes does, it presumes to speak in the name of God and to propound and advocate beliefs that are outdated, demonstrably untrue, and often, in their various manifestations, deleterious to individuals and to society."[9]

Templeton's apostasy is shocking. Like Judas Iscariot, he was a highly respected follower of Jesus. And, not just a follower, but also someone whom it seemed that God was working through to bring about significant advancement of his kingdom. And, like Judas, he not only came to a place where he lost his faith, he too turned on Jesus and betrayed him. Although a certain amount of shock and bewilderment at Templeton's loss of faith is understandable, in the light of Judas's betrayal of Jesus, it shouldn't completely surprise us that such things can happen.

Apostasy in the Epistles

The Bible is clear, there will be people who identify as Christians who will abandon their profession of faith, even those we would least expect. Perhaps that's why the writers of the epistles offer so many warnings and encouragements to persevere in faith. One of the major themes in the book of Hebrews is the warning that those who have committed their lives to Christ not return to Judaism. Six times in this book alone the writer warns the readers of the very real danger of deconverting from faith in Christ. The author of Hebrews says:

> See to it, brothers and sisters, that none of you has a sinful, unbelieving heart that turns away from the living God. But encourage one another daily, as long as it is called "Today," so that none

5. Templeton, Farewell to God, 229.
6. Templeton, Farewell to God, 218.
7. Templeton, Farewell to God, 232.
8. Templeton, Farewell to God, 233.
9. Templeton, Farewell to God, vii.

> of you may be hardened by sin's deceitfulness. We have come to share in Christ, if indeed we hold our original conviction firmly to the very end. (Heb 3:12–14 NIV)

Again, the author of Hebrews ominously speaks of the impossibility of "those who have once been enlightened, who have tasted the heavenly gift, who have shared in the Holy Spirit, who have tasted the goodness of the word of God and the powers of the coming age and who have fallen away, to be brought back to repentance." (Heb 6:4–6 NIV) What does it mean that such people have "fallen away"? It's debated among theologians whether these people were ever really born again. Some see in these verses the description of a true believer who had lost his salvation. Others take it as a description not of an individual who had been regenerated, but someone who only appeared to be among the redeemed. This person had come to hear the great truths of the gospel, experienced the ministry of the Holy Spirit as he worked in the community of believers, and been instructed in the word of God, yet had never truly committed to Christ. Such a person merely professed salvation, but didn't possess it. Regardless, whether they were truly saved or just individuals who made a profession and identified with a Christian community without ever having faith that resulted in salvation, the text leaves no doubt that there are, and will be, persons who identify as Christians but fall away. In this passage, the phrase "fallen away" is the Greek word *parapipto,* which means, "to abandon after being close beside." In short, the author of Hebrews was concerned that the believers to whom he wrote might not persevere in their faith. Therefore, he warned them to take care that they do not abandon their profession after being closely associated with Jesus and his church.

The Apostle Paul seemed to have such people in mind when he wrote to Timothy to encourage him in his pastoral duties. He instructed Timothy that to succeed as a minister of Jesus, he needed to do two things: hold onto his faith and maintain a good conscience. To highlight the importance of doing so, Paul then identified Hymenaeus and Alexander as two individuals who, regarding faith and a good conscience, "have rejected and so have suffered shipwreck with regard to the faith." (1 Tim 1:19 NIV) Men whom Timothy was shepherding and who at one time identified with the Christian community—spiritually speaking—had crashed and burned. They had shipwrecked their faith. We are not left to wonder what that means. In 2 Timothy, Paul provides a sad commentary on Hymenaeus when he identifies him as one who has "departed from the truth." (2 Tim 2:18 NIV) The word "departed" used by Paul carries with it the idea of pushing, repelling, and thrusting away. Hymenaeus, a man who identified as a follower of Jesus, chose to repel the gospel and the fellowship of believers. Hymenaeus deconverted.

In the same letter, Paul once again picks up on the theme of deconversion. He warned, "The Spirit clearly says that in the later times some will abandon the faith and follow deceiving spirits and things taught by demons." (1 Tim 4:1 NIV) He goes on to say that even some women who were part of Timothy's fellowship had fallen away. In reference to these women, he points out "Some have in fact . . . turned away to follow Satan." (1 Tim 5:15 NIV) I don't think this means that they actually became Satanists any more than when Jesus said to Peter, "Get behind me, Satan" that he was saying that Peter was actually Satan. Rather, I think it indicates that these women who once worked alongside Timothy were now tragically working against him and against the gospel in some capacity.

One of the gloomiest passages in the entire New Testament regarding apostasy is found in 2 Thessalonians. Paul's intention in writing to the Thessalonian church was threefold. First, he wrote to encourage the new believers who were experiencing trials (1 Thess 1:4–10). Second, he penned the epistle to correct a misunderstanding of the Lord's return (1 Thess 2:1–2). Third, he warned them about being idle. It seems that some in the church had quit their jobs because they were convinced that Jesus was about to return. This led to them becoming indolent and dependent on others to meet their needs. Paul wanted the Thessalonians to return to work and earn a living as they waited for the second coming of Christ.

The Thessalonians had been deceived into thinking that Jesus's return was the next event in the eschatological calendar. They were unaware that prior to that there were a number of events that would still need to occur. One of the events that would take place before Jesus returned is what Paul referred to as "the falling away." (2 Thess 2:1–3 NLT) The word Paul uses for "falling away" is *apostasia*. It's used only one other time in the entire New Testament, Acts 21:21. There, as here, it indicates a defection or a revolt. In this instance, Paul uses the definite article to indicate that he is referring to a specific event, not a general trend. A noteworthy loss of faith would occur in the believing community, and it would happen before Christ returned. Paul reminds the Thessalonians that he had previously warned them about the apostasy to come when he was with them in Thessalonica (2 Thess 2:5).

Paul expected that there would be those in the Christian community who would defect from the faith. He was so concerned that he warned the Thessalonians that before Christ returned "the apostasy" would occur. He knew that a time would come when those who identified as believers would depart in large numbers. Theologians and church historians are divided as to whether the event Paul prophesied has occurred. One thing is certain;

Paul did not assume that every person who claimed to be a follower of Jesus would remain one.

It is clear from his writings that Paul assumed that professing believers could fall away; he even said it would continue to happen. Likewise, Peter also warned his followers about the need to persevere in faith, the danger of falling away from the faith, and examples of false teachers who at one time professed to believe the gospel. In his second epistle, Peter told his readers to be on guard for false teachers who "have left the straight way and wandered off to follow the way of Balaam son of Bezer, who loved the wages of wickedness." (2 Pet 2:15 NIV) In a truly terrifying comment, Peter says of these people:

> If they have escaped the corruption of the world by knowing our Lord and Savior Jesus Christ and are again entangled in it and are overcome, they are worse off at the end than they were at the beginning. It would have been better for them not to have known the way of righteousness, than to have known it and then to turn their backs on the sacred command that was passed on to them. (2 Pet 2:20–21 NIV)

Peter wrote to his followers that he feared that false teachers (and those who follow them), those he described as having escaped the corruption of the world through their knowledge of Jesus, would return to the world, turn their backs on the truth, and be in a worse state than before they had claimed to be believers. Peter was well aware of the fact that not all who had joined the Christian community would remain faithful to their profession of faith.

The Apostle John warned about the danger of antichrists, those who actively oppose the teachings of Christ. Who are these people? They are individuals who at one time identified with the Christian community John is writing to. However, they had since departed and revealed their true nature as antichrists. John says:

> Dear children, this is the last hour; and as you have heard that the antichrist is coming, even now many antichrists have come. This is how we know it is the last hour. They went out from us, but they did not really belong to us. For if they had belonged to us, they would have remained with us; but their going showed that none of them belonged to us. (1 John 2:18–19 NIV)

Such individuals did not cease to exist at the close of the canon of Scripture; they continue with us today.

Some Things Never Change

Dan Barker, Charles Templeton, and many others at one time identified as followers of Christ, but, in the end, came to a place where they no longer believed. They fell away. They deconverted. While these stories may take us by surprise, they shouldn't catch us completely off guard. As we've seen, the New Testament not only assumes that a person who identifies as a Christian can fall away, it teaches that it will and does happen. The example of Judas, the words of Jesus, the author of the book of Hebrews, Paul, Peter, and John should prepare us for stories like Dan Barker, Charles Templeton, and others.

Apostasy in the first century was driven by many things; false teachers, persecution, and immorality are those most often mentioned in Scripture. While those temptations are still with us, the consistent testimony of contemporary apostates is that they left the faith because they encountered objections they could not overcome. Although the majority of deconverts point to intellectual problems for their loss of faith, that's only part of the story. It's not merely intellectual or emotional objections that are responsible for the loss of faith. It is the entire recipe, their own personality traits in combination with their religious training and cultural context, that gives the objections the required force to initiate a deconversion. Of these three, the preparation—or religious training—is the only aspect of the deconversion recipe that parents and church leaders have any control over and may be the most important element in the deconversion recipe. That's because four distinctive mistakes in how parents and church leaders socialize individuals into the faith prove to be disastrous in terms of deconversion. It is to these we turn.

Chapter 3

Hoping for the Best. Preparing for the Worst?

The difference between good and bad cooking can scarcely be more strikingly shown than in the manner in which ingredients are prepared.

Eliza Acton

The Thrill of Victory and the Agony of Defeat

Greg's family, growing up, was Catholic. In 1970, when he was thirteen, his parents divorced. At that time, his father announced he never really believed in the Christian message, so Greg decided neither did he. Shortly thereafter, he began experimenting with drugs. After experimenting with all that the counterculture had to offer, he found himself feeling empty and longing for more out of life. He found what he was looking for in a fundamentalist Pentecostal church, where at seventeen he converted to Christ. Looking back, Greg now sees that the church was "legalistic to the extreme"[1] and theologically shallow, but to him his encounter with Jesus was undeniably real. About that period of his life, he noted, "Words can't describe how good it felt to have the gnawing ache of emptiness in my soul replaced with a sense of joy and purpose."[2] Attending the church offered him the benefits of a community that provided him with emotional support and a worldview

1. Boyd, *Benefit*, 28.
2. Boyd, *Benefit*, 28.

that shaped his understanding of reality. He was convinced he had found the truth.

What Greg didn't understand at the time is that the "truth" was mediated to him through the interpretive grid of his fundamentalist Pentecostal church, an environment high on emotion and low on good theology. In particular, their understanding of the nature of biblical faith was naive and misguided. They valued a faith that was devoid of doubt and bursting with certainty. Furthermore, they expected believers to have certainty about a vast number of Christian teachings. Although the church acknowledged the differences between beliefs that are essential for salvation and those that are not, they were convinced that many beliefs were crucial to having a genuine Christian faith. If any one of these turned out to be false, the entire faith would collapse. One such teaching was that the Earth was created in six, literal twenty-four hour days, approximately 10,000 years ago. Greg recalled his pastor asserting, "that if Genesis 1 wasn't literally true, then 'the whole Bible is a book of lies!'"[3] Why in the world would he say such a thing and place the veracity of the entire Bible on such a precarious foundation?

The answer is that he held an unanalyzed assumption about what is required for a claim to be true. And that assumption was that speaking truly required speaking literally. Based on that assumption, if it turns out that the Earth is billions of years old, as contemporary science seems to show, then the Bible has a factual error in it and cannot be God's word. But why would a scientific error in the Bible lead to the conclusion that "the whole Bible is a book of lies"? Because the pastor also assumed that for the Bible to be the word of God, it must be without any errors whatsoever. Which of course meant the discovery of even one error in the Bible would demonstrate that it is not the word of God. The combined effect of the pastor's two assumptions was that the entire edifice of Greg's faith rested on the ability of Greg to maintain a belief in a literal creation account and to find an answer to every apparent biblical contradiction. Greg noted the problem these assumptions created for him: "Since we were taught that it had to be absolutely inerrant to be God's Word, our faith in it could be destroyed by one verse being proved to contain a mistake."[4] While the church didn't hold to believing in a literal creation account or the inerrancy of Scripture was required for salvation, they made them essential doctrines of the Christian faith. If just one of them proved to be in error, then Christianity was a sham.

In his first semester in college, Greg enrolled in a course on evolutionary biology. To prepare, he read several apologetics books arguing against

3. Boyd, *Benefit*, 29.

4. Boyd, *Benefit*, 158.

evolution and for young Earth creationism. Fully convinced of his position, he took it upon himself to regularly challenge his professor in class on what he perceived as the foolishness of evolution. To his utter dismay the professor was able to dismantle his arguments:

> The professor, who was always very gracious and seemed to welcome my enthusiastic pushbacks, would gently proceed to show how objections and counter interpretations were misinformed and/or wildly implausible.[5]

Despite his best efforts to show the professor the error of his ways, he lamented, "Without fail, the professor managed to gently expose the weaknesses of my objections."[6] Eventually, this took its toll, and by mid-term Greg doubted his faith. His description of it is vivid:

> The pain of the cognitive dissonance this doubt created in me was like nothing I ever experienced before . . . by the end of the summer school course on evolution I was a tormented young man who was slowly being ripped in two, with my longing for faith and the evidence for evolution pulling me in different directions.[7]

If that wasn't enough, Greg next enrolled in a class that studied the Bible from a historical critical perspective. Historical critical methodology is an approach to investigating the Bible from what is intended to be a position of neutrality. It does not assume the Bible is the inspired word of God, for that matter, it doesn't consider the Bible to be any different from any other ancient text. It approaches the Bible just as it would the works of the Jewish historian Josephus, the Roman historian Tacitus, or the Greek historian Thucydides. In doing so, it asks questions such as: who is the author of the text in question, how did the texts develop over time, and are the claims of the text historically accurate? The tools developed by the historical critical method are not in and of themselves necessarily problematic. Many evangelical scholars are open to the various ways that historical criticism can shed light on the Bible. At the same time, they are also quite aware that the overall impact of historical criticism on biblical studies has been overwhelmingly negative. That's because the ideology governing most historical critical scholars for over a century can be characterized as rationalistic skepticism toward the miraculous and supernatural.[8] The result in the secular academy has

5. Boyd, *Benefit*, 29.

6. Boyd, *Benefit*,

7. Boyd, *Benefit*,

8. This is very simple and there is more to be said about the problems with

been to completely undermine the historical accuracy of the Old Testament. For example, it is common for non-Christian biblical scholars to hold the following positions: the Pentateuch was not written by Moses, but several authors over at least 1,000 years and later combined into one book, and that the Israelites were a nomadic tribe living in the land of Canaan and were never slaves in Egypt. Therefore, the Exodus never happened, consequently Joshua never led the Israelites into the Promised Land. The conquest stories were compiled many years later, perhaps during the Babylonian exile to provide the people with a sense of identity. Furthermore, prophetic books, specifically the Book of Daniel, which seems to accurately predict the future, were actually written after the events occurred.

You don't need to be a prophet to see where all of this is heading. Already reeling from the disorienting experience in his evolutionary biology class, the full-on frontal assault leveled at the trustworthiness of Scripture eroded the little faith Greg had left. Unable to refute or even respond to the challenge of higher criticism, he was forced to admit to himself the Bible was not inerrant. But, doing so forced him into an uncomfortable position. He was now an evolutionist who believed the Bible was filled with historical errors, and, at the same time, a Christian who deeply loved Jesus. Difficult though it was, in the battle between what his heart wanted to believe and what his mind was convinced of, he was compelled to side with maintaining his intellectual integrity. Given that his church convinced him that literal six-day creation and inerrancy were essential Christian doctrines, what else could he do but abandon Christianity, since he no longer believed them?

And so . . . Greg deconverted. "I concluded my fight was hopeless. The obstacles to my faith were too formidable . . . I finally concluded that evolution was true and that the Bible was no different from other ancient works . . . I returned to the atheism I'd embraced in the four years leading up to my conversion."[9]

Four Perspectives On Deconversion

Why did Greg lose his faith? The answer might seem simple and obvious. He lost his faith because he became convinced that evolution was true and that the Bible had errors in it. But things are often not the way they seem. Greg's loss of faith appears to be underwritten by other more subtle factors.

---

historical criticism. For a thorough treatment see Eta Linnemann, *Historical Criticism of the Bible, Methodology or Ideology?* or Umberto Cassuto, *The Documentary Hypothesis and the Composition of the Pentateuch: Eight Lectures by U. Cassuto.*

9. Boyd, *Benefit*, 30.

Theologians are likely to point out that the problem wasn't that Greg believed in a literal creation account and inerrant Bible; many Christians share those beliefs and never are tempted to abandon their faith. Instead, Greg's problem was that his church elevated those beliefs to a place where the entire Christian religion depended on them being true. They leveraged his faith on being able to answer every possible challenge to the trustworthiness of the Bible. Why would they do such a thing? Because of their unexamined assumptions about what the Bible *had* to be. They assumed that if the Bible was the inspired word of God, it had to be inerrant. Therefore, any error in the text would immediately disprove it, resulting in the collapse of the entire edifice of Christianity. Moreover, they also assumed that speaking literally was the only way to speak truly, which is why Greg invested so much effort in demonstrating that evolution was false. He had to, if he was to maintain his belief in inerrancy. Theologians will argue that Greg's church was guilty of elevating far too many beliefs to the level of being an essential of the faith. Like Saul, who made David wear armor that was too big and burdensome for him when he went to fight Goliath, Greg's church required him to affirm numerous secondary and tertiary doctrines to be a true believer. And like David, who could not bear the weight of Saul's armor, Greg found the weight and narrowness of their theology too much to bear. Unfortunately for him, instead of questioning the assumptions he inherited from the church concerning what divine inspiration requires and what it means for the Bible to speak truly, he accepted them without question and followed them to their logical conclusion. In the end, he had little use for such a demanding set of doctrines and, like David who threw off Saul's armor, Greg threw off his church's take on Christianity.

The second interpretation of Greg's deconversion is sociological. Sociologists will also acknowledge that Greg's changing views on evolution and inerrancy did have a role in his loss of faith but like theologians they too point to other factors, which gave those beliefs their force. Coming from an unbelieving home meant that Greg's church community was entirely responsible for his socialization into the faith. It was from his fundamentalist Pentecostal church that Greg received his "take" on Christianity. They indoctrinated him into the faith by passing on their theology and their perspective on how to live as a Christian. In many ways, Greg's story is no different from thousands of individuals, who like, him came, from non-Christian homes and who were discipled by the church they came to know the Lord through. But, unlike Greg, many of those have not left the faith. What was it about Greg's experience that set him up for failure?

The sociological answer lies in two separate but intimately related factors. The first is the failure of Greg's church community to provide the kind of spiritual formation he needed to counter the formation he received at the hands of a secular culture that set the conditions for what he could reasonably believe. Second, and related, it also failed to pass on to him a version of the faith that was compatible with living in the twenty-first century. Instead of giving him a theologically robust set of beliefs that had a fighting chance against the challenges of an increasingly secular culture, they passed on to him an aberrant, shallow, emotional belief system that wilted in the face of its first encounter with opposition. Greg's fundamentalist Christianity was so intent on not compromising or being conformed to the world that it retreated from it socially and intellectually. In doing so, it created a cultural enclave that worked well for those who remained in it by reinforcing both the belief system and lifestyle. But if a member were to venture out and engage with the ideas and habits of the "world," it would lead to a collision of two radically different approaches to reality. As Greg's story illustrates, how his church community made sense of the world could not compete with the explanatory power that he encountered in the secular interpretation. From a sociological point of view, the issues of evolution and inerrancy were not the real reason that Greg lost his faith, they were simply the means by which the failure of the church's socialization became evident.

The third perspective on Greg's deconversion takes a more philosophical approach. The discipline of philosophy is concerned (among other things), with conceptual analysis. Concepts are abstract mental images we think *with* when we think *about* various aspects of the world. Philosophers analyze concepts to determine if they accurately describe the nature of the thing they represent. Concepts are vitally important to pay attention to because they operate on the unthought or presuppositional level of our noetic structure. We simply take our concepts for granted, which makes them so important. If we hold to an inaccurate concept of something that is crucial to a vibrant faith we might find ourselves in a crisis of faith that could have been avoided had we just engaged in a bit of conceptual analysis. A close reading of Greg's story reveals that the church instilled in him a distorted conception of faith that led him to experience a deep feeling of hopelessness, one that ironically only found relief by renouncing his commitment to Christ. Like the theological and sociological perspectives on Greg's deconversion, a philosophical take on his loss of faith agrees that it wasn't so much his belief in inerrancy and creationism that caused the problem. But, where the theologian sees assumptions about the *content* of the faith as the problem, and the sociologist sees the problem as a faith that was inflexible and out of touch with the culture, the philosopher sees Greg's deconversion as grounded in his conception of the nature of belief itself.

Greg was fully convinced that the Bible was inerrant and that, as a result, what it taught about creation was the literal truth. But, why was he so certain? One reason—as noted above—is that Greg's fundamentalist church made those two doctrines essential matters of the faith. They were non-negotiable. Meaning, if one is to be a Christian, then he must believe that the Bible is inerrant and that the Earth was created in six literal twenty-four-hour days about 10,000 years ago. But, that, in and of itself, doesn't account for the problem. Someone can believe something without being certain of it. Many Christians maintain their faith without being absolutely certain that it is true. In Greg's case, however, he was taught that real faith lacked doubt. In his church, the greater the degree of certainty a believer had, the greater and more genuine his faith was. Being certain of the truths of Christianity was an indication of deep faith. Of his experience at the fundamentalist church, Greg noted, "Questioning matters of faith was viewed with suspicion, and expressing outright doubt was considered positively immoral."[10] And, for a time, Greg fit in well at the church. He described himself as enjoying

> The euphoria of feeling absolutely certain I had found "the truth" through my senior year of high school. I was absolutely certain I had one single eternally important purpose in life, which was to help others discover "the truth."[11]

It makes sense that if being a Christian meant believing a certain set of truth claims, and believing meant being certain, why, then, Greg was so certain of inerrancy and creationism. He was convinced Christianity was true, and those doctrines (according to his church) were essential to Christianity, so, by extension, he was certain of them. The problem began when he lost his certainty in doctrines he took to be essential, and the process reversed itself. Doubting what he took to be essential doctrines of the faith meant doubting his entire faith. Doubt meant he wasn't certain, and, in his mind, if he wasn't certain, he didn't believe. When faith and doubt are seen as polar opposites, once doubt creeps in, faith ceases to exist. Why did Greg conceive of faith as being certain and lacking doubt?

Greg inherited his conception about faith from his church, which unfortunately equated faith with full mental assent. According to this view, being a Christian simply means affirming *that* certain doctrines are true. Admittedly, one has to affirm that certain doctrines are true to be a Christian. The problem lies in which doctrines and then equating faith with mental assent and mental assent with certainty. When one understands faith to

10. Boyd, *Benefit*, 11.

11. Boyd, *Benefit*,

be mental assent and mental assent to be synonymous with certainty, faith is reduced to a feeling or mere psychological state. The obvious danger is that psychological feelings naturally ebb and flow due to any number of factors. Greg's ebbed so low that he could not recover. Unable to retain his certainty, he concluded he no longer had any faith and acknowledged to himself he was no longer a Christian. From that point, it did not take long for him to return to atheism and a life of drugs and illicit behavior. Philosophically speaking, having an inadequate conception of faith played a major role in Greg's loss of faith.

A fourth perspective on why Greg lost his faith is existential in nature. This explanation emphasizes that the negative treatment Greg received from those within the church played a critical role in his deconversion. In other words, he lost his faith because other believers in the church hurt him. To see why, recall what happened when Greg confided in his Christian friends that his experience at university had resulted in a crisis of faith. When Greg was in the valley of despair due to his increasing doubts, he felt he didn't have anyone to turn to for help. According to him, he couldn't find an intelligent Christian he could go to and share his struggles with. The problem for Greg was twofold. One was finding an intelligent Christian that could address his questions in a thoughtful and caring way, but no one in his circles was up to the apologetic task. His second problem was finding a Christian he could open up to about his struggles. So, he turned to his friends from church, a church that, in his words, viewed doubt as "outright immoral."[12] Tragically, instead of being a source of comfort, they only made him feel worse by blaming him for bringing the crisis on himself. First, they chastised him for going to a public university. In doing so, he was just asking for trouble. Then, they charged him with "playing the Devil's poker"[13] by taking a class on evolutionary biology. In their minds, he had brought his troubles on himself, and they had no problem letting him know that. That was not exactly what Greg was looking for from his comforters. His cry for help elicited only chastisement. Greg was hurt and frustrated. The very people who should have brought him relief in his hour of greatest need added to his pain.

While sad, the fact that his church family wounded Greg isn't at all surprising when one considers other deconversion narratives. In doing so, it becomes apparent that a common thread woven throughout the stories of ex-Christians is the role of the church in their deconversion. Time after time, former believers claim that being wounded by church leadership

12. Boyd, *Benefit*,.

13. Boyd, *Benefit*, 30.

or rank-and-file believers was the catalyst that started their deconversion. Therefore, if deconversion necessarily means no longer believing the claims of Christianity are true, it appears being mistreated by fellow believers has the power to elevate doubts and uncertainties to critical levels. Undoubtedly, experience shows the body of Christ has an unfortunate practice of executing their own wounded. Rather than coming alongside struggling believers and helping to bear their burden, the testimony of former believers indicates that, all too often, we add to it.

Looking at the four different takes on Greg's deconversion, we see that although, on the surface, it looks like his loss of faith can be explained by simply pointing to a crisis regarding two doctrines, in reality there was much more going on. Greg's story shows, not surprisingly, that there is more than one way to lose one's faith. What makes his deconversion unique is that four notable factors came together in one person's experience. Those four factors were theological, sociological, philosophical, and existential in nature. Yet, the one thing all of the different factors share in common is that they all can be traced to the preparation stage of the recipe. The problems stem from Greg's religious socialization. His experience at the church left him theologically over- prepared, sociologically under-prepared, philosophically ill-prepared, and existentially painfully prepared when it came to his faith. One of these alone is enough to cause a spiritual crisis leading to the loss of faith, but all four in the life of one individual makes the loss of faith almost inevitable.[14]

Four Degrees of Preparation

Over-prepared

When I claim that a significant factor in Greg's loss of faith was that he was theologically over-prepared, I'm referring to the preparation that Greg received from his church in relation to what beliefs and behaviors were required for authentic Christian identity. The theological, doctrinal, and lifestyle assumptions that his church required him to hold about the nature of Christianity were inflexible and excessive. Assumptions, as I refer to them, are the taken for granted beliefs about a claim or aspect of reality. They are views regarding what is true about an aspect of the world, and they provide

14 Greg eventually came back to the Lord and today is a pastor of a large and vibrant church in Minnesota. He is the author of numerous books on theology dealing with a wide variety of theological issues. The story of his loss and eventual rediscovery of faith can be found in his book *Benefit of the Doubt: Breaking the Idol of Certainty*, Baker Books, (2013).

the starting point from which further reasoning is done. Assumptions can be caught and taught. But, either way, once a person assumes something to be true, it remains generally unquestioned and is taken to be "just the way things are." For example, growing up, all of the adults in my life had false teeth. Naturally, therefore, I formed the assumption that all adults had false teeth and that at some point in the future, so would I. That assumption played a role in how well I took care of my teeth as a kid. I had lots of cavities, and it seemed every time I went in for a check-up I ended up getting several fillings. I thought, what's the big deal with brushing and flossing and rinsing, I'm just going to get false teeth when I hit twenty anyway? I remember thinking, when I was twelve years old, why are my parents wasting so much money putting braces on my teeth when I will only have them for another ten years or so? You can imagine my surprise and relief when I found out that not all adults lose their teeth. I also started taking better care of my teeth, too.

Assumptions play a powerful role in all aspects of our lives. Which is why it shouldn't be all that surprising that assumptions play a significant role in deconversion. Marriage counselors are well aware of the damage that unacknowledged assumptions and unacknowledged expectations can have in a marriage. In their book *Saving Your Marriage Before It Starts*, psychologists and husband-and-wife team, Les and Leslie Parrot focus on the problem that unacknowledged assumptions can have in a marriage. They point out that both men and women come into marriages with unrecognized "ideas about what it would and should be like to be a married couple."[15] But, all too often, it doesn't occur to them that their spouse may not have the same ideas. They simply take for granted that they do, which often results in unmet expectations and feelings of disillusionment and resentment.

Early in our marriage, Nancy and I discovered the trouble that assumptions can cause. I was leaving for a week of teaching at a college about four hours from our home. After I had packed the car and was ready to go, I stood at the door to say goodbye to Nancy and waited for her to give me the bag of snacks she'd put together for me so I would have something to eat on the trip. The problem was that Nancy hadn't packed a bag of snacks. She hadn't even thought of packing a bag of snacks. So when I asked her where it was, she was a bit confused. She asked me why I would think she had a bag of snacks for me when I had never asked her to make one. Now I was the one who was confused. "Why should I have to ask?" I thought to myself, "You're my wife, that's just what you're supposed to do." Looking back on it now it seems silly (not to mention presumptuous, some may say sexist),

15. Parrot, *Saving Your Marriage*, 21.

but at the time I was upset. I was mad at Nancy for not doing something I had expected her to do based on what I assumed her role as a wife was. But, Nancy hadn't shared that same assumption about her role as a wife. My unrecognized and, therefore, unquestioned assumption led inexorably to my unmet expectations. This resulted in me feeling hurt, and it resulted in tension in our relationship.

Where had I gotten the notion that it was Nancy's job to make me a snack for the road? I got it from my own upbringing. As the Parrots point out, "Every person's expectation of who does what in their new marriage are shaped by the home they grew up in."[16] In my home, growing up, my mother always made me a snack for the road anytime I traveled. I never had to even think about packing a lunch, because I just knew she would. It was one way she expressed her love for me. I had unknowingly internalized the expectation that my wife would and should do the same. I never thought about it consciously, it was just something I expected based on what I assumed about her role as a wife and what I assumed about how love was expressed.

The fault for my assumptions and expectations lies entirely with me. My mother never taught me that if someone loves you they make you a lunch for the road! I had mistakenly formed that assumption on my own. However, all families do pass on or teach beliefs to their children that they internalize and which, for better or worse, become their assumptions about the world. The general beliefs that our parents either model or instill in us can set us up for success or failure. If they provide for us accurate assumptions about the world by which to guide our lives, then we have a good chance of being a flourishing person. If, on the other hand, they pass on to us beliefs we take for granted that are inaccurate, then we are likely to fall short of being a flourishing person.

I'm convinced that something similar is the case with our spiritual formation. In terms of deconversion, the content of one's assumptions plays a major role in leading to either a flourishing faith or a crisis of faith. Where do those assumptions come from? They come from parents and churches. The role of Christian parents and of the church is to disciple and train up those for whom they are responsible, whether that is their children or the members of the local church. A major aspect of that process is teaching them the essential doctrines of the faith. Parents and the church are to prepare believers by instructing them in the essentials of Christian doctrine and guiding them to live in a manner consistent with those teachings. But, just as a chef can over-prepare the ingredients of a

16. Parrot, *Saving Your Marriage*, 26.

recipe and negatively affect the meal, so too can parents and churches over-prepare those in their care.

Over-preparation occurs when parents or churches mistakenly equate their unique take on Christianity with the essentials of Christianity itself. They then require those for whom they are responsible to disciple to accept and maintain belief in the entire package to maintain an authentic Christian identity. Such an approach implants in believers a host of assumptions about what Christianity is and *must* be. This pre-packaged, overly specific, burdensome take on Christianity is assumed to just be Christianity. Which means that if one questions, doubts, or becomes convinced that a particular belief or interpretation is wrong, then the entire edifice of Christianity is in jeopardy of collapsing. The entire package stands or falls together. This is exactly the mindset that Greg had:

> While the fundamentalist church I came to Christ in acknowledged that there were certain beliefs that were "non-essential to salvation" and were okay to disagree over, we had a host of beliefs that we insisted were absolutely crucial. If any of these were removed, the whole edifice of our theology flattened out like a pancake.[17]

In short, over-preparation occurs when believers are taught that a specific take on Christianity is the true version of the faith. When believers assume that many, if not all, of their tradition's interpretations, theological positions, and secondary beliefs are in fact essential aspects of Christianity, they are over-prepared believers. A sign that a believer is over-prepared is the number of doctrines they take to be matters essential to be authentically Christian. The higher the number of doctrines they assume are essential to the faith, the greater the chances for a crisis of faith. It should be easy to see why. If an individual assumes that authentic Christianity is a set of prepackaged doctrines, then if one of those doctrines turns out to be wrong, Christianity is shown to be false. Over- prepared believers have a religious faith that stands or falls like a house of cards. Indeed, Greg described his early faith as a house of cards:

> I was taught that if the Earth was not created in six literal days and if Adam and Eve were not literal, historical people, then the whole Bible may as well be a book of lies. Flick this one card out, and the whole structure of faith collapses . . . Since we were taught that it [the Bible] had to be absolutely "inerrant" to be

17. Boyd, *Benefit*, 158.

> God's word, our faith in it could be destroyed by one verse being proved to be a mistake. The Bible itself was a house of cards.[18]

No doubt there are essential doctrines that constitute Christianity and which one cannot deny and still be a Christian. But in the case of many deconverts, it is clear that they equated many nonessential doctrines, interpretations, and theological positions as constituting the essence of Christianity. They assumed their set of beliefs, in total, constituted true Christianity.

Again, Greg's experience at his fundamentalist church serves as an example. After he became a believer, he was discipled by a church that passed on to him a set of beliefs that they identified as authentic Christianity. They mistook their take on Christianity for Christianity itself. They equated their entire set of beliefs with what was essential for Greg to believe and how he was to behave if he wanted to be a true Christian. Of course, Greg knew no better. He trusted the leadership in the church and assumed that everything they told him was true Christianity rather than their particular take on it. But, in their fundamentalist fervor they elevated so many doctrines, interpretations, and theological positions to the level of being essential to the faith that they set him up for a coming crisis. Why? Because it required him to continually believe and defend doctrines that in his mind were indefensible, both theologically and scientifically. Add to that the "all-or-nothing" ultimatum regarding the prepackaged faith they presented Greg with, and it's easy to see how the church set him up for a crisis of faith.

As mentioned above, there are essential doctrines that one must accept to be born again. There are several more that one must affirm to be a theologically orthodox Christian. But even combining the two categories of belief adds up to a relatively small number of beliefs that one must adhere to in order to be orthodox in one's beliefs. In the case of many former believers, the problem appears to be that they were expected to affirm not only the basic orthodox doctrines of Christianity but many secondary and tertiary doctrines as well, along with certain lifestyle expectations. Combined, they constitute what it means to be a "real Christian." This presented them with an all-or-nothing proposal.

> X constitutes authentic Christianity. Either you believe X or you are not an authentic Christian.

The above amounts to equating a particular take on Christianity rather than the essentials of Christianity itself. In Greg's church, the essential set of beliefs included not only those found in the creeds, but also inerrancy, creationism, specific baptismal formulas, and a long list of legalistic beliefs and practices.

18. Boyd, *Benefit*, 158.

For Greg, "Christianity" just *was* all of those things. He couldn't reject one belief of the total set of beliefs if he wanted to be a true Christian. So, it logically followed that when he became convinced that the Bible had errors in it and that evolution was true, he left the faith. His loss of faith can be clearly correlated with the fact that his church over-prepared him theologically by requiring him to accept their take on Christianity, burdening him with a host of doctrines that were non-essentials of orthodox faith.

Under-prepared

When I claim that a significant factor in Greg's loss of faith was that he was sociologically under-prepared, I'm saying that Greg's church failed to adequately provide for him the kind of effective and cognitive spiritual formation he needed to meet the challenges of the twenty-first century. This became painfully obvious during his first semester at university. The first two classes that he took shook his faith to the core. Although the experiences that caused Greg to doubt his faith were acute and sudden, they are indicative of the kind of challenges to the faith that educated, culturally sensitive Christians encounter over and over again as they make their way through the modern world. In that regard, Greg, a student at a major public university, was no exception. He was living in an environment that his Christian faith could not relate to nor meaningfully make sense of. Over time, the accumulated incongruity or disequilibrium that can build up between what one believes to be true about Christianity and the conflicting experience that living in our socio-cultural milieu can produce can be overwhelming.

One summer our family took a trip to the Pacific Northwest. One of the places we visited was the Ballard Locks, just outside of Seattle on Puget Sound. We happened to be there at the time salmon were spawning, and we were delighted to find out the Ballard Locks had a viewing station below the water line that allowed us to see hundreds of salmon migrating upstream to reproduce in the fresh waters of Lake Washington and Lake Union. Every year, salmon, after spending years in the Pacific Ocean and swimming thousands of miles, make the arduous trek back to the very freshwater spawning grounds, where, years prior, they hatched. To assist the salmon in this amazing voyage, the Ballard Locks built a salmon ladder, a series of low steps that allow the salmon to navigate upriver, avoiding the locks that otherwise would make their journey even more difficult than it already is. The last thing salmon need is more obstacles than they already have on their journey to the spawning grounds! Their trip is fraught with so many obstacles and challenges that it is amazing that any salmon reach their destination. For instance, some salmon swim over 900 miles and climb 7,000 feet before reaching their objective. On the way, they will encounter predators in the form of otters, bears, and bald eagles and have to surmount waterfalls and rapids, which they overcome by leaping through the air. The result of such an arduous journey is that many salmon never make it to the spawning grounds. In fact, only a small percentage of salmon do complete the trip. Those males that survive the trip are often haggard, having disturbingly humped backs, bent jaws, and torn fins. The females are bloated with a pound or more of eggs. Both have sizable white patches of bruised skin on their bodies. Those who are able to do so mate, reproduce, and then die of exhaustion shortly thereafter. It is an astonishing feat and a testament to the instinctual drive that the salmon have to reproduce that they will die to pass on their genes.

As we watched the salmon struggling up the salmon ladder against the unremitting current, it struck me how their struggle served as an illustration of how difficult it can be to maintain religious faith in the twenty-first century. Just as the salmon are besieged by and must fight against powerful natural forces that comprise the very environment in which they live, religious believers must struggle against powerful socio-cultural forces that are inimical to their faith. And, just as the turbulent current takes a devastating physical toll on the salmon, ultimately eliminating many from the spawning run, so, too, the socio-cultural challenges against religious faith that comprise our culture can take a spiritual toll on believers. While people often look for a specific cause for individuals losing their faith, in reality, it is almost never one cause. True, there is often a specific *reason* that deconverts identify as the final straw that broke the camel's back, but in many cases the loss of faith is the result of the cumulative effect of continually swimming culturally upstream. Exhausted and battered, many former believers eventually turn around and swim with the cultural current. Metaphorically speaking, western Christians, in the early decades of the twenty-first century, find themselves culturally swimming upstream, and the incline continues to increase.

Greg's story is a real-life example of a believer who was under-prepared to face the socio-cultural challenges to his faith. Due to his church experience, he was unable to integrate his faith with the world he lived in, and being out of step with culture took its toll. His fundamentalist Pentecostal church did not assist him in thinking well about the relationship between faith and culture. Instead it focused on having spiritual experiences with the Holy Spirit and being separate from the world. Rather than assisting the young believers in their church to engage with the cultural issues of the day that were challenging to the faith, they offered a version of Christianity that was simplistic and unrelated to the complexities of the modern world. Greg was forced to draw upon the resources of a Sunday school faith to respond to university questions. Those resources were found to be insufficient, and as a result, he, like the so many others who could not endure the socio-cultural challenges, floundered in his faith.

What Greg needed was a way to faithfully interact with the modern world, a world that is far different from the world of the Bible. The pages of Scripture record life in the ancient near east, a time and place with a radically different understanding of the world than that of our own. That world was enchanted, suffused with the supernatural. Gods, angels, demons, fantastic creatures, divination, and magic were normative features of the ancient worldview. Every aspect of the culture reinforced belief in a supernatural cosmos. From the king down through the priests to the prostitute, the sociological ordering principles of life were grounded in a religious mythology that gave each aspect of society its place and purpose. Our contemporary situation is far different. Nearly all major cultural institutions, including the education system, the courts, the market, the entertainment industry, and even the health care system are secular on principle. Religion plays little to no role in our public square. But, not only is the socio-cultural milieu of the ancient near east different than ours, its beliefs about the world are radically different from ours, as well. The ancient near eastern world, out of which the Old Testament emerged, held that the world was a flat disk sitting on four pillars and covered with a dome with holes in it that allowed rain to fall. It assumed the existence of a pantheon of gods who were in competition with one another. That the entrails of an animal could tell the future, and that the flight paths of birds were omens of things to come.[19] Famine, disease, and victories or defeats in war were seen as a direct result of the gods. Contrast that with our present situation.

Thanks to advances in science and technology, we have eradicated diseases that threatened to kill millions of people. We have not only landed on the Moon, but we have also put a rover on Mars. We have mapped the human genome and its 20,000 genes, allowing us to test and treat for specific illnesses in utero! We have engineered babies by combining the genetic material from three adults. And, we theoretically have the ability to create fetuses without the need of a male through a process that tricks the egg into acting like it has been fertilized. The result is a genetically identical clone of the mother. We have created self-driving cars and artificial intelligence. We can see almost back to the beginning of the universe and explain the mathematics and physics, which underwrite it with tremendous precision. How,

19. Alexander and Baker, *Dictionary of the Old Testament*, 193.

given all of that, are we to reconcile reality as we have come to know it with the Bible's claim that a talking snake tricked two naked people into eating a piece of fruit, and that is why the world is in such a mess? Does such a thing even make sense? How can any educated believer not ask themselves, "Have we not outgrown this stuff and come of age?" Can we really be sophisticated, educated individuals and still retain beliefs about such things?

Sustaining one's faith and being immersed in the socio-cultural milieu of the modern world is not easy. Like Greg, many young people are under-prepared to survive the challenges that our increasingly secular culture presents them with. Instead of developing a robust faith that can be articulated in contemporary terms, they have a malnourished faith that has not kept up with the times in which it exits and is, therefore, in danger of becoming culturally irrelevant. Believers are under-prepared when they are poorly socialized/discipled by the church. By that, I mean the church does not pass on to them a faith that can be made sense of in contemporary terms and is applicable to contemporary issues.

As a result, believers begin to see Christianity not only as outdated, but irrelevant. It's one thing to believe in a religion that is thousands of years old, as long as it has some cultural relevance. But when it becomes increasingly marginalized in the public square and relegated to a private faith that has no significance in the larger social context, maintaining faith becomes difficult. Perhaps that is why large numbers of former Christians identify their deconversion as a kind of "coming of age" story. Christianity, like Santa Claus, was fine to believe in as children, but not as educated western moderns of the twenty-first century. An ironic twist on the words spoken by the apostle Paul aptly expresses the sentiments of under-prepared believers, "When I was a child, I talked like a child, I reasoned like a child. When I became a man, I put the ways of childhood behind me." (1 Cor 13:11 NIV)

Ill-prepared

A significant factor in deconversion is being philosophically ill-prepared. By philosophically ill-prepared I do not mean that believers lose their faith because they enrolled in a philosophy course from a public institution, or that their church did not make them read philosophy from a Christian perspective. Rather, what I mean is that in terms of their noetic structure, they have internalized faulty conceptions of critical biblical issues. The faulty assumptions were either explicitly taught in their Christian sub-culture or they were unconsciously modeled in those sub-cultures. Either way, the damage that faulty conceptions can do is tremendous. Faulty conceptions lead to expectations, and when expectations go unmet it can open the door to a crisis of faith.

When I was growing up, every year my parents would take my brother and me to Florida for spring break. My grandmother, who lived next door to us in Canada in the summer months, would go to Daytona Beach to spend the winter in a beachfront condo. One of the things we always did when we visited her was to go to the local flea market to see what treasures we might find. While my parents looked at produce and practical items, I kept an eye out for novelties and random cool things to buy. I remember one time, when I was about fifteen years old, I was walking along looking at the various booths when I looked up and saw a man pouring water into a clear glass. He asked me if I wanted a drink but before I could answer he thrust the full glass of water at me as if he was intending to drench me with water. I ducked and covered, trying to protect myself from getting hit in the face with water. But, to my surprise, nothing came out of the glass! The water had somehow instantaneously solidified as he poured it in the glass and yet retained its transparent nature. When he thrust the glass at me, the now-transparent rubbery substance remained in the glass. It was the coolest trick I had ever seen. As it turned out, in the bottom of the glass—before any water had been poured in—was a substance that chemically changed the water from a liquid to a solid upon contact. The magician called it a superabsorbent powder. Needless to say, I bought the powder from him, and once I owned the trick, he quickly instructed me in how to use it. He handed me the bag with the powder and a set of instructions, and I was on my way, thinking about whom I would use my new and very cool trick on.

Later that day, when we got home from the flea market, my grandmother's friend, Mary, came over to visit. Mary, like my grandmother, was a snowbird. She came from southern Ontario to spend the winter in Florida. I had gotten to know Mary fairly well from seeing her for about two weeks a year over the last seven or eight years, so I knew she would appreciate a good magic trick. Excited to try out my new trick, I asked Mary if she would like a glass of water. She said, yes, she would and that she appreciated me asking her. I went to the kitchen and got a pitcher, filled it with water and then a glass, which I then poured the superabsorbent powder into just as the guy at the flea market had told me. I took them out to the living room where Mary was seated on the sofa. Sitting right across from Mary, I talked with her while I poured the water, making sure she could see the water going into the glass. Then, came the moment of truth. I looked at Mary and said, "You want some water, Mary? Well, here it is!" And with that, I thrust the open end of the glass at the kindly eighty-five-year-old lady sitting directly across from me. I was about to make her day by doing a magic trick she would tell her friends about for years. But, something quite unexpected happened. Something I will never forget as long as I live. To my horror, the water in the glass had not turned into a complete solid. Rather, it had gone from a liquid to the consistency of oatmeal. And instead of remaining in the glass as it was supposed to, it came hurling out and hit Mary right in the face. I can still see her sitting there, wiping slimy gel off her glasses and from around her mouth. My grandmother was mortified! Mary was in shock, and I was trying to apologize and explain what had happened. To make matters worse, Mary simply looked at me. Confused and hurt, she said, "Why would you do that to me?" I tried my best to explain, but there was no use. Nothing I said could make the situation any better. Mary went back to her condo to change her clothes, and I went to read the instructions to figure out why things had gone so wrong.

What I discovered when I read the instructions was that, although what the man who sold me the magic powder told me about using it was accurate, it was also incomplete. His directions had left me ill-prepared for pulling off the trick successfully. Yes, I had to put the powder in first, but what he didn't tell me was how much! I assumed that the amount that he showed me at the flea market was the standard amount. Although I used a bigger glass for Mary, I used the same amount of powder he had showed me at the flea market. Obviously, I hadn't used enough. If I had read the instructions before trying the trick, I would have discovered, as the instructions had made clear, that the bigger the glass, the more powder was required. It wasn't that the guy at the flea market had given me wrong information, it's that he hadn't give me enough information. I was ill-prepared to successfully perform the trick.

Like the magician who gave me correct but insufficient instructions for the trick, Greg's church gave him an incomplete notion of what "believing in Jesus" means. Being the good fundamentalist Pentecostal church that it was, the leadership rightly emphasized that salvation is secured not through good works but through belief in Jesus. Numerous times in the gospels and throughout the epistles it stated that believing in Jesus is the criterion for salvation. Jesus himself said, "For God so loved the world he gave his one and only son, that whoever believes in him shall not perish but have eternal life." (John 3:16 NIV) Paul explicitly affirmed that salvation comes through believing in Jesus when asked by the Philippian jailer in Acts 16, "Sirs, what must I do to be saved?" They said, "Believe in the Lord Jesus, and you will be saved, you and your household." (Acts 8:30–31 NIV) Salvation is dependent on believing in Jesus. Likewise, other writers of the New Testament, such as Peter, John, and Jude repeatedly state that salvation comes by way of believing in Jesus. The Scriptures are clear believing in Jesus is necessary for salvation. However, the question is, what does the Bible mean when it uses the word belief?

The church Greg attended assumed it knew what the Bible means when it uses the word "believe." Regrettably, as we will see, their assumption was only partially accurate. Although what they assumed about the biblical concept of "belief" was indeed a necessary component of biblical belief, it was not sufficient to encompass all that biblical faith is. Their understanding of belief lacked other necessary components to accurately reflect the Bible's teaching. In fact, it not only didn't accurately reflect the Bible's notion of belief, it significantly distorted it.

Even though Greg's faith community was fundamentalist and anti-intellectual, they unwittingly transmitted to him an unbiblical, overly cognitive conception of what it means to believe in Jesus. Their error was equating the rich biblical understanding of what it means to believe *in* Jesus with mental assent *that* propositions about Jesus are true. The logical conclusion of such a view ultimately ends up equating biblical faith with psychological certainty. Tragically, equating the two left Greg ill-prepared to deal with the doubts and intellectual struggles that he inevitably encountered. When Greg began doubting that the Earth was created in six, twenty-four hour days approximately 10,000 years ago and that the Bible was inerrant, it was equivalent to outright unbelief. It should be easy to see why; if believing in Jesus just *is* believing propositions about him are true, the more convinced one is that the propositions are true, the more belief one has. Having doubts and raising questions are antithetical to this notion of belief. According to this paradigm, the person who claims, "I am absolutely certain that Jesus rose from the dead!" is an example of robust, admirable belief. Whereas the person who says, "I am committed to the faith, but I am struggling with the idea that Jesus rose from the dead," lacks belief. In reality, both cases reveal much more about the psychological makeup of the individuals than it does the nature of their faith. The first may simply be a more confident person than the second, but confidence has little to do with biblical faith.

While genuine biblical faith does require believing certain propositions, it is much more than that. Genuine biblical faith is principally a commitment of oneself to the person of Christ, trusting in him and his work on the cross on our behalf. If trusting in Christ, as opposed to merely assenting to claims about him, is at the heart of what it means to believe in Jesus, then the individual who openly admits he is struggling with the resurrection but continues to give God the benefit of the doubt is exhibiting true biblical faith. On the other hand, the individual who has psychological certainty that Jesus rose from the dead but does not exhibit relational trust in God in the midst of an existential or intellectual test lacks biblical faith, regardless of how much psychological certainty he possesses at a given moment.

Ultimately, this view, that faith is a psychological state wherein one is certain about certain beliefs, was directly related to Greg's deconversion. As Greg became more and more convinced of evolution, his assumption that true belief meant being certain of essential biblical doctrines forced him into an untenable position. He would be forced to either acknowledge his doubt about young Earth creationism, a belief he took to be essential to the faith, or he could deny what he had come to believe about evolution at the cost of his intellectual integrity and live a lie.

Good intentions aside, from a philosophical perspective, the misguided understanding of faith that Greg's church taught him set him up for a crisis, because it confused faith (a commitment of trust) with a psychological state (certainty) that he could only maintain at the cost of his intellectual integrity. Not willing to pay such a high cost, Greg admitted he no longer believed in young-Earth creationism, which according to his church, meant he no longer believed in Christianity. Dejected, he left the faith and no longer identified as a Christian.

Churches produce ill-prepared believers and set them up for crises of faith when they do not provide them with biblically balanced notions about critical biblical concepts. For Greg, the erroneous assumption dealt with the notion of what it means to believe in Jesus; for others, it may have to do with the goodness of God, the efficacy of prayer, the relationship between virtuous living and being blessed, or any number of other issues. Believers are ill-prepared because their assumptions are only partially correct. Having wrong assumptions leaves believers prime candidates for deconversion, because it ultimately leaves them with unmet expectations of the way things should be and ill-prepared to deal with them.

Painfully Prepared

When I say that a significant factor in the process of deconversion is being painfully prepared, I mean that the emotional hurts experienced by former believers at the hands of their fellow Christians either created serious doubts about Christianity or was the catalyst that allowed them to open themselves up to investigating whether the nagging doubts they already had carried any weight. Moral failures, hypocrisy, spiritually abusive leadership, being let down or feeling unsupported in a time of need, a lack of forgiveness, judgmentalism, and self-righteousness are just of the ways that former believers have been mistreated at the hands of those who were supposedly their brothers and sisters in Christ. The wounds they received were so significant that it caused them to wonder if Christianity were true. They reasoned that if it were, why hadn't it made more of a difference in the lives of those who had mistreated them? In some cases, they reasoned that if this is what Christianity is, then who needs it?

As we have seen in cases of being over-prepared and ill-prepared, a number of assumptions deconverts uncritically adopted from their upbringing are often unwarranted or outright false. But in the case of their expectations that Christians should act like Christians, they are on more solid ground than many of their other assumptions. In fact, the expectation is grounded in the very words of Jesus himself. On the night before his trial and execution, Jesus hosted a meal for his disciples. At that meal, he shared with them his final instructions, those things that they needed to hear in order to endure through the difficult days ahead and fulfill the mission he had called them to.

One of the most important teachings that Jesus left them with that night was a litmus test for how the world would know that they were truly his disciples. In John 13:34, Jesus gave them a "new commandment."

> A new commandment I give unto you, that you should love one another as I have loved you. By this everyone will know that you are my disciples, if love one another. (John 13:34 NIV)

Their identity as Jesus's followers wasn't in how much of the Torah they could quote. It wasn't how much they tithed. Nor was it how often they prayed and fasted. Rather, it was the love that they had for one another. A love that was patient, kind, enduring, and resilient. A love that wasn't easily irritated, arrogant, rude, or resentful. Given that those character traits should identify God's people, it's no wonder that former believers were devastated when other Christians treated them poorly. I suppose one could argue that it might be a bit naive to expect Christians to always act with grace and love. But reading deconversion stories gives one the impression that it wasn't merely naive expectations that were the problem. The problem, in many cases, is that former Christians really were treated shamefully by those who identified as followers of Jesus.

There are two reasons why being wounded by other Christians is so significant in instigating deconversions. The first is that when Christians mistreat one another it casts doubt on the claims they make regarding Jesus. Jesus himself actually gives the watching world the right to call into question those claims based on how Christians treat one another. The same night he commanded the disciples to love one another, he prayed to his father on their behalf. Among the things he prayed for them—perhaps the most important—was that they would be one, just as he and the father are one. Jesus prayed, "My prayer is not for them alone. I pray also for those who will believe in me through their message, that all of them may be one, Father, just as you are in me and I am in you. May they also be in us so that the world may believe that you have sent me." (John 17:20–21 NIV) Jesus desired that his people would be a unified, loving community of individuals from all walks of life. But being at one with each other was not an end in itself; it was the means to an apologetic end, which was that the world would know that the father had sent him.

According to Jesus, Christian unity would result in what Francis Schaeffer called the ultimate apologetic:

> Yet, without true Christians loving one another, Christ says the world cannot be expected to listen, even when we give proper answers. Let us be careful, indeed, to spend a lifetime studying to give honest answers. For years the orthodox, evangelical church has done this very poorly. So it is well to spend time learning to answer the questions of men who are about us. But after we have done our best to communicate to a lost world, still we must never forget that the final apologetic which Jesus gives is the observable love of true Christians for true Christians.[20]

In other words, the way we treat each other is the primary manner by which the non-Christian world will be able to discern whether Jesus is who we claim him to be. The reason why is simple; if Jesus really is who we say he is, then the difference he makes in our lives should be easily recognizable. We, as Christians, should live in loving unity with each other just as he did with his father. Christ's love should overcome ethnic, economic, social, gender, and nationalistic differences. In a world fractured by racism, sexism, economic inequality, and xenophobia, it would take a supernatural act to overcome such things to the point where people of such vast differences and historic hostilities toward one another could not only peacefully coexist in the same group, but actually love one another. The authors of *Total Church*, Chester and Timmis, put it this way:

> What will commend the gospel are lives lived in obedience to the gospel and community life that reflects God's triune community of love. People will not believe until they are genuinely open to exploring the truth about God. They become open as they see that it is good to know God. And they see that it is good to know God as they see the love of the Christian community.[21]

20. Schaeffer, *The Great Evangelical*, 164–65.

21. Chester and Timmis, *Total Church*, 175–76.

If Christians living in love and unity, supporting and being supported, sharing each other's burdens, and building each other up is the most powerful and persuasive apologetic, then how damaging is it to the cause of Christ when Christians treat each other in unloving and divisive ways? The damage done to the witness of the church by its division and lack of love gives the world the right to question the claims we make about Christ. And, often the verdict they arrive at is that "If Jesus really is true as you say, then why doesn't he make a bigger difference in how you treat one another?" But it's not just the outside world that raises that question. Many times, it is believers themselves who have been hurt by other Christians and begin to wonder if they have bought into a lie. Time and time again, former Christians identify the less than loving ways they were treated by other believers as the catalyst for their doubts that eventually culminated in their loss of faith.

The second reason mistreatment by other Christians is a significant factor in the loss of faith has to do with the important role that interpersonal relationships play in both who we are and what we believe. The influence of interpersonal relationships and group dynamics deeply impacts our mental and emotional development and what we believe about ultimate questions, such as the existence of God. To see how, consider the 2013 study conducted by the Commission on Children at Risk entitled *Hardwired to Connect: The New Scientific Case for Authoritative Communities.*[22] The commission was comprised of thirty-three pediatricians, research scientists, mental health professionals, Dartmouth Medical School, and the YMCA of the USA. The study noted that despite the fact that children in the United States live lives that rate among the best in the world in terms of material standards of living, they exhibit higher levels of mental and emotional disorders than any time in history. And, although society has sought to address the problems through psychotherapy, medications, and special programs for at-risk children, they have by and large missed a crucially important environmental factor in mental and emotional development.

The study shows that humans (especially children and adolescents) have a biological need to be in meaningful connection with others. The report maintained "science is increasingly demonstrating that the human person is hardwired to seek connection with each other . . . beginning with mothers, fathers, and extended family, and then moving out to the broader community."[23] According to the report, we are not only hardwired for connection with

22. Kline, *Hardwired to Connect.*

23. Kline, *Authoritative Communities*, 9.

others, it appears we are also hardwired to seek "for meaning . . . and drive to search for purpose and reflect on life's ultimate ends."[24]

The above facts lead to the conclusion that if we are to see an improvement in the emotional and behavior profiles of adolescents that, along with therapy and medicine, we must emphasize the role of what the lead researcher for the Commission on Children at Risk, Kathleen Kline, refers to as "authoritative communities" in the socialization process of children. Authoritative communities are groups of individuals that are "committed to one another over time and who model and pass on at least part of what it means to be a good person and live a good life."[25] It is within such groups that children develop their identity in relation to others in the group and in such groups that a picture of the good life is modeled. Authoritative communities meet the hardwired needs we have to connect to others for moral and spiritual meaning.

Without authoritative communities in their lives, children suffer from a disconnectedness that in turn negatively impacts their mental and emotional well-being. But there is a caveat. Not all communities are conducive to producing flourishing individuals. Rather, it is those communities that exhibit characteristics such as being warm, nurturing, loving one's neighbor, and delineating clear expectations and limits that contribute to flourishing. Communities that do not express and promote these characteristics not only fall short of contributing to well-being, they harm it.

If authoritative communities that are warm and nurturing and focus on love of neighbor are vital environmental factors in children and adolescents becoming flourishing individuals, then one can imagine the potential damage that can be done by communities that in reality are either *authoritarian* communities or characterized by vices such as self-righteousness, judgmentalism, and hypocrisy. Sadly, one does not have to imagine too hard; many former Christians describe their church experience in just those terms and associate their deconversion with it. To be clear, I am not claiming that churches that behave in those ways are responsible for the emotional and behavioral problems of individuals in their sphere of influence. I am merely pointing out the fact that if the communities (churches) in which we are socialized play a pivotal role in shaping us in deep and lasting ways, we should not be surprised when former believers refer to their negative experience of the church as a contributing factor in their spiritual crisis. Therefore, we cannot underestimate the role that negative community experiences—and for Christians the community is the church—play in the loss of faith.

24. Kline, *Authoritative Communities*, 9.

25. Kline, *Authoritative Communities*, 9.

Churches as authoritative communities not only shape who we are by contributing to or detracting from our flourishing, but they also play an equally important role in what we believe. They do so because they act as the primary means by which we consider our beliefs credible. Sociologist Peter Berger argues that all beliefs are held and persist through the influence of socio-cultural institutions and processes. Therefore, if beliefs and practices are to retain their legitimacy, it is essential that they be anchored in a structure that gives them plausibility. Plausibility structures, according to Berger, are particular groups of people. If knowledge claims are going to be accepted, the groups who represent them must be viewed favorably. For example, an individual is likely to believe the claims of a political party if they view the party and those who lead it as good. But once the structure or institution is no longer viewed as either credible or good, the rationale for maintaining the belief it provided as foundation is weakened. When the political party betrays the voters and the leader has a moral failure, supporters and rank- and-file members may begin to question whether the platform of the party really is correct after all.

The parallels between the church and the example of the political party should be obvious. When confidence in the church (universal or local) is shaken through competing plausibility structures or through disenchantment at being mistreated by other Christians, it can result in a spiritual crisis. This shouldn't come as a surprise given what we have seen about the importance of the church. According to Jesus, it is the means by which his claim to be the unique Son of God can be evaluated. According to psychology, the church plays the all-important role of being an authoritative community, impacting our emotional and mental well-being for good or ill. And, according to sociology, the church functions as the plausibility structure that either gives or detracts from the credibility of the gospel. It is little wonder, then, why those who perceive their experience with the church in such negative terms identify that as a spark that ignited their deconversion.

An Invitation

Deconversion from the faith is a growing reality. Similar to a recipe, deconversions are comprised of three aspects: the ingredients, their preparation, and the environment in which they are cooked. Parents and church leaders can do little about the first and third aspects of the recipe. The personality of individuals and the socio-cultural world in which they live are, for the most part, beyond of the church's ability to influence. The second aspect, however, the preparation stage, is crucial in the deconversion recipe. If the church and the parents mishandle the raw ingredients of believers, they can unintentionally contribute to deconversion. The good news is that if churches and Christian parents take heed to the stories and insights in the following chapters, they can not only avoid setting up believers for deconversion, but also provide for them a solid foundation from which they can flourish as followers of Christ.

Join me as I introduce you to an over-prepared future preacher turned best-selling atheist author and historical Jesus skeptic, an under-prepared fighter pilot turned atheist activist, an ill-prepared worship band member turned atheist radio show host, and a painfully prepared youth pastor turned atheist porn star. In hearing their stories and those of others—whose deconversions are by comparison more mundane—we will be able to see just how important a role that their spiritual and religious preparation played in their loss of faith. Doing so will provide us with concrete examples of what not to do as we disciple believers. In the final chapters, I will offer *A Recipe for Success* for how we can faithfully train up believers to be faithful disciples.

Chapter 4

Over-prepared

I believe all that God ever revealed, and I never heard of a man being damned for believing too much.

Joseph Smith

The Theologian and the Historian

Stretching north from the shore of Lake Ontario, eventually turning into Highway 11, Yonge Street is Canada's longest roadway at a whopping 86 kilometres (53 miles). It's also one of the most famous and historical streets in the country. In the heart of downtown Toronto, Yonge Street has been home to Santa Claus, the World Series, and Gay Pride parades. It's hosted concerts by R.E.M., Beyoncé, John Mayer, and others. During the 2010 Winter Olympics, Yonge-Dundas Square was crammed beyond capacity to watch the men's hockey final between the United States and Canada on a giant screen. Canada won in overtime and Yonge Street became Ground Zero for a massive celebration.

But, there's a darker side to Yonge Street. For all of its history and cultural relevance, it's also home to a large number of homeless who populate downtown Toronto. Whether it's because of poor choices, unfortunate events, or mental illness, Toronto, like all major cities, has its share of people living at the margins of society. Often the homeless are either looked down on as unsightly nuisances or ignored altogether, but, not at Sanctuary. Tucked away just a block off Yonge Street sits an old, red brick church building that houses one of the city's most unique congregations. Sanctuary is a church that reaches out to the lost and broken in downtown Toronto by intentionally creating a community comprised of the well to do and the down and out. Prostitutes and police officers, drug addicts and business owners, the mentally ill and elementary school teachers meet each Sunday and break bread together. Through sharing their lives and resources with the homeless and outcasts of downtown Toronto, the individuals at Sanctuary have created a community that is truly the hands and feet of Jesus. It is a church made up of unlikely members. One of those unlikely congregants is my friend Rachel. Sanctuary is not only Rachel's church, it's also where she works as part of the staff, caring for the homeless. But, Rachel is not an unlikely member of the church because she has an amazing story of how she got off the streets and now serves in Christian ministry. In fact, just the opposite is the case. Rachel was never down and out on the streets of Toronto. On the contrary, she lived a comfortable life growing up in a Christian home on an island in rural northern Ontario.

It's unlikely that Rachel is a member of the church and on staff because according to the deconversion profile, Rachel probably shouldn't be a Christian at all. Why? Because she scores highly in all four personality traits exhibited by deconverts. For starters, she's above average in intelligence. In college she was accused by her philosophy professor of having a senior student write her freshman paper on the philosophy of Immanuel Kant. For a time, she was the lead Canadian apologist for one of the most well-respected evangelistic/apologetic organizations in the world. Her job was to articulate and defend the claims of Christ in some of the most intellectually challenging environments one can imagine. At the time of this writing, she is in the final stage of completing her PhD in theology. There is little doubt that Rachel, like most deconverts, is above average in intelligence. Furthermore, on tests measuring an individual's openness to experience she scores high, particularly as it relates to intellectual openness to new and unusual ideas and debating and dialoging about ideas. She also scores high as it relates to being open to psychological liberalism (being willing to challenge authority and traditional values). On the other hand, she has little time for either right-wing politics or fundamentalist mentalities, scoring a low twenty-four percent on the Right-Wing Authoritarianism scale (fifty-five is average). She differs from most deconverts, scoring slightly below average for tolerance for ambiguity and uncertainty. Like many deconverts, Rachel wrestled with her faith for a period of her life as she entered the fourth stage of Fowler's development framework. Where she differs from deconverts is that she was able to push through from the fourth to the fifth stage. That she shares so many traits with those who are prone to deconvert raises the question, why did Rachel manage to maintain her faith while so many others like her don't?

In the Sierra foothills near Nevada City, California, is a summer camp at which my friend Dave is a speaker. Each year, kids from all over the western half of the United States come to Camp Quest for a wilderness experience and to be exposed to great speakers like my friend Dave. Unlike many summer camps across the nation, Camp Quest is not religiously affiliated. Unless, of course, you consider atheism, agnosticism, secular humanism, and naturalism to be religious designations, because they are the worldviews that Camp Quest promotes. Described by the Washington Post as "atheists' answer to Bible school,"[1] Camp Quest has multiple sites across the United States where they promote, among other things, free thought and empiricism for children of atheists and agnostics. Camp Quest isn't the only venue where Dave speaks; for instance, he is also on the Speakers Bureau for the Center for Inquiry, a secular think tank that "promotes and defends reason, science, and freedom of inquiry in education" and is "committed to the enhancement of freethought, skepticism, secularism, humanism, philosophical naturalism, rationalism, and atheism on college and high school campuses throughout North America and around the world."[2] And when he isn't speaking about atheism, Dave is writing books. He is an award-winning author of sci-fi, paranormal erotic fiction, and three scholarly works arguing that the Jesus of the Bible never existed but was only a fictional character made up by early Christians. In the world of atheism, Dave is becoming a big name. But, it wasn't always that way. For much of his life, his family thought he was going to be a minister.

Dave grew up in central California, and, like Rachel, he grew up in a Christian home. Dave's family regularly went to church twice on Sunday and to a mid-week prayer meeting. The church, for Dave's family, was their "major social environment." Dave described himself as very devout all the way up to college. Like Rachel, Dave is very intelligent, as his speaking and writing career aptly testify to. He is also highly open to experience and equally highly opposed to right-wing authoritarianism. On the Openness to Experience scale, Dave, like Rachel, scored high. On the Right-Wing Authoritarianism scale, Dave's score was 6.8 percent, meaning that he has almost no affinity for that kind of mentality. His tolerance for ambiguity and uncertainty, on the other hand, is very high. Given those personality traits, it shouldn't come as a complete surprise that he is no longer a Christian. Interestingly, Dave's deconversion happened as he was talking with a girl about religious matters. Her responses collapsed his house of cards by pointing out to him that one of the beliefs that he had assumed was true,

1. Hesse, "Camp Quest."

2. Center for Inquiry, "About CFI on Campus," lines 1–3.

vitally so, was in fact false. In that moment, Dave realized that his entire worldview was crumbling.

> So one day we're having an argument and she said, "Well Dave, you know the Hindu religion is 3,000 years older than Christianity." I was all set to jump on her case and say "Oh, no. It's not . . . " and I stopped. And, before a word came out of my mouth, I realized, "You know, I have no idea if Hinduism is older than Christianity." And at that moment, it was like bolt of lightning from the blue. I realized, I'm just like the Mormons and the Jehovah's witnesses; I'm just parroting what I was taught. And from that millisecond, on catching myself in a need of response, Christianity never looked the same to me after that. It was just boom! Christianity just seemed so obviously made up from that point on. I've never had such a visceral . . . Boom! It was a moment that changed my whole life ever since.[3]

Not long after, Dave stopped going to church and began his journey to atheist rock star status. Why did Dave and Rachel, two people that have many of the important deconversion indicators in common, take such different paths? I suggest that, among the many contributing factors, one that stands out is that Dave was over-prepared and Rachel wasn't.

Beth's Pies

My friend Beth is a pie expert. Not far from where Lake Erie cascades over Niagara Falls into Lake Ontario is Beth's successful and growing bakery, Sweetie Pies, where she bakes up some of the best pies, breads, and butter tarts in Southern Ontario. In the competitive world of bakeries, where overhead can be high and profit margins low, Beth is a success, in part due to her business savvy, but mostly because of her product. She is one mean baker with hundreds of catering successes under her belt. For instance, every Thanksgiving she bakes over 900 delicious pies for the pastry-loving people of the Niagara region. But, even experts make mistakes, and Beth, as good as she is, is no exception. Shortly after opening the bakery a number of years ago, Beth received an order for one hundred pies. Unfortunately for her, due to circumstances beyond her control, she was left with insufficient time to fill the order. Not wanting to let her customer down, she did what she could to make it happen. In order to make up for lost time, she rushed the preparation of the dough. In doing so, she worked the dough so hard

3. Dave in discussion with the author, January 2014.

it overheated and lost all its flavor. The result was a disaster. Although she delivered the pies, they were so bad that she decided to give the customer a complete refund.

Pie crust is made with a delicate combination of fat, starch, and shortening, along with an acid such as vinegar. A good baker will gently combine the fat and flour until the shortening pieces are pea-sized. Then, the wet ingredients are added and gently folded in with a fork. The dough is gently kneaded into a circular shape and allowed to rest before use. The two biggest factors in preparing dough that result in light, flaky, and flavorful crust are gentle handling and rest. The quickest way to ruin dough is by over-preparing it. This happens when the dough has been over-mixed and the rising temperatures from the mixing cause the gluten that holds the dough together to overheat. When that happens, the crust becomes tough, pale, pasty, and flavorless. Another way of saying it is that over-preparing the dough can ruin a pie. Just ask Beth!

As strange as it may sound, flavorless pie crusts and former Christians like Dave share something in common; both are often the unfortunate result of being over-prepared by well meaning "chefs." In the case of pie crust, over-preparation puts too much strain on the dough by overheating it. In the case of former Christians, over-preparation, as it were, happens when churches or parents put too much strain on them as well. The strain in the case of former believers came in the form of trying to maintain a take or perspective on Christianity they were taught was necessary to be an authentic "biblical" Christian. Usually, the take or version of Christianity was assumed to simply be Christianity, but in reality, it included a large number of beliefs that—although not essential to Christianity—were elevated to the level of nonnegotiable dogmas. This produced an inflexible and fragile belief system that was susceptible to collapse due to its all-or-nothing nature.

Consider how Rachel and Dave describe their religious socialization. Even though they share similar personality traits, traits that many deconverts also share, Rachel remains a Christian while Dave does not. The greatest difference between Rachel and Dave occurs in their religious socialization. By that, I mean how their families or church communities communicated to them what Christianity is.

Ask Rachel what her religious socialization was like, and she describes it occurring "in a church and family with fairly conservative theological and political views," and yet she "always considered my parents to be very open in their approach" to new ideas and ways of following Jesus more faithfully." As a young child she "asked a lot of questions and often struggled to make sense of the things [she] was taught." Contrary to what one might expect from her theologically and politically conservative parents, they "always encouraged this questioning" and "urged [her] to think for herself" about what she believed and why. In Rachel's words, "It was more important to them that I had integrity in my faith and character than that I accepted a certain set of beliefs." Not only did her parents encourage her to be open-minded, she witnessed her "parents grow and change in their own perspectives over time, mostly because they were open to learning from others and did not assume they already had everything right."[4] Her parents' instruction and example had a significant impact on how she viewed being a Christian. She noted that, "This was very formative for me as I learned from them that faithfulness to God is not about rigid obedience to a system but about honesty, integrity, humility, and love, and these virtues are far more likely to lead one closer to the truth than an unquestioning acceptance of specific beliefs will."

Now consider Dave's story. Ask him what his religious socialization was like and he describes it primarily in terms of narrow thinking that was governed by rules and regulations. "I grew up Southern Baptist, so we definitely had rules," he said. "We couldn't cuss; smoking, no. We never listened to secular music at home . . . Some music was okay but most was very suspect." His natural stance toward those outside of his Baptist tradition could be characterized as suspicious, noting that his parents "had a laundry list of the right churches and the suspect churches." Most notably, "anything Roman Catholic was suspect." He and his family had to be "at church every time the door opened, which was three times a week." He came to believe that as a Christian he needed to be baptized according to a certain formula, have daily devotions, actively share his faith, and go on mission trips. In terms of how he would describe the mindset of his Christian experience, he says that it was "a siege mentality, we felt like we were the only ones who had it right and the whole world was messed up in one way or another." It bred in him an attitude that he described as "very judgmental" and lamented that it "took a long time to get over the xenophobia" he developed "toward others who were outside his denomination." When he came into contact with a new idea, he "had to check it first to make sure it didn't conflict with what [he] already knew" from the Bible. If it didn't match with his Southern Baptist interpretation, it was rejected. There was, in his words, a "raft of beliefs you have to accept" to be a Christian. But, "trying to make that work" created in him an overwhelming sense of "cognitive dissonance and a lot of compartmentalization growing up."[5] Eventually, it all became too much.

4. Rachel in discussion with the author, December 2017.

5. Dave in discussion with the author, March 2017.

The Tyranny of the Necessary

Over-prepared individuals like Dave suffer from a theological condition I call the *Tyranny of the Necessary*. Believers who suffer from the *Tyranny of the Necessary* are the product of a particular kind of religious socialization process. This process requires them to affirm and defend an excessive number of theological beliefs to maintain their identity as a genuine biblical Christian. Churches inflict believers with the *Tyranny of the Necessary* and thus over-prepare them when they implicitly or explicitly communicate that the Christian faith is a package deal of biblical truths that must be affirmed to be a genuine, "biblical" Christian. They then identify those truths with their own take that includes a whole host of doctrines and theological positions. Doing so saddles believers with having to affirm and defend all of the teachings they have been taught Christianity is or reject it. Even though it's the job of churches and parents to prepare (disciple) believers so that they will grow into mature believers, they set them up for a crisis of faith by requiring them to believe far too many teachings to be a "biblical" Christian.

These beliefs are considered essential to authentic biblical Christianity and denying one of them may be seen as denying all of them. In reality, however, they are usually only essential to the take or interpretation of Christianity that their family or church community has mistaken for Christianity itself. Christianity, for those laboring under the *Tyranny of the Necessary*, is a bloated system of beliefs and practices that is in danger of collapsing under its own weight. Former managing editor at *Prism* magazine Fred Clark expresses the *Tyranny of the Necessary*:

> Fundamentalist Christianity is a package deal—an inseparable, all-or-nothing bundle of teachings and ideology that says every piece depends on every other piece. If any one piece of it isn't true, fundamentalism insists, then it all falls apart and *none* of it is true . . . from the *inside,* within fundamentalism, this all-or-nothing message is pounded home again and again with such frequency and urgency that it seems true to those shaped by that world. Belief in Jesus, in forgiveness, or in faith, hope and love, really does come to seem contingent and dependent upon all those other beliefs in inerrancy, literalism, creationism, and whichever weird American variant of eschatology your particular sub-group of fundies subscribes to.[6]

If that's true, then what is it that constitutes the *Tyranny of the Necessary*? What's the difference between a healthy socialization that passes on to

6. Clark, "The All-or-Nothing Lie," lines 48–56.

believers a solid foundation for their faith and one that sets up believers for a crisis of faith?

The *Tyranny of the Necessary* is driven by three assumptions:

- A particular assumption about the nature of the Bible and the role it plays in the family and/or the community of faith.
- An assumption about God's intention for giving us the Bible.
- An assumption that one's interpretation of the Bible is Christianity itself.

In the first instance, the nature of the Bible is understood to be an inerrant, supremely authoritative standard of truth, which serves as the foundation of an individual or community's meaning making system. The emphasis here is on the Bible as the source of objective, absolute propositional truth. In the second instance, the Bible is viewed as a comprehensive collection of facts given by God so that we may believe correct theological truths. The emphasis here is on our duty to discover the objective, absolute truths contained in the Bible. In the third instance, one is unaware of the role that interpretation plays in our encounter with the Scriptures. Being ignorant of the necessity of interpretation can lead to mistaking one's construal of Christianity with Christianity itself. The emphasis here is on the perspicuity of Scripture and our ability to know the objective, absolute truths of the Bible. These three assumptions nearly always result in a rigid, prepackaged version of Christianity that constitutes the *Tyranny of the Necessary*, an all-or-nothing proposal that all too often leads to a crisis of faith. As we look at the three assumptions below, it will become clear why.

The B-i-b-l-e, Yes, That's the Book for Me.

Psychologists have long maintained that a fundamental aspect of being human is the need to make sense out of our world. Psychologists often use the term "meaning making system" to describe the different ways we go about trying to make sense of the fragmented world that we live in. We are, by nature, storytellers, and the stories we tell are motivated by our desire to make sense of the world around us. A meaning making system, then, can be understood as a set of beliefs about reality that includes beliefs about ourselves, others, and a vast number of situations.[7] Another, perhaps more common, word for a meaning making system is "worldview." A worldview answers the big questions of life such as: why is there something rather than nothing,

7. Hood et al., *Psychology of Religious Fundamentalism*, 14.

what is the nature of ultimate reality, who are we, and why are we here? The answers to these questions directly impact how we live, including: what we choose to invest our time and money in, what goals we decide to pursue, our political affiliations, and so on. There are at least three basic needs that a meaning making system needs to satisfy if it is going to successfully create meaning: 1) A unifying philosophy of life; 2) a sense of coherence; and, 3) a sense of meaning that is identified as possessing a feeling of purpose, value, and self-worth. The unanswered question is: What is capable of providing our lives with that kind of significance?[8]

For many, the answer is religion. Given the role of a meaning-making system, it's not hard to see why. Religions offer a robust unifying philosophy of life that impacts the cognitive, affective, and behavioral facets of life. In doing so, it provides a coherent account of the world by telling a story that weaves together the disparate aspects of the world into an intelligible story that is comprehensive in nature.[9] In other words, religions are big stories that make sense out of a confusing world. Finally, religions have unique resources to provide adherents with a deep sense of meaning by offering a community to belong to and a set of beliefs that originate from the divine, providing a sense of purpose, value, control over events, and self-worth.[10]

In 2005, three prominent psychologists of religion, Ralph Hood, Peter Hill, and Paul Williamson, suggested that of all the religious meaning making systems, one of, if not the most powerful is that of fundamentalism. "Fundamentalism," said J.I. Packer, is for many a "theological swear-word."[11] Packer, it seems to me, is correct. Today, not even fundamentalists want to be identified as fundamentalists. The president of what may be the best-known fundamentalist school in the United States, Bob Jones University, suggested that faculty and students label themselves "biblical preservationists" rather than "fundamentalists,"[12] and for good reason. No longer is the term "fundamentalist" understood in its historical context, as a Christian who affirms a number of nonnegotiable, fundamental doctrines. In our cultural moment, being a fundamentalist has less to do with the content of one's belief and more to do with how one holds one's beliefs. Today, fundamentalists are regarded as unintelligent, intolerant, narrow-minded bigots that in some cases will resort to violence in defending or promoting their beliefs. If that's what fundamentalism means, then who can blame

8. Hood et al., *Psychology of Religious Fundamentalism*, 15.

9. Hood et al., *Psychology of Religious Fundamentalism*, 18.

10. Baumeister, *Meanings*, 201.

11. Packer, *Fundamentalism*, 30.

12. Hood et al., *Psychology of Religious Fundamentalism*, 12.

Bob Jones III for not wanting his university to be labeled fundamentalist? If you're wondering how on Earth, with all the negative connotations that fundamentalism has, it can prove to be such an effective meaning making system, Hood, Hill, and Williamson offer an answer, and it lies in the role that Scripture plays in fundamentalist thought.

According to Hood, Hill, and Williamson, fundamentalism's power to create meaning is due to the preeminence given to the sacred text, interpreted literally as the sole source of meaning. Fundamentalists accept the basic truth that "there exists an objective truth—revealed, by God recorded, and adequately preserved—illuminating an original intent that can be grasped and valued as the foundation for understanding all of life."[13] Moreover, since God's intention is to communicate his mind to us, as a general rule, the Bible should be taken literally unless there are good reasons within the text to do otherwise. The sacred text alone specifies what absolute truths are, and, as such, it alone becomes the ultimate criterion of truth. No truth claims from outside sources, such as science or history or common sense, can ever call into question the absolute truth claims of the sacred text. "The fact that the text is authoritative, inerrant, and without contradiction means that the believer is capable of knowing, with total certainty, how fellowship with the Divine Being is to be achieved. No other source of knowledge shall in any way alter the true meaning of the text."[14]

It needs to be pointed out that Hood, Hill, and Williamson's conception of what constitutes fundamentalism also applies to the attitude of many evangelicals toward the Bible. That being the case, just because one identifies as an evangelical and not a fundamentalist doesn't mean they do not share important fundamentalist presuppositions with their more conservative Christian cousins. Popular evangelical pastor and commentator John MacArthur provides an excellent example of what might be called "evangelical fundamentalism" in relation to the priority given to the Bible:

> Unbelievers put no stock in the divine authority of God's word, and believers should put no stock in the presumed authority of men's words. No matter how biblically sound their arguments may be in themselves, Christians who debate with unbelievers inadvertently allow Scripture to be considered on the same level as human wisdom . . . Because the Bible is God's inerrant, authoritative, sufficient, and sole source of His divine word of truth, every other truth rests on that truth. [15]

13. Hood et al., *Psychology of Religious Fundamentalism,* 22.
14. Hood et al., *Psychology of Religious Fundamentalism,* 37.
15. MacArthur, *Second Timothy,* 72.

For fundamentalists, the popular declaration, "God said it. I believe it. That settles it" is not quite correct. A more representational slogan would be, "God said it. That settles it whether you or I believe it or not." For Hood, Hill, and Williamson, fundamentalism isn't a set of specific beliefs about doctrine or behavior, nor is it characterized by negative militant attitudes. Rather, it is a way of thinking, a process and structure where the claims of a sacred text are elevated to the status of the ultimate criterion of truth unchallenged by any other source.

That the text plays such a central role for fundamentalists is the key to explaining why it is such a powerful meaning making system and consequently so attractive for many. It's the text that's the source for the three essential requirements for a meaning making system: a unifying philosophy, a coherent account of the world, and the satisfying of personal needs.[16] The text answers the big questions of life, stipulates moral codes, and provides descriptions about reality (doctrines) in absolute terms. Furthermore, the text does not contradict itself.[17] As the word of God, the Bible is viewed to be inspired and, therefore, internally consistent with itself and the narrative that brings the fragmented nature of reality into a coherent whole. "The fact that the text is authoritative, inerrant, and without contradiction means that the believer is capable of knowing, with total certainty, how fellowship with the divine being is achieved."[18] In short, the answer to the question of why fundamentalism, with all of its cultural baggage, is such a powerful meaning making system is that an all-authoritative text containing absolute transcendent truths from God revealing the nature of reality can be a pretty attractive source of meaning.

There are, however, consequences for making the above assumption about the nature of the Bible. First, if the text teaches absolute and objective truth, what could ever justify not affirming a truth revealed by God himself? In order to be authentically biblical, shouldn't Christians affirm everything the Bible teaches? So, whatever the word of God teaches concerning belief and practice, authentic Christians must affirm. As we will see, this assumption will play a significant role in the *Tyranny of the Necessary*. Likewise, because of the important role the Bible plays as the foundation of a believer's meaning making system—giving him a unifying philosophy of life, a sense of coherence, and a sense of value and worth—when an aspect of it gets called into question, it can have catastrophic

16. Hood et al., 34.

17. Hood et al., 36.

18. Hood et al., 37.

consequences. As the Psalmist said, "When the foundations are destroyed, what can the righteous do?" (Psalm 11:3 NIV)

Assume the Position

It is sometimes said of theology that where you start determines where you end up. That means your theological assumptions will determine your theological conclusions, which in turn impact how you live. Our deeply held basic beliefs, regardless of whether we are aware of them or not, direct the shape and content of our theological conclusions in the same way the set of the sail directs the course of the boat. Perhaps there is no more important theological assumption than what we assume the Bible is and how it works, because the Bible is the authoritative source of information about every theologically important question we can ask. As we have seen, the Bible is the means by which many believers make sense of their world. It's the foundation of the Christian's meaning making system. Therefore, what we take the Bible to be and how we make sense of it will have a major impact on what we believe and how we live.

New Testament scholar Scot McKnight has identified a number of mistaken assumptions about Scripture that are commonplace among conservative evangelicals and that have negative implications for theological conclusions.[19] Two of these mistaken assumptions about Scripture appear repeatedly in the narratives of former believers. The first is the assumption that the reason God gave us the Bible is so that it can act as a source of information in order that we would have correct beliefs. On this view, the Bible is a storehouse of facts scattered throughout the sacred text like puzzle pieces, and our job is to fit them together to map God's mind. Puzzlers begin with the belief that the point of the Bible is correct, if not precise, beliefs about truths of history, science, and theology. These individuals are divine cartographers creating maps that become systems.[20] The problem, as McKnight points out, is that we don't have the top of the puzzle box to look at to compare our efforts with. Unfortunately, that doesn't stop us from identifying our map with God's mind and requiring others to adopt it for their spiritual journey if they are to be biblical Christians.

The second unhelpful approach to Scripture that McKnight identifies is what he refers to as morsels of law. Individuals who approach the Bible from this perspective see the Bible not so much as a source of knowledge but

19. McKnight, *Blue Parakeet.*

20. McKnight, *Blue Parakeet,* 50.

a collection of laws of what to do and not to do.[21] As McKnight points out, it's not hard to see how this can happen. The Bible is filled with commands regulating behavior. The Old Testament, in particular, can seem like one massive legal code covering every aspect of life from the mundane to the bizarre. And, even though the New Testament doesn't prescribe laws and commandments like the Old Testament does, there is no shortage of admonitions and commands that prohibit or proscribe certain behaviors and practices for followers of Jesus. The upshot of seeing the Bible as primarily a legal code concerned with how we live is that it makes God out to be a judge with unrealistically high expectations and unreasonably low tolerance for our shortcomings. Unless, of course, you think that you are one of the "Obedient Ones,"[22] those self-righteous, smug believers who are zealous for wholehearted obedience to God. And, by obedience, McKnight means obedience to a long list of "thou shalt nots" that convince these people that before God and the world they had joined an elite fraternity.[23]

Just as there are consequences for assuming what the nature of the Bible is and its role in the life of the Christian community as the foundation of the meaning making system, there are consequences when we make assumptions about God's intention in giving us the Bible. When we assume that the Bible is given to us so that we can map God's mind or discover morsels of the law, we will tend to over intellectualize the Bible by seeing it as a storehouse of facts to be plundered in order to have correct beliefs. Doing so reveals that we assume God's primary reason for communicating to us is that, more than anything, he wants our mental assent. Such reasoning inevitably leads to a diminished spiritual formation that produces brains on a stick, rather than robust disciples. It also tends to produce argumentative, contentious believers willing to wage theological war with their brothers and sisters over what are, in reality, minor theological differences. If we over-emphasize the truth component of God's word and see the acquisition of true beliefs as the sole or primary end of why God inspired the Bible, we are in danger of forgetting that according to 1 Timothy 3:16, God inspired the Scripture, so we would be a certain kind of people, ones prepared to do good work. There is no doubt that to be doers of the word we need to know what it teaches. I am not advocating that we ignore orthodoxy and focus on orthopraxy. What I am proposing is that we approach the Bible from a different perspective, one that sees it primarily as the story of God's redemption of humanity. By doing so, I believe we will be in a better position to

21. McKnight, *Blue Parakeet,* 44.

22. McKnight, *Blue Parakeet,* 44.

23. McKnight, *Blue Parakeet,* 44.

affirm those important truths and practices in a way that avoids the pitfalls of the approaches that see the Bible as a puzzle to be solved or a law code to be legislated. More on what that looks like in chapter 9.

My Bible Clearly Says . . .

While there does seem to be an internally consistent logic to the above reasoning, there's only one problem, and that is the question of what the Bible actually teaches. Many believers, especially those who fit the above model, either shun the need for interpretation or are unaware that they are doing it as they read the Bible. In doing so, they mistake what they take as the "clear" or "plain" teaching of Scripture for uninterpreted Scripture itself. Gordon D. Fee points out that some people "tend to think *our understanding* is the same as the Holy Spirit's or human author's intent."[24] An example of Fee's point can be seen in a blog discussion I came across, where the issue being debated was the legitimacy of divorce. "I don't interpret Scripture, for Scripture is of no private interpretation . . . Scripture interprets Scripture . . . either you believe and obey what the Scriptures says or you don't."[25] While the person who posted the comment expressed a common belief among Christians, it is nevertheless false. Fee says, "we invariably bring to the text all that we are. With all of our experiences, culture, and prior understandings of words and ideas."[26] In doing so, what we take to be clear and plain may reveal more about ourselves than the meaning of the text. Merold Westphal maintains that among some, interpretation is seen as the means by which the uncommitted attempt to get around the plain meaning of Scripture.[27] In other words, faithful students of the Bible read it and accept it at face value. Only those who are looking to get around what it plainly says "interpret" it. Interpretation on this view only obscures what simple reading and common sense make self-evident. A prime example of this attitude toward interpretation is seen in the final episode of the PBS Evolution series. In the episode, Ken Ham, president of Answers in Genesis, a young earth creation ministry, tells his audience, "I don't interpret Scripture; I just read it." Ham's claim expresses what many fundamentalists and evangelicals believe is the proper approach to the Bible. Such statements are enthusiastically received by

24. Fee and Stuart, *How to Read the Bible*, 2.
25. McCray, "The Divorce Is Final," lines 41–42.
26. Fee and Stuart, *How to Read the Bible*, 2.
27. Westphal, *Whose Community?*, 18.

certain audiences who affirm claims that we should "take God at his word" or "trust the clear message of God" rather than the "interpretation of men."[28]

But, if there is one thing that contemporary philosophy has demonstrated, it is the naiveté of the idea that we discover the meaning of the text simply by reading it. Rather, we interpret it according to a host of presuppositions. In fact, there never is simple seeing of anything without interpretation, let alone simply reading the Bible.[29] Contemporary psychologists, philosophers, and physicists are inclined to agree that even simple observations are always "theory laden."[30] That means what we see is always shaped by our assumptions, making all bare impressions an illusion. Consequently, reading is always up to its eyeballs in hermeneutics. Discovering what the Bible teaches requires more than simple seeing; it requires interpretation, and interpretation always adds to or takes away from the pristine meaning of the text. Our engagement is always mediated by a number of factors or lenses through which the text provides its meaning for us. Some of those lenses are our own finitude and situationality (such as culture, history, and tradition) and the unspoken rules by which our unique Christian community reads the text.[31]

James K.A. Smith puts it nicely:

> We never simply have "the Scriptures, pure and uninterpreted; every appeal to "what the Bible says" is an appeal to an *interpretation* of the Bible. Whenever someone promises to deliver "the Scriptures alone," he or she has already delivered an interpretation that is carried out within an interpretive community."[32]

Kevin Vanhoozer agrees with Smith, saying that the view that we immediately apprehend reality or the text without mediation "has been effectively refuted from a number of quarters. The notion that the mind simply apprehends the world as it is overlooks the way in which theories shape our observations."[33] It needs to be noted that the above quotes by Smith and Vanhoozer do not preclude the existence of objective truth or the possibility of having an interpretation that approximates the meaning of the text. There is no denial of a real world beyond interpretation or the denial of meaning in a text beyond interpretation. What it does rule out are phrases such

28. Stephens and Giberson, *The Anointed,* 48.
29. Placher, *Unapologetic,* 24–38.
30. Placher, *Unapologetic,* 27.
31. Smith, *Fall,* 51.
32. Smith, *Fall,* 53.
33. Vanhoozer, *Is There a Meaning?,* 300.

as those used by World Bible publishers concerning their new translation, God's Word: "Now no interpretation needed. The Bible: the all-time best-seller—but hardly the best understood. God's word the revolutionary new translation that allows you to immediately understand exactly what the original writers meant."[34]

It's hard to imagine how an advertising campaign for that translation ever received approval from the head office. A translation is by its very nature an interpretation! Such reasoning is not only philosophically naive, it is demonstrably false. When we mistake our interpretation of the word of God for *the* word of God, we are guilty of mistaking the map for the terrain itself. Sociologist Christian Smith argues the mistaken notion of simply reading the text without interpretation can be easily demonstrated. "On most matters of significance concerning Christian doctrine, salvation, church life and morality, different Christian—including different Biblicist Christians—insist that the Bible teaches positions that are divergent and often incompatible with one another."[35] As support for his claim, Smith lists no fewer than thirty-four volumes, each comparing and contrasting different positions on doctrine, theology, and practice. The doctrinal debate ranges from the days of creation to the book of Revelation and touch on just about every major doctrine in between. Surely, if all that were required to discover the "clear" teaching of the Bible is to simply read it, there should be greater unity among theologians, let alone the average believer. All of which goes to show the hermeneutical nature of all reading. Despite the evidence to the contrary, the belief that Scripture need not be interpreted, just read, persists in evangelicalism. Christian clichés such as "God said it. I believe it. That settles it," imply that if one were to read the text of Scripture it should settle all matters of debate, if only one is willing to submit to its teachings. If we were being honest, the bumper sticker should read, "God said it. I interpreted it according to my presuppositions. That settles it for me." But, I suppose that wouldn't sell as well.

Being unaware of the factors that impact our reading of Scripture has significant consequences. First, it can trick us into thinking that what we "just read" is simply what is "just there," when in fact it's the *product* of what is there in the text and those things that constitute our finitude, acting as the lenses through which we "just read" the text. Interpretive ignorance can and regularly does lead to mistaking our "take" of Christianity for Christianity "plain and simple." When we believe that we possess *the* correct meaning of the text unadorned by our own interpretative practices,

34. Westphal, *Whose Community?*, 18.

35. Smith, *The Bible Made Impossible*, 22.

we are set up for both arrogance and inflexibility. We can become arrogant and dismissive of those who do not read the text as we do, ascribing to them any number of nefarious motivations for not obeying what the Bible "clearly teaches." We can become inflexible because we fail to see how our interpretation of the text is conditioned by numerous factors. Not realizing this fact can trick us into thinking that our take just *is* what the Bible teaches. In such scenarios it's not difficult to see how that assumption leads to mandating that if others want to be authentic biblical Christians, they must adopt our take on Christianity.

Three Assumptions and You're Out

Combining the above three assumptions about the role of the Bible, the nature of the Bible, and the "no interpretation needed" approach to the Bible constitutes the *Tyranny of the Necessary*. It's easy to see how Christian communities that burden believers with the *Tyranny of the Necessary* tend to produce over-prepared believers who are ripe for a crisis of faith. Follow the logic: If one begins with the Bible as the means by which they make sense of the world (the role of the text) and with the Bible as the ultimate, inerrant source of absolute truth (the nature of the text), then one is obligated to believe what it teaches, no compromise.

Second, if one assumes that God's purpose in communicating through the Bible is that we can believe the right things about doctrine, the emphasis will be on getting "it right." Theological precision and accuracy will become a priority. The more accurate people are in their beliefs, the more of a genuine, biblical Christian they are. Practically speaking, this tends to elevate secondary and tertiary doctrines to the level of the essentials, because all truth is God's truth. Combining assumptions one and two will give you a long list of beliefs and behaviors that believers assume need to be affirmed to be a genuine biblical Christian.

Third, assuming that one's "take" on Christianity *is* Christianity—because one can discover the truths contained in the Bible by simply reading it without the process of interpretation—results in cognitive rigidity and an inflexible prepackaged version of Christianity. If I, or my community, read the Scriptures and simply see what it teaches, then we have discovered the essence of Christianity. If that is the case, how can we compromise on absolute, objective truth? Others may believe differently, but they are simply wrong. That is the reason that God gave us the Bible in the first place, so we would know the truth. It is clear to us, untempered by the realization that our beliefs are interpretations of the text and, as such, can be bad or wrong.

Combining these three assumptions results in the *Tyranny of the Necessary,* an all-or-nothing ultimatum about a particular take on the faith. Absolute and objective truth is communicated in a supremely authoritative text that originated with God. God's intention in communicating was so that we would be "in the truth" and possess correct beliefs about reality. The text speaks to many aspects of reality from the theoretical to the concrete. What it teaches, we are obligated to believe. We do not have the luxury of picking and choosing which truths we like. All truth is God's truth, and, as such, all truths found in the Bible are nonnegotiable. Admittedly, conservative evangelicals and fundamentalists will acknowledge that there is a difference in importance between what the Bible teaches about the number of horses Solomon owned and the deity of Christ. But practically speaking, it can be a difference without distinction because both are absolute truths and biblical Christians affirm all that the Bible teaches without exception. This effectively erases the important theological difference between essential and secondary doctrines. This is a problem because an essential doctrine of the faith is one that a believer must affirm to be a believer and one that, if proven false, invalidates the entire edifice of faith. The *Tyranny of the Necessary* hands believers a prepackaged set of beliefs, a "take" on Christianity, which their community has mistaken for Christianity itself. They, likewise, mistake the "take" for the real thing and, given their operating assumptions, accept the ultimatum that requires an all-or-nothing buy-in to be a genuine, biblical Christian. At this point, the only thing standing between a believer and a former believer is being convinced that one aspect of the "take" is wrong.

Lake Wobegon Daze

A humorous but sad example of the above mentality is found in Garrison Keillor's classic fictional memoir, *Lake Wobegon Days*, based on the fictional town of Lake Wobegon, Minnesota. In his chapter titled "Protestant," Keillor tells the story of growing up among the closed Brethren, a small fundamentalist group of Christians scattered throughout the Midwest. Although the novel is fictitious, Keillor's description of the Brethren is largely based on his own experiences as a member of the group during his youth.

> We were "exclusive" Brethren, a branch that believed in keeping itself pure of false doctrine by avoiding association with the impure. Some Brethren assemblies, mostly in larger cities, were not so strict and broke bread with strangers—we referred to them as "the so-called Open Brethren," the "so-called" implying

> the shakiness of their position. Whereas we made sure any who fellowshipped with us were straight on all the details of the Faith, as set forth by the first Brethren who left the Anglican Church in 1865 to worship on the basis of correct principles . . . Unfortunately, once freed from the worldy Anglicans, these firebrands were not content to worship in peace but turned their guns on each other. Scholarly to the core and perfect literalists every one, they set to arguing over points that, to any outsider, would have seemed very minor indeed but which to them were crucial to the Faith.[36]

Growing up in the so-called Open Brethren, I can confirm that Keillor knows whereof he speaks. Even though my experience with the Open Brethren in my youth and twenties was largely positive (and one for which I am deeply grateful), it was also, in part, responsible for instilling in me a large number of assumptions about what being an authentic Christian entailed, namely a long list of beliefs I felt I needed to affirm to be a biblical Christian. Most of those assumptions related to ecclesiology, which is where the Brethren derive their identity. As a reform movement that originated in Plymouth, England, in response to the high church practices of the Anglican Church, the Brethren sought to worship the Lord according to Scripture alone, not as they considered the unbiblical practices of the established churches of the day.

Being involved in the Brethren assemblies from my childhood, I adopted many "truths" through instruction and osmosis. I came to believe that to be a truly biblical Christian you had to meet according to the New Testament pattern, which was clear to anyone not already deceived by denominationalism. The pattern included that the local expression of the church was completely autonomous and unconnected to any manmade denomination. We gathered unto the name of the Lord only, not a man like the Lutherans or Wesleyans did. We also believed in being governed by a plurality of elders, not a senior pastor. Pastors were an example of the professionalization of the ministry that could not be found anywhere in Scripture. Furthermore, paid pastors made congregants passive consumers instead of active members of the assembly.

We broke bread weekly in an open forum where all the men could participate by expressing a short thought on the death of Christ, pray, or give out a hymn. When I once asked why we did it once a week and other churches broke bread once a month or once a quarter, I was told that it was because they chose to follow their denominational policy rather than the

36. Keillor, *Lake Wobegon*, 105.

pattern of the Scriptures. Our ladies were silent in church, and most wore head coverings following the instruction of Paul in 1 Corinthians 11. Head coverings are a distinctly Brethren practice that I felt a sense of pride in. Probably because even among conservative denominations, the Brethren were the only group of believers that I knew of who held fast to the "truth" of Scripture on that issue. As a teenager, my wife once wore a tissue on her head because she forgot to bring her covering. For her commitment to the Scriptures, everyone roundly praised her!

We even had a biblical argument for how we referred to ourselves. We did not call ourselves Brethren, that was just the name that was given to the movement by those outside of it. We simply considered ourselves as Christians gathered unto the name of the Lord Jesus. We referred to our Sunday morning gathering as "the meeting" or "the assembly," because the church is the universal body of Christ, not a building on the corner of McNabb and Pine Street. Add to the above beliefs a long list of doctrines such as a literal six-day creation, inerrancy of the Scriptures, eternal security, dispensationalism, the pretribulational rapture of the church, and forbidden practices such as no dancing, no playing cards, no going to movies, no drinking alcohol, which I felt I needed to affirm and defend to be genuinely biblical, and you can see how it was that I thought, quite possibly, no one outside the Brethren were saved. If they were, I didn't think they cared very much about what the Bible had to say since they ignored so much of what it "clearly" taught.

Not everyone, or even the majority of people in the assembly I attended, affirmed the above beliefs. There were, to be sure, a number who did, and those would have been the ones I gravitated toward. In my youthful zeal I was committed to the truth, even down to the smallest jot and tittle. There were many patient and gracious believers in my local church. I have fond memories of it and much to be thankful for in terms of my experience growing up there. Nevertheless, in hindsight, it was my experience among the Open Brethren where I first experienced the *Tyranny of the Necessary* to a degree.

Believers suffering from the *Tyranny of the Necessary* result from Christian communities that mistake their "take" on Christianity for Christianity itself, and thus require believers in those communities to affirm a long list on nonnegotiable beliefs and practices to be an authentic biblical Christian. The theological edifice that is built on the foundation of the above assumptions about truth, the word of God, and simple reading is, by nature, rigid. If all truth is God's truth, it means that all truth is nonnegotiable. Communities that are unaware of the lenses through which they interpret Scripture mistake their interpretations for *the* truth, which is why deconverts mistakenly assume their community's take on Christianity *is* Christianity. Furthermore, the take is a package they must take as a whole, because to reject one aspect of it is to reject it all.

House of Cards

C.S. Lewis is revered by many Christians, and for good reason; he was a brilliant thinker with the ability to communicate difficult theological truths in clear and winsome ways, whether it be his allegories like the *Chronicles of Narnia* series or his more theological works such as *Mere Christianity* and the *Abolition of Man*. From his conversion in 1929 to this very day, it's hard to overstate Lewis's impact on Christians. In 2005, *Christianity Today* polled over one hundred of its contributors and other Christian leaders concerning the most influential Christian books of the twentieth century. C.S. Lewis was by far the most popular author, and *Mere Christianity*, his exposition and defense of the essentials of the Christian faith, was number one on the list. No doubt his position is well earned. But, what many don't know is that Lewis, the apologist, went through a crisis of faith of sorts when his wife Helen Joy Davidman passed away. In *A Grief Observed*, Lewis recounted what the experience of losing the love of his life was like and how it revealed to him the nature of his faith. Surprisingly, what he discovered was that his faith wasn't as robust as he thought.

> From the rational point of view what grounds has Helen's death given me for doubting all that I believe? Should it, for a sane man, make quite such a difference as this? No. And it wouldn't for a man whose faith had been real faith. The case is too plain. If my house has collapsed at one blow it is because it was a house of cards. Indeed, it's likely enough that what I shall call, if it happens, a "restoration of faith," will turn out to be only one more house of cards.[37]

Lewis's faith was restored, and thankfully not to the "house of cards" that he feared. Still, the question remains about just what exactly Lewis meant when he identified his faith as a "house of cards." The answer is quite simple; he realized that despite all of his rational arguments, the edifice of his faith wasn't what he thought it was, a robust fortress able to withstand any attack. In reality, it was so frail that one blow from the vagaries of life knocked it over. One emotional, existential crisis revealed to Lewis that his faith was as frail as a house made of playing cards. Like a house of cards that only needs

37. Lewis, *A Grief Observed*, 37.

one card to fall to bring down the entire edifice, it took but one negative experience to bring down the edifice of his faith. Even though Helen's death didn't cause him to lose his faith in its entirety, the doubt that it produced concerning the goodness of God nearly shipwrecked him.

Something similar happens to believers laboring under the *Tyranny of the Necessary* and who have been over-prepared by well-meaning Christian communities that hold the above three assumptions about the Bible. In Lewis's case, his house of cards nearly collapsed because of his doubts about a crucial aspect of the faith, the goodness of God. In the case of over-prepared believers, due to the nature of their faith, it need not be something so significant. Given their underlying commitments to the Bible and to truth, believers are in danger of their house of faith collapsing from even the simplest truth being called into question. If a community assumes the Bible is the ultimate source of absolute truth, that it is a depository of truths about what to believe and how to behave, and that one's take of Christianity is Christianity itself, the result is a prepackaged, rigid, system of nonnegotiable truths that must be affirmed. If even one of them proves to be false, the entire structure collapses, because if all truth is God's truth, then there can't be errors. Not recognizing that perhaps the error is in their take or their assumption that the text has to be inerrant, what options are left? If one doctrine is wrong, then it isn't God's word. Again, Fred Clarke:

> For those shaped by fundamentalism, belief in Jesus, faith, hope, and love are all constantly imperiled by even fleeting glimpses of reality. Some such glimpse will eventually penetrate the protective fundie shell—the recognition that maybe all sedimentary rocks didn't come from Noah's flood, the realization that the Synoptic Gospels can't be easily "harmonized," the attempt to evangelize some Hell-bound Episcopalian that results in them getting the better of the conversation. And when that happens, the whole edifice threatens to topple like some late-in-the-game Jenga tower. At that point, the reality-punctured fundie is trained to believe they have only two choices. Either they can fiercely decide to pretend it never happened and that they never caught such a glimpse—thus becoming the sort of person who is increasingly capable of such pretense and denial. Or they can chuck it all and embrace the nihilism and meaninglessness that they were always taught was the only alternative to this fragile fundie faith.[38]

38. Clark, "The All-or-Nothing Lie," lines 41–55.

Reading the narratives of former believers offers insights of the kind of "cards" that cause the structure of faith to collapse when they are no longer believable. These include:

- A literal account of creation
- An inerrant Bible
- A literal Hell
- Penal substitution atonement theory
- An historical grammatical hermeneutic
- A dispensational eschatology
- Premillennialism
- A Pretribulational rapture
- Speaking in tongues
- A particular Bible translation
- Abstaining from work or play on Sunday
- A particular ecclesiology
- Beliefs about what is inappropriate for a Christian to do
- Playing cards
- Dancing
- Drinking alcohol
- Going to movies
- Listening to contemporary music
- Getting tattoos

As you can see, there are two kinds of beliefs that need to be affirmed. One has to do with doctrine, the other with practice. Christians, according to each particular *Tyranny of the Necessary,* need not only affirm all the correct doctrines, but also a list of beliefs about which practices are prescribed and which are taboo. For example, it is common to hear from former believers that the church they attended emphasized its own unique beliefs and practices as true Christianity.

A Crisis in the Making

The combination of the fundamentalist understanding of Scripture and being blind to one's own interpretive lenses results in the rigid, prepackaged faith that is an all-or-nothing proposition, I have called the *Tyranny of the Necessary*. The *Tyranny of the Necessary*, then, tends to generate a sense of cognitive dissonance leading to ego depletion and ending in a loss of faith.

When someone like Dave encounters what he takes to be contrary evidence to a belief he takes as crucial and his system is so rigid that he can't adjust it to fit the new information, the system is in trouble. Dave, very early on in his journey out of Christianity, came to realize, in his words, that "evolution was obviously true." And, according to his operating assumptions, accepting that evolution was true effectively meant he had denied his faith. Why? Because for Dave, the take on Christianity that he had adopted allowed no room to fit evolution into the belief system. If evolution was true, then the Bible (or more accurately, their reading of the Bible) was falsified. In the mind of Dave's faith community and of young Dave, the Bible clearly taught that God created life by speaking it into existence, fully formed.

As he wrestled with the claims of evolution and what he took the Bible to teach about origins, he experienced what psychologists have identified as cognitive dissonance. In 1957, psychologist Leon Festinger proposed a theory arguing that people have a deep need to have coherence and consistency in their beliefs. Therefore, when two beliefs contradict one another, a sense of discomfort is produced that needs to be resolved. In order to relieve the discomfort, individuals have three options. First, they can give up one of the beliefs. Second, they may look for more information that will reduce or eliminate the tension. Third, they can reduce the importance of the conflicting beliefs, in effect, finding a way to see the beliefs as not in contradiction with one another. Dave was a young Earth creationist; he believed that God made the universe in six literal twenty-four-hour days approximately 10,000 years ago. Then, he encountered persuasive evidence for evolution. Holding both the evidence for evolution and the belief that God specially created all life created a sense of psychological discomfort for him. To relieve it he could either abandon his belief in young Earth creation or abandon the evidence for evolution. Second, he could look for new information to reinforce his belief in young Earth creation. He might tell himself that evolution is just a theory, only an interpretation and not empirically provable. Third, he could attempt to reduce the discomfort by telling himself that, on balance, believing in young Earth creationism is the safe choice. If he accepts evolution and he is wrong, then there are serious negative eternal consequences. But, if he chooses to remain a creationist and he is wrong, then there are no eternal consequences for him, since he believes that if evolution is true then God does not exist and there is no life after death. One thing he can't do is continue living with the tension.

Believers inflicted with the *Tyranny of the Necessary* can either deny the data, evidence, or beliefs that are inconsistent with their faith commitments, or they can look for new information that will allow them to tell themselves that the contrary data, evidence, or beliefs are not really a problem. Or, they can try to convince themselves that there are other reasons why retaining their faith is justified. Each option has difficulties. In the first scenario, the believer simply eliminates the contrary data that counts against his belief. But, doing so may not be so easy. At some point, it may be impossible. At some point, we all gave up the idea of Santa Claus, because the data became undeniable. We can't believe in Santa Claus no matter how hard we try. When the evidence against a position is seen as conclusive, no amount of determination will allow people to believe in what they have been convinced is false. The second option is one that most individuals pursue. Naturally, we want to retain those beliefs that are the most meaningful for us. In the face of contrary evidence, we instinctively look for evidence that confirms what we already believe. On one hand, this strategy may resolve the tension, allowing us to retain our original belief by giving us a sense of confidence that the evidence does support it. On the other hand, it may only be effective for so long. Finding information that confirms one's original belief may not be so easy. Sometimes, it may not be forthcoming, and, in a worst-case scenario, contrary evidence may be the result. When that happens, the original belief is in jeopardy of being jettisoned. The third option requires that the believer be willing to place a pragmatic choice over concern for truth. According to William James, this is a completely reasonable option but only if the evidence is inconclusive. If the evidence tilts one way or the other, however, an individual is obligated to follow it.

Cognitive dissonance is a state of affairs that everyone, not just believers suffering from the *Tyranny of the Necessary*, experiences. But, it can be much more acute and threatening to such believers because of the number of beliefs they must maintain and the nature of those beliefs as nonnegotiable absolute truths revealed by God. But, doing so can lead to what is known as ego depletion. Ego depletion is the controversial theory that an individual only has so much willpower, and it is reduced with overuse. Social psychologist Roy Baumeister proposed the idea that self-control is like a muscle that can become fatigued with overuse.[39] When the reserve of self-control has been depleted, the ability to persist in activities or beliefs

39. Baumeister et al., "Ego Depletion," 1252–65.

that require intentionality can become difficult or impossible. An important experiment that Baumeister conducted in support of his theory required participants to exercise self-control by resisting the temptation to eat chocolates. Doing so required them to draw on their limited pool of mental reserves. Upon successfully resisting the temptation, they were then given the task of a frustratingly difficult puzzle that required a significant amount of determination to complete. What Baumeister discovered was that those who successfully managed to resist the temptation of the chocolates were less able to persist in working on the puzzle. He concluded that the reason why was because they had depleted their limited resources of self-control and didn't have the mental fortitude to resist the temptation to quit. Baumeister's ego depletion theory sheds light on what it is that finally pushes believers suffering from the *Tyranny of the Necessary* to give up their faith. At some point, they simply have no more energy or mental resources left to fight the good fight. By that, I mean they no longer can continue seeking resolutions to the cognitive tensions created by the sheer number of theological and doctrinal beliefs they feel the need to affirm and defend to be genuine biblical Christians and the data that call those beliefs into doubt. Eventually, a tipping point is reached in their experience and the cognitive dissonance is so great that they simply no longer have the ability to rationalize their faith commitment. It is psychologically easier to relieve the tension by exercising option one for dealing with cognitive dissonance, but in this case, it is not the beliefs that challenge Christianity that are rejected as the problem, it is Christianity that is rejected.

Perhaps this is why so many former Christians describe their deconversion as being set free.[40] Over and over again, the stories of former Christians repeat the refrain that despite the cost of losing their faith, it was well worth it for the freedom they gained; freedom from trying to justify beliefs they felt they had to affirm but no longer could with intellectual integrity. Dan, a former Christian, now atheist, articulates it well:

> In my ten years between my baptism at eleven and my deconversion moment at twenty-one, I was always rationalizing trying to rationalize my faith. That's how faith, i.e., a willful commitment to believe in things either under-supported by evidence or refuted by evidence, corrupts reason so badly. It teaches you to accept a tradition's beliefs as true no matter what, as a matter of identity and morality, and allows doubting and reasoning (even highly sophisticated forms) to only operate as part of an entire spiritual life ultimately only interested in defending and developing the initial

40. Marriott, *The Cost of Freedom.*

> commitments . . . Faith is a ***deliberate commitment to rationalize*** rather than rationally criticize when it comes to your core beliefs. Religious faith is not just a matter even of ordinary susceptibility to confirmation bias, it goes much further and perversely makes willful rationalization a moral ideal.[41]

Is it any wonder so many individuals feel a sense of liberation when they walk away from the faith? In doing so, they relieve themselves of the burden of what, for them, can feel like the continual need to justify their beliefs to themselves, against themselves! Tragically, it was well-meaning mentors of the faith who placed such heavy burdens on them. Just as David was weighed down with Saul's armor as he went out to fight Goliath—armor that Saul thought was necessary but David could not support—might it not be the case that former believers were burdened with an inflexible take on Christianity that was bloated with beliefs that must be affirmed but which deconverts, for various reasons, could not? That is the tyranny of the unnecessary.

Conclusion

Churches and parents are responsible for the spiritual formation of their members and children. This means that they are to train them up in the way that they should go, in the hope that in the future they will not depart from it. Part of that is by teaching them what it is that Christians believe. Former believers, those who have deconverted, are often over-prepared believers, Christians whose spiritual formation took on a theologically bloated, inflexible version of the faith, what I call the *Tyranny of the Necessary*. By requiring believers to maintain beliefs that are unnecessary to be a Christian, families and churches set up believers for crises of faith as they struggle to affirm beliefs that they no longer believe but feel they must in order to be a Christian. Eventually, the house of cards can no longer withstand the strain and comes crashing down.

By being aware of the negative impact that burdening believers with doctrines and theological positions that are not essential for being a genuine biblical Christian, we can avoid preparing believers for crises of faith that can lead to disaster. But, being aware of what not to do is insufficient. We also need a positive alternative to the *Tyranny of the Necessary*. We need an approach to spiritual formation that is both faithful and avoids the pitfalls of the *Tyranny of the Necessary*. In chapter 9, I will offer a way forward and present a strategy for faithfully preparing believers.

41. Finke, "Since My Deconversion," lines 102–12; 116–22.

Chapter 5

Under-prepared

By failing to prepare, you are preparing to fail.

American proverb

The Philosopher and the Fighter Pilot

Located on the edge of the hill country region of southern Texas, Austin is not only the capital of Texas, but also the home of the flagship campus of the University of Texas. UT Austin boasts one of the highest ranked philosophy programs in the country. Which is why, every year, hundreds of prospective graduate students apply there, hoping to be selected into the PhD program. Only a select few make the cut. One of those who did is my friend Craig. Craig grew up in the Midwest in a Christian home, was homeschooled until his senior year in high school, and then attended Southern Illinois University, Edwardsville, where he majored in philosophy. After graduation, he and his wife moved to China for two years, where they served as missionaries. Upon returning to the United States, he spent five years working on a master's degree in philosophy before enrolling at the University of Texas in the philosophy PhD program. Today, he is finishing up his PhD by investigating the relationship between evolution and ethics. He also serves as the worship leader at the church he and his family attend. Needless to say, Craig is pretty intelligent. He also is open to experience, scoring high on the Openness to Experience scale. And, as you might expect, he scores far below average on the Right-Wing Authoritarianism scale, at thirty-three. Regarding his tolerance for ambiguity and uncertainty, he scores as average. In his teen years, Craig arrived at the fourth stage of

Fowler's faith development model, where he began trying to make sense of a faith that at times seemed at odds with the world around him. Through college, Craig searched for answers to vexing questions he had about his faith. And, although the questions were challenging and at times threatening to what he believed, he managed to find a way to advance to the fifth stage of the faith development model and retain his faith.

Whereas Craig grew up in the Midwest and pursued philosophy, Alan spent his youth in the Rust Belt around Ohio. When it came time for him to go to college, he ventured to Michigan and studied physics. After graduating, he enlisted and served his country for twenty-one years in the United States Navy. In that time, he was a nuclear submarine officer and a fighter pilot, flying more that seventy missions over Iraq and Afghanistan. He retired from the Navy with the rank of Commander, in charge of a strike fighter squadron of F-18 jets. In retirement, he attended Stanford University and received a master's degree in business management and accepted an executive position at a *Fortune* 500 company. He's also a member of Mensa, which means his IQ is in the top two percent in the nation. Alan scores above average in terms of being open to experience, very low in his appreciation for right-wing authoritarianism, and above average in his toleration for ambiguity and uncertainty. However, as we will see, Alan could not find a way to move from the fourth stage of faith development to the fifth.

Although not raised in an overtly Christian home, Alan never doubted the existence of God. And, even though he didn't receive explicit religious teaching from his parents, he believed in a number of Christian doctrines such as Heaven, Hell, and that Jesus is the Son of God. Throughout his childhood, Alan considered himself a believer in Jesus. But, at the age of fifteen, Alan had a spiritual awakening of sorts. During a meeting of his high school's Christian Fellowship Club, Alan asked Jesus to become his Lord and Savior for the first time in his life. Alan had become born again:

> I *knew* it, *accepted* it, and *felt* it in my very soul. It was an awakening—a rush of overwhelming clarity in the recognition that God loved me so much that he actually suffered and died as a human in order to save me from my sins. I felt, all at once, an intense combination of gratitude, joy, relief, calm, and awe. I was *born again* in Christ.[1]

From that moment on, Alan's life was focused on living for Jesus. Studying the Bible, evangelizing, and participating in prayer meetings were regular aspects of his life. In recounting that time period, he said, "As I look back on those heady days of religious zeal, to say I was really into my

1. Jeskin, *Outgrowing God*, 6.

Christianity would be an understatement."[2] However, somewhere between his high school days as a zealous Christian and his life in the business world, Alan outgrew his belief in God. Today, the once-zealous Christian is an outspoken atheist and the author of two books, each making the case that God does not exist, Christianity is untrue, and the world would be better off if religion came to an end.

Craig, for all his questions and doubts, still identifies as a Christian. He has kept the faith despite swimming in the deep end of the philosophical pool, a pool where he is the minority. A recent study surveying 3,000 philosophers from around the world reported that 72 percent of respondents identified as atheists.[3] Yet, Craig is committed to Christ and to intellectual integrity. It's not always easy, but he seems to have weathered the storm of intellectual doubts and come out on the other side with a faith that not only makes sense of the world but also provides him a foundation from which he engages in philosophy. Alan, on the other hand, asked many of the same kind of questions that Craig did but found Christianity to be intellectually unsatisfying and incapable of making sense of the modern world. In fact, the modern world made Christianity look foolish and false to him. Assuming that Alan and Craig are committed to the pursuit of truth and intellectual integrity, what might have contributed to their different appraisals of Christianity? I maintain that a clue lies in their religious socialization. In each case, their Christian communities provided them with an understanding of Christianity that set them up to either successfully integrate their faith with life in the twenty-first century or see them in conflict with one another. Craig's socialization allowed him to retain his faith in the face of contemporary challenges, while Alan's apparently did not. In short, Alan was sociologically under-prepared by his church community to keep his faith in the face of the challenges arising from living in the twenty-first century.

Cookie Dough

Given the choice between cookies and cookie dough, it's a toss-up as to what many people would choose. When I was young, I looked forward to eating the dough left in the bowl as much as I did the cookies. Who would have ever guessed that eating the leftover scraps of cookie dough was putting me in mortal danger? The federal Food and Drug Administration, that's who. According to the FDA, eating raw dough, whether it's for

2. Jeskin, *Outgrowing God*, 7.

3. Bourget and Chalmers, "What Do Philosophers Believe?," 465–500.

cookies, pie crust, pizza, or bread, can make you sick.[4] Why? The answer has to do with the dangers that may be lurking in the under-prepared ingredients in the dough, specifically the flour. That's because untreated flour can be infected with the E. coli bacteria. E. coli is a natural bacterium lining the intestines of animals. When it comes into contact with wheat from which flour is made, the wheat is contaminated and so is the flour. Unless the flour is treated with what is referred to as a "kill step" (exposing it to high temperatures), it will remain contaminated with E. coli, thus contaminating the dough. Eating even the smallest bit of dough made from contaminated flour is enough to cause a person to become seriously ill. Symptoms of E. coli poisoning include severe abdominal cramps, bloody diarrhea, fever, and vomiting, and can potentially lead to death. No wonder the FDA recommends not eating cookie dough.

All of this sounds quite alarmist, doesn't it? Kids have been eating cookie dough since there have been cookies. Do people actually get sick from eating under-prepared cookies? It appears that they do. In 2016, General Mills recalled ten million pounds of flour due to E. coli contamination that caused dozens of people in twenty states to become ill.[5] In Canada in 2017, the Canadian Food Inspection Agency recalled flour produced by Ardent Mills because of E. coli contamination. People across the country became ill after they ingested raw dough made with the flour. Although no one died, six people were admitted to hospitals and treated for severe symptoms.[6] Tragically, in 2013 one woman died from complications due to E. coli that she contracted after eating Nestle's Toll House cookie dough that was later recalled due to E. coli contamination.[7] Under-prepared ingredients, such as cookie dough, as harmless and delicious as it may seem, can in fact be dangerous. As we have seen, the way ingredients are prepared has consequences.

The same is true in the case of many contemporary believers. It's clear from reading and listening to the stories of many former believers that they were unprepared to live out an ancient faith in the modern world. Their religious socialization failed to help them bridge the gap between the world of the Bible and their lived experience at the beginning of the twenty-first century. As a result, the Christian faith began to look and *feel* completely out of step with modern life, both rationally and morally. For educated, intelligent, reflective Christians, believing the Bible with its stories of giants,

4. Stearns, "FDA: Raw Dough's a Raw Deal."

5. Weise, "General Mills Recalls."

6. Cotter, "Investigation Into E. Coli."

7. Murray, "How Eating Raw."

talking animals, chariots of fire, angelic visitations, and resurrections can be as difficult as believing in Santa Claus. Likewise, the violence commanded by God in the Old Testament is, for many contemporary believers, nearly impossible to harmonize with their modern moral sensibilities. Commands ordering genocide, slavery, bodily mutilation, stoning, burning individuals alive, slaughtering livestock, and destroying entire towns are, to say the least, deeply troubling. In short, for many modern believers, it is a struggle against feeling that the Bible is irrational and immoral.

This is precisely the way that Alan looks at Christianity today. His experience living in the modern world made the narrative of the Bible, steeped as it is in the premodern worldview, appear ridiculous.

> As a navy submarine officer, I had harnessed the power of nuclear fission to propel an 8,000-ton submarine hundreds of feet beneath the surface of the ocean. As a naval aviator, I routinely flew faster than the speed of sound in combat aircraft launched from, and recovered to, a ship hundreds of miles from any landmass. I was experiencing, firsthand, the incredible power of the human mind in understanding, transforming, and directing the tremendous forces extant in nature. This power was a human privilege that only science could deliver. If we could make such significant technological strides in understanding and mastering the physics of our world, why then were we still clinging to unreasonable and arcane 2,000-year-old ideology concerning the metaphysics?[8]

It isn't just the irrationality of the Christian story that he objects to, but the ethics of the Bible as well.

> As a Christian, my construct of morality began with a walking, talking snake giving bad fruit to a naked couple in a garden. The "Original Sin" of the couple accepting and eating the bad fruit then set off an incredible chain of events beginning with a disappointed vengeful deity immediately evicting the couple from the garden and promising that life would be an unpleasant experience for the couple and all their progeny until the end of time. It also included ten rather random edicts divinely inscribed on ancient stone tablets, a virgin-born hybrid god-man tortured and killed to appease the vengeful deity for all mankind's sins (including the initial eating of the bad fruit), and finally, celebrating the torture and death of the god-man with an ornate, cannibalistic ritual of symbolically eating the flesh and

8. Jeskin, *Outgrowing God*, 16.

> drinking the blood of the tortured god-man. Self-loathing guilt, repentance, redemption, eternal bliss or damnation, and other complicated ideas were also thrown in as part of the equation.[9]

Social Insecurity

To socialize individuals is to prepare them for life in a social setting. This usually involves teaching them through active and passive means an entire "form of life," including a governing narrative, what beliefs and behaviors are obligatory and which are taboos, and vision of the good life. When I refer to religious socialization, I am meaning the process that Christian families and churches engage in as they train up believers for life as a Christian within the social setting of the church. In doing that, it is crucial that they keep in mind that the church is embedded in the larger social setting of the surrounding culture. To avoid setting up believers for a crisis of faith, the church needs to socialize believers in such a way that they can live in both social settings without a sense of vertigo as they simultaneous indwell each. The problem is that the narrative that governs the church and the narrative that governs the culture are radically different and that difference can make people feel that they must choose one or the other as the governing narrative of their life. Looking closer at Alan and Craig can help us see the importance of how the church goes about socializing believers.

Alan's religious socialization was radically different from Craig's. The question is, did the way they were socialized play a role in their ability to maintain their faith in the modern world? Craig says that, for him, it most certainly did. Looking back, Craig speaks fondly of his upbringing in terms of his family and his church experiences. Raised in a conservative evangelical home that placed a great deal of importance on the Bible, Craig was well acquainted with its content from a young age. In his home, his parents encouraged critical thinking about the Bible. Sundays, around the dinner table, they discussed the message they heard in church and engaged in constructive critique. According to Craig, this practice nurtured in him "a healthy practice of evaluating and being open to questioning the teachings he heard in church."[10] When he went through a period of doubt in high school, his parents encouraged his intellectual curiosity by affirming the need to think well about his faith, acknowledged that the Bible contained many stories that sounded strange, and directed him to resources

9. Jeskin, *Outgrowing God*, 30–31.

10. Craig in discussion with the author, September 2017.

they thought would be helpful. Although they were conservative in their doctrine, they were aware of the complexity of, and the challenges posed, by Scripture. This was evident to Craig in their "openness to new ways of understanding the text."[11] They made no secret that Christians often disagreed with one another over how to interpret biblical passages. They modeled intellectual humility by acknowledging that "despite their best efforts, it was always possible they had misunderstood the text."[12] Although not perfect, Craig's religious socialization appears to have provided him with a means by which he could reconcile his religious faith with the challenges posed by living in the modern world. A strong commitment to the Bible as God's word was complemented with an attitude of humility and open-mindedness. An awareness of the role that culture plays in either supporting or challenging faith was acknowledged, and critical evaluation of doctrine and church teaching was encouraged. Appreciating the complexity, strangeness, and difficulty of believing the Bible in the twenty-first century freed Craig up to find ways of reading it that were consonant with being a modern day Christian. As a result, he has remained one.

In contrast to Craig, consider Alan's experience. He grew up in a nominal Christian home and was exposed to the story of the Bible through his surrounding culture.[13] Growing up in the United States exposed Alan to the basic storyline of the Bible but not much more. His family didn't attend church, and he had little interest in reading the Bible. When he did, he had a difficult time resolving what he took to be contradictions between his "religious concepts" and "the physical realities of nature."[14] He recalls that "the process of revising my religious beliefs so they not conflict with my expanding knowledge of reality was easy enough to do early on, but became exceedingly challenging as I matured."[15]

Alan's primary spiritual formation came when he moved to Liberia, West Africa, during his high school years. Liberia is predominantly a Christian country and in Alan's words, a "very fundamentalist"[16] environment where they "took the Bible as the truth, literally."[17] In Liberia his family attended a Presbyterian church pastored by his grandfather, and he was a member of his high school Christian club. Neither of these environments enriched the

11. Craig in discussion with the author, September 2017.
12. Craig in discussion with the author, September 2017.
13. Jeskin, *Outgrowing God,* 2.
14. Jeskin, *Outgrowing God,* 2.
15. Jeskin, *Outgrowing God,* 3.
16. Alan in discussion with the author, September 2017.
17. Alan in discussion with the author, September 2017.

intellectual aspect of his faith. The onus was on him to deal with the challenges of how to read the Bible in light of his modern knowledge. To maintain his faith, he continually modified it to fit with his growing knowledge of the world. His primary strategy for dealing with conflicts between articles of faith and the facts of science and history was to adopt the scientific view as true and take the Bible as allegorical. But he could only allegorize so much with intellectual integrity. Eventually, he came to the conclusion that the Bible was not what he was taught that it was.

When asked about his Christian experience, Alan acknowledged that his Christian club at the high school and his church had a very simplistic understanding of the Bible. They were largely unaware of, or ignored, its various genres and, as a result, they did not appreciate the complexity and nuance in the text. They overlooked or ignored difficult passages or simplified them rather than facing up to the difficulties and discussing them. According to Alan, neither his church nor his Christian club appreciated the need for reading the Bible as a literary work or as a work of history. Rather, they were guided by thin theological readings that were beholden to fundamentalist assumptions resulting in a flat, literalistic approach to interpreting the Bible. They seemed to be generally unaware that they interpreted the Bible according to a number of assumptions. Moreover, they imposed a modern criterion of truth on the claims of the Bible not recognizing that it assumed an ancient one. They assumed that the Bible had all of the answers to life's questions and humanity's problems and could not possibly contain any errors. Serious attempts at connecting the Bible, and thus Christianity itself, to life at the end of the twentieth century were sorely lacking. Critical thinking that brought the Bible and the broader culture into dialogue with one another never occurred. In the end, the cognitive dissonance proved to be too much, and Alan abandoned his faith. Interestingly, the phrase he uses to characterize his deconversion is "outgrowing God." In other words, he came to believe that belief in God is childish for an educated person to affirm on intellectual and moral grounds. Just as he had outgrown belief in Santa Claus, he had outgrown belief in God. Did his socialization play a role in his loss of faith? There is no way to know with certainty. However, he is a prime example of a person who couldn't take the Christian message seriously living in the twenty-first century. In his book *Outgrowing God: Moving Beyond Religion*, he clearly articulates his reasons for abandoning his faith. He leaves no doubt that he lost his faith because he no longer could believe it was true, and what led him to that conclusion was that he couldn't reconcile the problems he saw between his understanding of Christianity and his beliefs about the modern world. The question is, had he been socialized in an environment that had done a better job of preparing him to live as a Christian at the cutting edge of the modern world, would he have still lost his faith? He emphatically claims that, regardless of how he was socialized or what version of Christianity he was presented with, he would have "eventually climbed out of it" and become an atheist. According to him, no matter how well he had been prepared, he would have come to see the truth that Christianity is, at its core, "fantastical and immoral."[18] Maybe he would have rejected Christianity no matter how well he had been socialized. Nevertheless, it's not surprising that, given the kind of Christianity he was socialized into, he left the faith. He was completely under-prepared to live as a Christian in the twenty-first century.

If over-prepared believers suffer from the *Tyranny of the Necessary*, which, if you recall, has to do with what one needs to *believe* to be a Christian, under-prepared believers struggle with how to *be* a Christian in the twenty-first century. They suffer from what I call *Spiritual Culture Shock*.

Spiritual Culture Shock

What we normally think of as culture shock is sociological in nature. It is a sense of "confusion and uncertainty sometimes with feelings of anxiety that may affect people exposed to an alien culture or environment *without adequate preparation*."[19] In the same manner, believers exposed to the formative influences of contemporary culture who have not been adequately prepared to understand and respond to it can experience uncertainty and disillusionment with their faith. Believers who experience *Spiritual Cultural Shock* often emerge from Christian communities that do not appreciate the challenge of being a believer in the twenty-first century. Consequently, they have failed to equip believers to remain faithful in an increasingly secular age. The socio-cultural conditions in the United States that made Christian belief seem not only plausible but also reasonable and good have been undergoing rapid change. The church has been the cornerstone of American life for centuries, but in just the last thirty years much has changed.[20] These changes have made being a Bible-believing Christian harder, especially for well-educated, intelligent, and reflective individuals. If that's true, where has the church dropped the ball in preparing believers to live *as believers* in the broader culture? Three ways that the church contributes to *Spiritual Cultural Shock* are:

18. Jeskin, *Outgrowing God*, 24.
19. *Merriam-Webster*, "Culture Shock."
20. The Barna Group, "The State of the Church," lines 1–3.

- Not understanding the role that culture plays in belief formation.
- Not appreciating the shift to a secular culture.
- Not communicating the Bible in a manner that is culturally suitable.

Deconversion narratives of many former believers appear to reveal they were nurtured in a faith community that was largely unaware of the formative role that the surrounding culture has on faith development. As such, they couldn't appreciate or adequately respond to the challenges it creates. Second, their church environment did not appreciate the unique cultural shift that has been taking place across the religious landscape of America. The United States, like Canada and Europe before it, is becoming increasingly secular. For an increasing number of Americans, Christianity is no longer the default position. But, perhaps even more important, Christianity is not the guiding narrative of those who have the greatest influence over the accepted definition of reality. Cultural elites sitting atop the most influential of the culture-producing institutions are decidedly secular. Their ascendancy correlates with a decrease in church attendance, an increase in the numbers of those who no longer identify as belonging to any religion, and an increase in those who claim atheism. Third, failing to appreciate the power and increasingly secular nature of contemporary culture, the church has not figured out a way to faithfully make sense of the Bible for intelligent, well-educated believers. At one time in our history, a "Sunday school flannelgraph" conception of Christianity could survive, given that, for most Americans, Christianity was the default option. Such is no longer the case. The combination of the first two failures combined with a shallow and simplistic version of Christianity results in many believers who are wrestling to maintain a faith they feel they have outgrown, intellectually and morally.

Culturally Insensitive: Appreciating the Role and Power of Culture

Before we can begin to discuss the relationship and the impact that culture has on how we think, we need to know what culture is, and, as with any abstract concept, it's difficult to define culture in a manner that will satisfy everyone. Culture, like the terms "religion" and "society," isn't a concrete object that we can simply point to and say, "There it is; that's culture," in the way we can with a tree or a dog or a building. And yet, in spite of that, we all seem to have a workable understanding of what we're talking about when we use the word "culture." But can we say more about the nature of culture than "we know it when we see it"? Can we know more about it than merely how to correctly use the term? Can we come up with a helpful definition to have a better, more precise understanding? I think we can.

Theologian Kevin Vanhoozer defines culture as "the distinctly human world that humans create by doing things not by reflex but freely as expressions of desire, duty and determination."[21] Culture, according to Vanhoozer, is a human product, the result of the universal human need to make sense of the world of experience. To help us get a better handle on the role that culture plays in ordering our social worlds, Vanhoozer suggests that we think of culture as analogous to the software operating systems that run the hardware of a computer. Software, much like culture, operates in the background, largely unnoticed by the individual but indispensable for the operation of the computer. And, in the same way that a software operating system provides the information required for the computer to run, culture is the operating system providing the information for the overall way of life of a given group of people, including its beliefs, customs, and meaning making systems.[22]

Sociologist James Davison Hunter adds to our understanding of culture by identifying four important aspects of the abstract nature of culture. To begin with, Hunter says that culture is the comprehensive set of assumptions about how we take the world to be and how we understand others. It's a system of truth claims about moral obligations and the essence of reality that we have in common with a group of people. These assumptions exist prior to us even thinking about them. They are so taken for granted that they are, for us, self-evident truths. For example, in America, the framers of the Declaration of Independence believed that it was ". . . self-evident, that all men are created equal, that they are endowed by their Creator with certain unalienable Rights . . ." Self-evident, in this context, means the equality of all men was obvious, and needed no further demonstration or argument.[23]

Second, Hunter maintains that culture is a product of history. It's the slow outcome of how groups of people understand the world around them

21. Vanhoozer, et al., *Everyday Theology*, 9.

22. Culture is more than just located in the abstract world of beliefs and meaning making systems. Theologian David Hegman (*Plowing in Hope*, Canon Press, 2007) notes that Scripture affirms that culture is also a concrete phenomenon that is produced by human actions, which in turn transform the Earth. Artifacts, the things that people make, things that they invent, like cell phones and disposable diapers, *are* culture in that they directly impact how we live and the kind of world we live in. What we create flows from our desires and in turn creates a space for our values and beliefs to become externalized. All of this is grounded in the fact that, as humans, we bear the image and likeness of God.

23. Hunter, *To Change the World*, 32–33.

and pass it on to succeeding generations. Over time, we take these understandings not as perspectives on reality, but as *reality itself*. Which is to say, our understanding of the world seems natural. For example, many ideas that we take today as simply reflective of the way the world really is can be traced back to thinkers hundreds of years ago with ideas that would have seemed radical to their contemporaries. But, given the slow march of time, those ideas gained traction, were eventually adopted by social elites, and ultimately have become part of our natural understanding of the world.[24]

Third, Hunter persuasively argues that institutions produce culture. Ideas and obligations are generated by institutions and the elites who lead them. Institutions such as the market, the state, the education system, the media of mass communication, and the products of scientific and technological research are all carriers of ideas and obligations that form culture. Culture, then, is manufactured. Tech firms like Apple, Microsoft, and Google; entertainment companies such as Disney, Universal, and MGM; along with elite educational institutions like Harvard, Princeton, and Yale are the epicenter of cultural manufacturing.[25]

Fourth, not all institutions have the same influence in the production of culture. The institutions that have the greatest influence in manufacturing culture exist at the center, not the periphery, of the institutional landscape. What places an institution at the center? The answer is prestige. Institutions, such as Stanford, have much more prestige and, therefore, much more cultural capital, than the local college. While it's possible that students might get an excellent education from their local college, it won't come with the opportunities or influence that a Stanford education will afford. Stanford is at the institutional center of prestige while the local community college is on the periphery of prestige. Therefore, it has much more cultural capital, or impact, on the shape that culture takes.[26]

Culture, then, is a comprehensive, shared set of largely subconscious assumptions and values of a group that are the product of both history and institutions, and which constitutes for them a social "reality." It is the space in which we live and move and have our being. As such, it has incredible power to shape the kind of people we are and what we accept as reasonable and moral. The church has not always appreciated this fact.

Not recognizing the power of culture to influence our beliefs is not something that is unique to the church. Probably most people, Christian or not, assume that reason is the primary element that determines what

24. Hunter, *To Change the World*, 33–34.

25. Hunter, *To Change the World*, 34–35.

26. Hunter, *To Change the World*, 36–37.

claims we are willing to believe. In other words, we think we believe what is rational and that we discover that by using our cognitive faculties. But that is only one part of the story. Although reasoning is involved in our belief formation, so is our cultural context. The cultural setting we find ourselves in has an underlying and subversive power to imperceptibly influence what we find believable. While it's tempting to think that we believe claims about the world based primarily on their inherent plausibility and rationality, that conclusion would be wrong. It is true that two of the primary reasons we accept a claim as true have to do with its plausibility and rationality but not its *inherent* plausibility and rationality. Few, if any, claims possess what could be called *inherent* plausibility or rationality. All claims are made by someone living somewhere, at some time, who possesses a web of beliefs that are often taken for granted but which determine whether a new claim is plausible or rational. A claim's plausibility—and, to a lesser extent, rationality—are relative to the background beliefs of an individual. The question is, what shapes and provides the conditions for these background beliefs? There are a number of factors, but it is one's culture that serves as the primary ground for a belief's plausibility. Ideas do not originate, seem reasonable, and find acceptance in a vacuum; they do so within social settings and conditions that make them seem either plausible or not. But, and this is crucial, the role of culture in influencing claims as plausible or rational is subversive. By that, I mean that the plausibility and rationality of claims is felt, not apprehended, cognitively. Culture does its formative work at the affective level of the gut, not the intellectual level of the head. Sociologist Peter Berger once claimed that if you were to put people behind a screen and tell him nothing about them except their income and occupation, he would be able to make accurate predictions of their beliefs regarding religion and morality, voting behavior, and lifestyle choices, including sexual practices. That's because income and occupation are primary indicators of where individuals are likely to reside on the social landscape. And where they reside influences what they believe. In Berger's words, "Beliefs that people hold always have a sociological address."[27] It's undeniable that the cultural and social worlds we inhabit shape us in ways that are as powerful as they are surreptitious. We simply can't escape the power of culture and are largely unaware of the degree it impacts what we value and what we believe to be true about the world. It shapes our perceptions, attributions, judgments, and ideas of self and others.[28]

27. Berger, *A Far Glory*, 12.

28. Livermore, *Cultural Intelligence*, 84.

To see this, consider the change in attitude that has taken place among Americans concerning slavery. At one time, for many Christians in the South, slavery was taken for granted as the natural state for a certain group of people. Moreover, to them, not only was it natural, it was biblical. Defenses of slavery abound which appeal to natural law and to the Bible. But prior to the Civil War, for many in the south no argument was needed because few questioned it. But prior to the Civil War, for many in the south no argument was needed because few questioned it. Today, virtually no one in America, Christian or otherwise, believes that slavery is moral. In fact, it's painfully obvious to us that it is evil. That we so strongly believe slavery is wrong is interesting, given the fact that our belief that slavery is wrong is not one we have come to by way of argument. We believe it not because we have arrived at that conclusion after a process of reasoning but as a result of living when and where we do. It has become implicit knowledge, implanted deep in our psyche by the formative power of culture. Consequently, we are left to wonder how anyone, let alone fellow Christians, could have ever believed slavery was moral. So, why did many Christians in the Antebellum South, who read the same Bible we do, see slavery as quite natural, whereas we see it as obviously wicked? The answer is that, for a number of reasons, the cultural milieu of the United States has changed concerning slavery. In doing so, the conditions of belief, as they relate to the morality of slavery, have changed. As a result, it is nearly impossible for us to see slavery as moral; we just know in our bones it's wrong. Had we lived in the Antebellum South, no doubt we would have had a different attitude. That's the power culture has to influence what we believe.

There is little doubt that cultural patterns have a significant impact on our behavior and our thinking. But, in all likelihood, we don't appreciate the degree to which they do so. The way we see things seems "natural" or "just the way things are." But, in reality, the culture in which we live influences what we assume about gender and sexuality, race and ethnicity, wealth and poverty, production and exchange, authority and power, kinship and marriage, and even the categories by which we order reality. If culture plays such a powerful role in what we are willing to find believable, how does it do so? The answer, according to Peter Berger, is via what he calls *plausibility structures*. In *The Sacred Canopy*, Berger argued that humans are, by nature, "world-builders." By this he means that, unlike every other species, humans have a need to make sense of, and give meaning to, reality. In doing so we construct a "world" to live within. Thus, every society, large or small, is a "world" that has been constructed by humans. These "worlds" include the way individuals view themselves, others, their roles, and their values.[29] In doing so, the world or society or culture they create becomes "objective" in that it exists apart from themselves as a creation. Culture and society exist and stand external to humans, although they are creations of humans. When individuals who live in the "world" forget or do not recognize their social structure as a creation but take it as a natural reflection of "just the way things are," they have internalized the "objective," yet constructed "world" into structures of their subjective unconsciousness.[30] Because of the vital function they perform, "worlds" must be maintained. But, because they are constructions, "worlds" are precarious and unstable. In danger of collapse, they must be legitimized by something that gives their "world" its plausibility.[31] Berger posits that what gives a "world," or interpretation of reality, its plausibility/security is a social base. Each "world" requires a social base for its continued existence. Those who have been effectively socialized into seeing the world in a particular way constitute the base. The base then acts as a plausibility structure for the "world."[32] By that, Berger means that the social base gives a sense that the "world" is discovered or given, as opposed to constructed and, therefore, open to challenge.

"Worlds," or interpretations, whether religious or not, are only as strong as the plausibility structures that underwrite them. Naturally, then when an entire society accepts, or buys in, as it were, to a world interpretation it serves as a powerful plausibility structure and legitimizes that "world." When this happens all the important social processes within it serve to confirm the reality of this "world." [33] Instead of being seen as a social construct it is taken as simply a reflection of reality. A perfect example of this is Europe in the Middle Ages. Nearly all of Europe held a Christian interpretation of reality that was constructed and legitimized by the existence of a massive social base. Indeed, Christianity was the most distinctive and powerful component of medieval civilization.[34] The church played a fundamental role in every aspect of life and every level of society during the Middle Ages. Christian teaching influenced the economic, social, intellectual, cultural, and daily lives of all Europeans.[35] The "world" of the average European living in the late 1500s was a Christian one. The prevailing Christian culture

29. Berger, *Sacred Canopy*, 8.

30. Berger, *Sacred Canopy*,

31. Berger, *Sacred Canopy*, 9.

32. Berger, *Sacred Canopy*, 27.

33. Berger, *Sacred Canopy*, 29.

34. Spielvogel, *Western Civilization*, 208.

35. Spielvogel, *Western Civilization*, 206.

reinforced the rationality of the Christian worldview. Being a Christian in such an environment was the norm and therefore relatively easy. Such is no longer the case. Europe today is thoroughly secular. By which I mean it has undergone a process by which the presence and influence of religion and religious institutions have been relegated to the margins of society. This has resulted in a state that, for the first time in history, individuals look upon their own lives and the world without the benefit of religious interpretations.[36] Religious interpretations have lost their credibility not only for a few intellectuals and cultural elites but also for entire societies. Statistics show that the United States is following in Europe's footsteps.

Not recognizing the influence that culture has in shaping the kind of people we are and the beliefs we are prone to accept is fine when the culture is largely Christian. However, when it is not, being in the dark concerning the formative power of culture is problematic because it tends to lead to stunted Christian socialization. It does so primarily because of a misdiagnosis of sorts. A misdiagnosis made by a doctor will ultimately lead to the wrong treatment and not cure the malady. And, in the same way, when the church fails to appreciate the impact culture has on belief formation, it will apply an inappropriate treatment. Which is why the default move in addressing doubt is apologetics. Instead of addressing the underlying affective factor in bringing about a crisis of faith, the church tends to address the cognitive symptoms. We have primarily focused on apologetics to the exclusion of formative practices. We have addressed our response to the mind and ignored the gut. We have preached worldview to the exclusion of social imaginary. Apologetics can be useful, as can worldview talk. But I am not convinced that either gets to the root of the problem.

Culture Shift: From the Sacred to the Secular

If the first factor contributing to *Spiritual Cultural Shock* is not appreciating the formative power of culture, the second contributing factor is not appreciating the degree to which our culture has moved from one that was respectful of religious faith to one that is increasingly challenging toward it. Today, in the modern West, although Christianity has a veneer of plausibility, it is no longer the dominant "world" interpretation. The dominant "world" interpretation is an increasingly secular one. This may come as a surprise to those who are familiar with the data that shows belief in God among Americans at nearly 70 percent. But numbers can be deceiving. When it comes to the impact that the secular narrative has on culture, it's

36. Berger, *Sacred Canopy*, 108.

not so much how many people are secular, but who those people are. Recall James Davison Hunter's definition of culture. Culture is a product of elites who possess power at institutions that are at the center of cultural production. Culture is not the result of the hearts and minds of enough ordinary people being calibrated toward the same end. It is a top-down production, not a bottom-up one. When it comes to cultural influence, we are talking in terms of class, not numbers. Berger puts it this way:

> There exists an international subculture composed of people with Western-type higher education, especially in the humanities and social sciences that is indeed secularized. This subculture is the principle "carrier" of progressive, enlightened beliefs and values. While its members are relatively thin on the ground, they are very influential, as they control the institutions that provide the "official" definitions of reality, notably the educational system, the media of mass communication, and the higher reaches of the legal system.[37]

Referring to the United States, Berger wryly states, "If India is the most religious country in the world and Sweden is the least, the United States is a nation of Indians ruled by Swedes."[38] In other words, even in the United States, a nation that has a long Judeo-Christian heritage and large numbers of professing Christians, religion no longer legitimizes the dominant "world" interpretation. Therefore, those who continue to adhere to the "world" as defined by the religious traditions find themselves in the position of cognitive minorities, a status that has social-psychological as well as theoretical problems.[39]

Conservative political commentator and former legal counsel in the Reagan White House Hugh Hewitt provides an example of what Berger is talking about:

> What had in the U.S. long been an alliance between faith and intellect—between reason and revelation—became at first a split, then a chasm. Today it is a battle. Intellectual elites have never been so far removed from the normal distribution of religious attachment or practice as they are today. And no segment of the intellectual elite is more estranged from faith, and specifically from Christianity, than the media elite—the collection of professionals who write, edit, program, or produce the nation's prestige media: *The New York Times, The Washington Post,* the

37. Berger, *The Desecularization of the World*, 10.
38. White, *A Mind for God*, 27.
39. Berger, *Sacred Canopy*, 152.

> *Los Angeles Times, The Christian Science Monitor, The Wall Street Journal, Time, Newsweek, U.S. News & World Report, Fortune, Forbes, Business Week, Harper's, Atlantic, The Nation, The New Republic,* the *Weekly Standard, The New York Review of Books, The American Spectator,* CBS, ABC, NBC, CNN, Fox, PBS, and the major movie studios.[40]

Secularists, not the church, control and write the accepted definition of reality. The narrative shaping culture is no longer that of the Bible but a cocktail of Enlightenment rationalism, humanism, and scientism. The result is that religious expression and belief are marginalized and excluded from public discourse, legal reasoning, and the political process. Whereas the West once looked to the Bible as the standard of truth, today we "know better." Religious belief may have been okay for our unenlightened ancestors, but it should play no role in shaping society today. Science and reason are the tools for shaping society in the secular age.

How has that happened? How have we moved from a culture that was largely supportive of the faith to one that is secular? Those are the questions that Canadian philosopher Charles Taylor sought to answer in his magisterial work *A Secular Age*:

> So what I want to do is examine our society as secular . . . which I could perhaps encapsulate in this way: the change I want to define and trace is one which takes us from a society in which it was virtually impossible not to believe in God, to one in which faith, even for the staunchest believer, is one human possibility among others.[41]

Taylor is not so much concerned with the content of belief, or even the lack of belief, as much as he is discovering the conditions that make belief in the sacred difficult. Taylor argues that specific changes and events over the last 400 years have weakened the plausibility structures that legitimized belief in God and provided the cultural underpinnings of the West. The changes in the plausibility structures in turn brought about a change in the prevailing social imaginary, which in turn have brought about what he refers to as *A Secular Age*.

What then is the *Secular Age*? And how is our contemporary social imaginary related to it? We now live in an age when religious belief is no longer viewed as the default option. On the contrary, religious belief is optional in the modern West. There has been a massive shift from "a society where

40. Hewitt, *Embarrassed Believer*, 1.

41. Taylor, *A Secular Age*, 3.

belief in God is unchallenged and indeed, unproblematic, to one in which it is understood to be one option among others, and frequently not the easiest to embrace."[42] Today, as opposed to in the 1500s or even the 1950s, belief in God is always plagued by doubt for all but the most hardcore fundamentalist and the unreflective and naive believer. In the words of James K.A. Smith:

> Even as faith endures in our age believing doesn't come easy. Faith is fraught; confession is haunted by an inescapable sense of its contestability. We don't believe instead of doubting. We believe *while* doubting. We're all Thomas now.[43]

Taylor wants to know why this has happened and argues that the reason has not so much to do with a change in belief per se, but a change in the *conditions* that make beliefs believable. Like Berger, Taylor maintains that social conditions are the key to understanding why people believe what they do. It is not just a matter of becoming more enlightened or rational, but of being socialized into seeing the world differently.

A key to comprehending Taylor's argument is to understand what he means by the term social imaginary. Taylor describes the way persons construe life as a social imaginary. For Taylor, the social imaginary is not mere ideas but the background understandings that provide the framework for social life and shape the way humans conceptualize the world they inhabit. These are understandings that humans take for granted as a result of being socialized into a take on the world.[44] Social imaginaries have a tacit quality, meaning they are comprised of implicit understandings that are shared by a group of people.[45] They are "the way that ordinary people 'imagine' their social surroundings, and this is often not expressed in theoretical terms, it is carried in images, stories, legends, etc."[46] Taylor goes on to describe it as "the way we naively take things to be. We might say: the construal we just live in, without ever being aware of it as a construal."[47]

It is important to understand that when Taylor refers to social imaginaries he is not talking about the cognitive construct that often goes by the name "worldview." While worldviews are both powerful and subtle, at their deepest presuppositional level, they are cognitive in nature. Social imaginaries are more connected to the affective nature of our being than

42. Taylor, *A Secular Age*, 3.
43. Smith, *How Not to Be*, 4.
44. Coulter, "Wrestling."
45. Nerlich, "Imagining Imaginaries," 17–19.
46. Taylor, *A Secular Age*, 171–72.
47. Taylor, *A Secular Age*, 30.

the cognitive. The difference between the two concepts was brought home to me after speaking to a Christian high school group. After my talk, a young man approached me and asked if we could talk about the issues of same-sex attraction and same-sex marriage. Although it had nothing to do with my talk, I was happy to oblige him. When I asked him what it was that he wanted to discuss, he pointed at his head and said the following: "I believe the Bible is God's word. And I believe 'up here' that it teaches that same-sex attraction is not God's intention for people and that same-sex intercourse is sin." Then he pointed to his heart and said, "But I just can't shake the feeling that two people who love each other should be allowed to express that love towards each other. I believe it's wrong, but I feel that it's not." I would be willing to bet, had he lived in the 1950s when there was a general consensus among Americans that homosexuality was wrong, the conflict he was experiencing between his head and his heart would not have manifested itself. Unless this student works hard to maintain his belief, he will change his mind. That is because, regardless of how rational we may think we are, we always reason according to our most deeply held values.[48] And our values are significantly impacted by our social imaginary, which is a product of our culture.

Taylor argues that the contemporary social imaginary of the West is characterized by immanence and coins the term "Immanent Frame," by which he means that we live at a time in the history of western civilization where the transcendent has been excised from the *lived experience of society*. Practically speaking, we live in a world where God plays no active role in the social fabric of society. Our social imaginary doesn't include him, and it seems we get along pretty well on a daily basis without him. God, if he exists, is largely irrelevant to our lived experience. Individuals in the Immanent Frame may continue to *believe* in God, but the plausibility structures that once supported that belief have eroded and been replaced with ones that make maintaining belief in God more difficult. In contrast with the Immanent Frame of our age, consider the lived experience of individuals in the Middle Ages.

In the Middle Ages, God was everywhere. A sense of the transcendent infused the daily life of nearly everyone in the premodern period. They lived within a transcendent frame, by which I mean the social imaginary of premoderns was constituted by assumptions about an enchanted cosmos and the daily grind of life. Each reinforced belief in God. In medieval Europe, the existence of God was not only taken for granted, but it was also the foundation upon which society was built.

48. Haidt, *The Righteous Mind*.

> If we go back a few centuries in our civilization, we see that God was present in . . . a whole host of social practices—not just the political—and at all levels of society. You couldn't engage in any kind of public activity without "encountering God" in the above sense. But the situation is totally different today.[49]

Taylor describes the shift as a "titanic change in our western civilization."[50] That change is not just in what individuals believe but what they are capable of believing under the present conditions of their lived experience as twenty-first-century westerners. "We have changed not just from a condition where most people lived 'naively' in a construal (part Christian, part related to 'spirits' of pagan origin) as simple reality, to one in which almost no one is capable of this."[51]

The lived experience of our present cultural moment is largely absent of the transcendence that characterized the Middle Ages. We are still free to choose to believe in God or not. But now it is understood *as a choice.* There are other options, ones that are easier to embrace, given our lived experience in the Immanent Frame of the twenty-first century. Our age is what Taylor describes as "cross-pressured," where we feel the echo of transcendence but aren't sure how it fits within our immanent frame. And, even though we live in an age where belief in transcendence is possible, there is no denying that, culturally, another option is on hand, one that Taylor labels as "Exclusive Humanism." Exclusive Humanism, for Taylor, is a way of being in the world that sees neither need nor relevance for the transcendent. Exclusive Humanism is becoming an attractive option for many living in the Immanent Frame, void as it is of transcendence. Exclusive Humanism offers significance and meaning without the need of appealing to otherworldly entities. Atheism is now a live option and one that aligns with our lived experience in the Immanent Frame. For this reason, the question of God's existence and his role in the life of the individual and society are questions that, according to Taylor, our neighbors are no longer concerned with.[52]

Taylor's account of *how* the shift from a world dominated by an awareness of transcendence—one in which belief in God was naively easy—to the Immanent Frame of our contemporary world where belief comes hard, is beyond the scope of my present purpose. What is important to grasp is that he grounds the increase in the loss of faith that we see in late modernity not primarily in the cognitive realm of ideas. He does not argue that atheism

49. Taylor, *A Secular Age*, 2.
50. Taylor, *A Secular Age*, 12.
51. Taylor, *A Secular Age*, 12.
52. Smith, *How Not to Be Secular*, viii.

became fashionable because it was clearly more rational, or that atheists won more debates over theists, or that theism was proven to be irrational. No, he locates the radical shift from a time in western civilization where belief in God was ubiquitous and unavoidable to one where it is contestable and difficult in *social conditions* that laid the groundwork for the cognitive shift to occur. Assumptions about the nature of reality, along with social structures and institutions that comprised life in the Middle Ages such as marriage, the monarchy, the family, the education system, religious feasts, and festivals contributed to a social imaginary or set of background conditions that made belief in God a given. Why? Because beliefs held by individuals or groups are sustained through socio-cultural institutions and processes.[53] And all of the socio-cultural institutions and processes of the Middle Ages reinforced belief in God by either presupposing his existence or implying it.

Not so anymore; the existence of our institutions and social systems no longer presuppose God nor find their legitimacy by appealing to his existence. Embedded in modern institutions, traditions, and habits of thought is the tacit belief that God's existence is irrelevant. Practical atheism is for all intents and purposes the de facto religion of contemporary secular society and culture. The central institutional realities of our society and culture in political life, science and technology, economics, education, and the production and transmission of culture itself have neither need nor room for God. At no other time in history has the structural coherence of a social order depended less on religious understanding than today.

But it is not just that we live within the Immanent Frame where belief is optional. We live in a culture that makes belief in Christianity a real challenge. As Berger, Hunter, and Hewitt have pointed out, liberal elites control the institutions at the epicenter of cultural production. What this means is that they have the power to influence culture in the direction they want it to go. A look at recent statistics shows that the secular narrative is having a major impact on the religious landscape of the United States. There is little doubt that Christianity in the United States is on the decline. Ed Stetzer laments that "Americans have given up on God, and the 'Nones'—those who have no religious ties—are on the rise. It is indeed true that parts of the Christian Church in America are struggling, while a growing number of Americans are far from God."[54] Albert Mohler, president of the Southern Baptist Theological Seminary, is even more pessimistic, arguing that "a remarkable culture-shift has taken place around us. The most basic contours of American culture have been radically altered. The so-called Judeo-

53. Swatos, *Encyclopedia of Religion and Society*, "Plausibility Structures."

54. Stetzer, "Churches in America," lines 1–4.

Christian consensus of the last millennium has given way to a post-modern, post-Christian, post-Western cultural crisis which threatens the very heart of our culture."[55] David Davenport, writing for *Forbes* magazine, agrees, arguing that, "This historic shift will affect everything from elections to education to ethics and beyond."[56] Showing this shift has and is occurring is quite easy to do. Consider the following.

In 1996, the Barna Research Group published a study entitled "Christianity Has a Strong Public Image Despite Fewer Active Participants." Among other things, Barna discovered that 85 percent of outsiders had a favorable view of Christianity.[57] Ten years later, a massive change in perception had taken place among 16- to 29-year-olds.[58] The numbers are as shocking as they are disheartening. According to Barna, young people see Christianity as:

- 91 percent Anti-homosexual
- 87 percent Judgmental
- 85 percent Hypocritical
- 75 percent Too Political
- 72 percent Out of Touch with Reality
- 78 percent Old-fashioned
- 70 percent Insensitive to Others
- 68 percent Boring

Barna's findings reflect not the cognitive evaluation of Christian belief, but the affective feeling, the gut-level reaction that people have toward Christianity. In 2016, Barna reported that 76 percent of Americans identified as Christian, which sounds like a high percentage. But, when Barna asked how many self-identifying Christians went to church at least once a month, the number dropped to 31 percent. Furthermore, when Barna included a set of factors measuring traditional Christian beliefs and practices in relation to American adults, the number of those Barna identifies as post-Christian is an astonishing 48 percent.[59] At the same time, those who profess no religious affiliation, the so-called "nones," has tripled since the early 1990s and now make up 24 percent of the population. For 13- to 29-year-olds, that

55. Mohler, "Transforming Culture," lines 15–20.

56. Davenport, "Elites and Courts," lines 5–6.

57. Kinnaman and Lyons, *UnChristian,* 24.

58. Kinnaman and Lyons, *UnChristian,* 28.

59. The Barna Group, "The State of the Church," line 41.

number jumps to 38 percent.[60] Consider the fact that in 1967 only 2 percent of Americans identified as "nones."[61] And, although only about 10 percent[62] of Americans identify as atheists, some argue that the number is likely higher, perhaps as high as 26 percent.[63] And, for every adult raised without religion who joined one, four adults raised in a religion have dropped out. That means that for every adult who joined a Christian group, four left.[64] Today in the United States, nearly two-thirds of seniors are white Christians. Simultaneously, however, less than a quarter of Americans under age thirty are white Christians.[65]

If plausibility structures and social imaginary set the conditions for belief, the above statistics give us good reason to believe that it is becoming, and will become, increasing difficult to maintain faith in our secular age. Again, this is not because in the twenty-first century we have discovered that Christianity is irrational or false. Rather, it is because the cultural conditions that shape the way we feel about Christianity have changed. I strongly suspect that for many deconverts who tell "coming of age" stories to describe their loss of faith, it is in part the result of the changing cultural ethos. Christian communities that do not effectively counter this change in plausibility structures and social imaginary tend to produce believers who are unprepared to live as Christians in the *Secular Age*.

That's Incredible: The Problem of the Bible

The third aspect that contributes to *Spiritual Cultural Shock* is the incongruity felt between the content of the Bible and the modern world. If believing in God in contemporary culture is hard for educated moderns, believing in the Bible, with all of its supernatural strangeness, can feel downright impossible. Believers can experience *Spiritual Cultural Shock* when their understanding of the Bible is left at a "Sunday school" level, while in every other area of life their intellectual development rises to the level of knowledge in the twenty-first century. The Bible makes some very fantastic, hard to believe, and, quite frankly, embarrassing claims to modern sensibilities. There is a radical dissimilarity between the world of the Bible and the contemporary world, both in what we know about the world and how we live. Charles

60. Public Religion Research Institute, *America's Changing*, 11.

61. Stetzer and Schooten, "The State of the Church," 20–21.

62. Gallup, "Most Americans Still Believe in God."

63. Resnick, "How Many Americans," line 58.

64. Wormald, *America's Changing*, 12.

65. Public Religion Research Institute, 11.

Taylor argues that a major reason we feel the difference between our world and the world of the Bible is that the world of the Bible is an enchanted world, and ours is decidedly not. Our world is radically disenchanted. By that, he means we no longer indwell a world that is infused with essences, substances, spiritual forces, witches, fairies, spells, or immaterial beings that we appeal to to make sense of the world around us. Thanks to Newton and his discovery of the three laws of motion, differential and integral calculus, and universal gravitation, we no longer need enchanted explanations for events. There are neither fairies in the garden nor an immaterial essence that causes the acorn to grow into an oak tree, only the mechanistic and deterministic laws of physics and chemistry. The Enlightenment and the scientific and technological discoveries that developed out of it denuded the enchanted elements from the world. In that sense, our culture has changed from the world the Bible and the premodern era, which were enchanted worlds, infused with the mystical. The modern world we inhabit at the beginning of the twenty-first century looks at the enchanted world of our ancestors as attempts by our unenlightened forebearers to explain the world with the limited prescientific knowledge they had. We know better. The Enlightenment and the Scientific Revolution have shown us the world as it is, and, although it is fascinating and awe inspiring, it is not enchanted; quite the contrary, it is a thoroughly naturalistic disenchanted space. Given that the Bible speaks of the world as a thoroughly enchanted space, much of it sounds strange, primitive, and false to modern ears. This is why it can be quite embarrassing for many, in our scientific and technologically advanced age, to admit to believing a talking snake tricking two naked people into eating a magical piece of fruit is the reason our world is so broken. And that's just for starters. The Bible also speaks of a tree whose fruit bestows immortality (Gen 3:22); a voice coming from a burning bush (Exod 3:4); rods turning into snakes (Exod 7:10–12); water changing into blood (Exod 7:19–22); the parting of the Red Sea (Exod 14:21–22); water coming from a rock (Num 20:11); a talking donkey (Num 22:28); the sun standing still (Josh 10:13); a witch bringing the ghost of Samuel back from the dead (1 Sam 28:3–15); a dead man reviving when his corpse touched the bones of a prophet (2 Kgs 13:21); iron floating (2 Kgs 6:5–6); the sun's shadow going back ten degrees (2 Kgs 20:9–11); disembodied fingers writing on a wall (Dan 5:5); a man living for three days and three nights in the belly of a fish (Jonah 1:17); people walking on water (Matt 14:26–29); a virgin impregnated by the Spirit of God (Matt 1:20); a pool of water that can cure ailments of those who dip in it (John 5:2–4); and angels and demons influencing earthly affairs (e.g., Acts 5:19; Luke 11:24–26).[66]

Such fantastic stories often feel more like the tales we read in primitive religions than they do sober accounts of history. And if we have little doubt about the falsity of those religious accounts—due in part because we doubt their outlandish claims—then how, with intellectual integrity, can we make an exception for the stories in the Bible, which seem just as fantastic in nature? Part of the problem is that how we teach the Bible in the early years of the twenty-first century is no different from how we taught it in the eighteenth century. Then, a "Sunday school" understanding of the Bible may have been sufficient for adult Christians. It is sufficient no longer. Churches contribute to *Spiritual Cultural Shock* when they pass on a flannelgraph, Sunday school version of the faith to university-educated, intelligent believers living in the modern world.

By not cashing out the strangeness of the Bible in ways that mitigate the radical difference between the world of the Bible and our own, the church can inadvertently set up believers for a crisis of faith. It is what sociologist Robert Wuthnow refers to as "the God Problem." The problem, according to Wuthnow, is that "in the past, before the advent of scientific medicine, people who held superstitious beliefs could perhaps be excused for the false ways of thinking, critics argue. But in the contemporary world, being superstitious is a sign of stupidity. Thoughtful, educated people should know better."[67]

For Wuthnow, there is a prevailing idea in culture that:

> An educated person should understand that the Scriptures were not really divinely inspired, that sacred texts contain errors, and that there are naturalistic explanations for religion itself. People living several centuries ago may have read the biblical story about the world being created in seven days and have little trouble believing that this really happened in space and time. They may have heard that God created Adam and Eve about 6,000 years ago and figured it was exactly when it happened. A person nowadays with no education might have heard these yarns from a family member and had no reason to question them. A child could learn the story of Noah's ark in Sunday school and think how nice it was that all the animals were saved from the flood. But educated people should have reasons to question all of this.[68]

66. Adapted from Sommers, "Some Reasons Why."

67. Wuthnow, *The God Problem*, 8.

68. Wuthnow, *The God Problem*, 11.

In other words, the Bible, with its fantastic stories, was well and good for our distant relatives. They knew no better, but we do. Thanks to advances in science and technology, we have culturally come of age and see through the childish beliefs of our ancestors. We have abandoned them in much the same way we have outgrown and abandoned our belief in Santa Claus.

Galen, a former believer and contributor to a popular website for ex-Christians, is a prime example. He contends that the Bible can't be the word of God because the authors of Scripture believed in patently obvious myths. He argues, "We could begin by considering some of the creatures they wrote about in the Bible such as witches, wizards, sorcerers, spirits, ghosts, giants, dragons, sea monsters, satyrs, and unicorns. Modern science can't come up with the slightest trace of evidence that any of these creatures exists or has ever existed. This stuff was just made up."[69] He goes on to argue that not only is the Bible filled with mythical creatures, it is also filled with outlandish stories that any rational person would reject. "Other mythical oddities of the Bible include a talking snake, a talking jackass, a talking bush, 900-year-old men, a man whose super-human strength resided in his hair, three men who walked unharmed through fire, a man who lived three days in the belly of a whale, a wandering star which somehow led to one building, and a corpse which stood up and walked away after three days in a tomb."[70] He concludes that "No half-educated adult living today, who was not indoctrinated in this stuff since childhood, could take it seriously or would consider even for a moment that this stuff is really history."[71]

Former Christian John Loftus echoes Galen's incredulity toward the Bible. He challenges Christians to face up to the fact that they believe primitive superstition rather than historical truth. He presents them with what he calls the "Outsiders Test for Faith." Loftus encourages Christians to "test or examine their own religious faith as if they were outsiders with the same presumption of skepticism they use to test or examine other religious faiths."[72] If Christians think that Scientology is bizarre and untrue based on its tenets, and if they apply the same standard to what they themselves believe, Christians should come to the same conclusion about their faith as they do about Scientology. I remember once in my mid-twenties, reading an unflattering *Los Angeles Times* article on Scientology. I had previously heard of Scientology, but I was unfamiliar with just what it was that they believed. The article was stunning in what it revealed about Scientology. The beliefs

69. Rose, "Primitive Nonsense," lines 10–13.

70. Rose, "Primitive Nonsense," lines 14–18.

71. Rose, "Primitive Nonsense," lines 19–20.

72. Loftus, *The Christian Delusion*, 84.

struck me as absurd and therefore obviously false. That was until I got to the end of the article, where the author made an unexpected turn. In her final paragraph, she pointed out that as strange as Scientology sounds, it wasn't any stranger than the biblical narrative, which taught that human suffering and natural disasters are the result of two naked people who lived in a garden and were tricked into eating a magical fruit by a talking snake. That hit me like a ton of bricks. For the first time, I saw the biblical story from the outside, and it looked just as silly as Scientology.

It is not just the content of what the Bible claims that is challenging to affirm, but also justifying its ethics. Former believers felt the intense discomfort of having to accept that God is the paradigm of goodness and love but that he killed all of the innocent first- born Egyptians, commanded that adulterous young women be burned alive (Lev 21:9), required the bodily mutilation of a woman who shamelessly intervenes in a fight involving her husband (Deut 25:11), and called for the genocide of the Canaanites and the taking of virgins as war booty (Num 31:7–18). Whether such criticisms can be justified is not my concern. I simply want us to stop for a minute and ponder what God commanded the Israelites to do. To the above list there could be added more horrifying commands God gave the Israelites. It is quite easy to read such commands and not think about what the reality of carrying them out would be like. But just imagine what burning a young woman alive would be like and see if you can come up with any reason that doing so could be reconciled with your contemporary modern ethical sensibilities. If any other religion or religious text advocated such things, we would take such commands as evidence of its obvious falsity. For many former believers, the multiple violent commands of God look indistinguishable from the barbaric and demonically inspired atrocities of ISIS. Luke, a former Christian and popular blogger, wrote of his deconversion:

> The Bible revealed an ugly, evil God not worthy of worship even if he did exist. This God overturned free will, caused disaster, lied to his people and instructed them to lie, dismembered forty-two children for calling Elisha bald, and murdered or ordered the murder of millions of innocent people (in the conquest of Canaan, the death of Egyptian firstborns, the Amalakite genocide, the 50,000 Beshemish people killed for looking into the ark of the covenant, and the great flood).[73]

We may quibble with the lack of context and the way Luke frames his examples of God's "immoral" character. What we can't quibble with is that he and many other contemporary modern readers of the Bible feel the same

73. Muehlhauser, "Live Blogging," lines 34–39.

way Luke does about the Bible. I contend part of the reason they see God in such an unflattering light is that they have not been socialized into a faithful reading of the Bible that addresses these points of tension. More often than not, for many former believers, these "darker passages" of Scripture were ignored or glossed over, doing more harm than good. We need to do better at presenting the "enchanted" and "morally suspect" elements of Scripture in ways that are faithful to the text and intelligible to modern readers.

From Religion to Reason?

Seth Andrews is a former radio personality who at one time was the morning host of one of the most successful Christian radio shows in the United States.[74] Today, however, Seth is no longer a Christian. He chronicled his loss of faith in his book *Deconverted: My Journey from Religion to Reason.* Seth's story has much in common with what we have discussed in this chapter. He could not reconcile his belief in the Bible with his life in the twenty-first century. The long quote that follows expresses precisely the problem I have been trying to bring to the forefront in this chapter.

> Religion is the slammed door that keeps humankind from entering and enjoying this incredible age of discovery. It must be broken down and broken through. After all, shouldn't our goal be to live truthfully? Shouldn't we embrace a difficult fact over an easy fantasy? Won't humankind's problems be better addressed with our eyes facing forward instead of toward ancient texts and an empty sky? Aren't we better off as a species rejecting primitive books of magic and embracing our amazing technological age? After all, we're more equipped to examine our bodies, our minds, our origins, our planet, and the cosmos than any generation of humans in history.[75]

He continues:

> I'm alive in a time where, every day, humans transport themselves to faraway destinations via flying machines traveling hundreds of times faster than a human can walk. We predict storms days before they occur. We drive to faraway destinations as GPS systems guide us through every turn. Our TV remotes, our power tools, and our telephones have no cords. We can emulate an entire orchestra artificially with a single instrument. We put

74. Andrews, *Deconverted*, 34.
75. Andrews, *Deconverted*, 179.

> tracking devices in our pets so we can find them with satellites. We're touching the bottom of our deepest oceans. We cook our meals with one touch. We prevent pregnancy with one pill. We pay our bills with one click. We experience motion pictures in three dimensions. We're using stem cells to dramatically change the treatment of disease. We're snapping photographs on the surface of Mars. And who knows what the coming years will bring? Instead of clutching onto the ham-handed explanations, doctrines, solutions, and instructions of ancestors who were essentially feeling their way in the dark, it's time to embrace the more satisfactory evidence that science provides and be grateful that we're alive to see in action the microscope, the telescope, the video camera, the vaccine, the computer, the laser, the x-ray, the spacecraft, and so much more.[76]

Seth's story is another "coming of age" tale. Like Alan, Galen, John Loftus, and Luke, Seth outgrew his faith. He couldn't reconcile his understanding of the Bible with the technologically and scientifically advanced secular age he lives in. For him, Christianity, like all other religions, is the product of primitive minds that told superstitious and patently false stories to explain their world. But no grown adult living this side of the Enlightenment could believe such things unless they were self-deceived. For Seth, the choice was irrational faith or objective reason. Given that choice, who wouldn't choose reason? The problem is that no one needs to feel that is the only choice. But, if you have been handed a "Sunday school flannelgraph" version of Christianity that forgets the radical cultural, epistemological, and technological differences between the world of the Bible and our own, one that fails to acknowledge the strangeness of much of the Bible rationally and morally, you are susceptible to experiencing *Spiritual Culture Shock.* In short, by not appreciating the strangeness of the Bible, the church sets believers up for a crisis of faith in an increasingly secular culture.

Bringing it All Together: The Combined Effect

I have argued that a good number of former believers who could not maintain their faith suffer from *Spiritual Culture Shock. Spiritual Cultural Shock* occurs when believers are underprepared to meet the challenges presented by living in the modern secular age. Their Christian socialization did not adequately prepare them to handle the influence that an increasingly secular culture has over how they perceive their own faith. This occurs for

76. Andrews, *Deconverted,* 181.

three reasons. First, the church is largely unaware of the formative power of culture and how it determines the conditions for belief. This formation happens at the affective, gut level and not at the cognitive level. The surrounding culture will either make Christianity "feel" plausible and attractive or implausible and repulsive to varying degrees. The plausibility structures and social imaginaries of our age are subtly working below the surface. The symptoms that counter-formative plausibility structures and social imaginaries produce may appear in the form of cognitive doubts and objections. But don't be deceived; the real problem can be much deeper. Second, the church has not fully appreciated that the cultural underpinnings of the West have been changing. We are living in what Charles Taylor has called *A Secular Age* where the plausibility structures and social imaginary challenge religious faith rather than support it. The "official" description of reality is one that is devoid of God. Both culturally and practically in our daily lives, God has little importance. Worse, religion itself is increasingly seen as not only irrational, but dangerous. Third, without being able to explain the biblical narrative with all of its strangeness in ways that were nuanced and sophisticated, rather than simplistic and woodenly literal, made it difficult for now-former believers to maintain. Put simply, when the church's process of socialization into the faith does not respond to the formative power of culture, the cultural conditions, and the strangeness of the Bible, it makes belief in the twenty-first century difficult. Unless we are prepared to address this problem, we will produce believers who are unprepared to encounter it. In chapter 9 I will suggest ways to do just that.

Chapter 6

Ill-prepared Part 1

Expectation is the mother of all frustration.

Antonio Banderas

High School Converts

Not far from the golden beaches of Orange County in sunny Southern California lives Derek. Orange County just might be the most politically conservative and religious area in Southern California, if not all of California. Not only are there many churches in Orange County, there are some of the largest and most well-known churches in the country. And yet for all that, Derek's exposure to Christianity was almost nonexistent. Both his parents were raised in religiously nominal families, his father Jewish and his mother Christian. The combined effect of their nominal religious upbringing resulted in a home devoid of any religious sentiment at all. Growing up, Derek celebrated Christmas and Hanukah with his family, but he never made any religious connections with either of them. His parents believed that Derek and his sister should be allowed to decide for themselves what they believed when it came to religion. And so they did. Derek's sister has followed in her parents' footsteps and is irreligious and leans politically to the left. Derek, on the other hand, is the Bible teacher at an international Christian high school and a pastor of a growing church in the heart of Garden Grove, California. But Derek, like Rachel and Craig, is an unlikely convert, given the deconversion profile. He has above-average intelligence, scoring high on the SAT and having a GPA of 3.87 despite not trying because he didn't care about school. Even though he didn't have a heart for academics, his grades got him accepted into an elite honors institute at a private university. For several years, he has been a panelist on a program that broadcasts on the largest Christian radio station in the United States, discussing theology, culture, and the rationality of faith. His score on the Right-Wing Authoritarianism scale is low at forty-three, and his level of Openness to Experience is about average. Knowing Derek as I do, I can testify to the fact that he has a high tolerance for ambiguity and doesn't slavishly crave certainty and security in his belief system. Derek is brighter than the average person, has a low tolerance for religious fundamentalism and right-wing authoritarianism, scores average in openness to experience, and has a moderate tolerance for ambiguity. Given that he scores high on the deconversion profile, what is it about him that has kept him from deconverting?

Deep in the heart of Texas lives Richard, one of the most prolific anti-theists on the scene today, utilizing multiple platforms to make his content available. He is the host of a popular radio show extolling the virtues of irreligion and the folly of Christianity. He has produced and starred in a documentary about the loss of faith, published a book about his own deconversion and also a children's book about the wonders of science. His weekly podcast, on which he debates matters of faith and reason, has 30,000 weekly subscribers, and five-and-a-half-million downloads. He also speaks at free-thinker and skeptic conferences across the United States. Yet Richard wasn't always an activist on behalf of atheistic humanism. Once he identified as a follower of Jesus Christ, played in his church worship band, and was an active member of his youth group. He engaged in evangelism and desired to know and serve God. Like Derek, Richard is a sharp thinker. He regularly debates professional philosophers, theologians, and apologists on his radio program and engages with brilliant thinkers such as astrophysicist Neil De Grasse Tyson, theoretical physicist Lawrence Krauss, philosopher Daniel Dennett, biologist P.Z. Myers, and magicians Penn and Teller. He is articulate, well read, and thoughtful. When it comes to being open to experience, Richard, like Derek, scores average. On the Right-Wing Authoritarianism scale, however, he scores very low at eleven; likewise, with the Religious Fundamentalism scale, coming in at thirteen. Overall, Richard's scores correspond to scores that make him fit the deconversion profile.

Richard's deconversion began, of all places, in the baptismal tank during his baptism! When the day came for him to be baptized, he stood in the baptistery and the pastor asked him the customary question; are you trusting in Christ for salvation? At that moment, a terrifying thought occurred to him; "Why do I believe this stuff?"[1] Richard realized he was about to commit to something he felt he hadn't done due diligence in researching, and the

1. Richard in discussion with the author, May 2013.

weight of that hit him like a freight train. He knew he believed that God existed and that Jesus had died on the cross for his sins. But, what his baptism made him realize was that, if he was going to be a follower of Jesus, then he'd better know what it was he was getting himself into. Too late to back out, he was baptized. Upon leaving the church that day, Richard went home, cracked open his Bible, and began to read it. His intention was to get close to the God he had committed himself to by learning more about him. Just the opposite happened. Not long afterward, he lost his faith.

Given their similar backgrounds and personality traits, why has Derek remained a Christian, but Richard has not? Like the other faithful believers and deconverts contrasted in the previous chapters, I'm sure that emotional, intellectual, and experiential dynamics are all contributing factors. At the same time, there is something that repeatedly stands out in deconversion narratives that seems to be characteristic of Richard's experience but not of Derek's, and that is Richard was ill-prepared.

Left Out

Recently, I came across a video produced by the Bristol Science Center in England that seeks to educate children on the chemistry of baking. They did this by baking several cupcakes, each missing a different ingredient. The purpose of leaving out the ingredients was to show the importance of each component in making a good cupcake. Leaving out just one of the ingredients was enough to ruin each of the cupcakes. The cupcake that was missing the egg was soggy because eggs have proteins, which contribute an essential component to the structure of the cake. Without eggs, the cupcakes lacked the air bubbles that are produced when heated, which in turn makes the cake light and fluffy. The cupcake without margarine lacked fat, resulting in a dry cupcake due to the fact that the margarine coats the proteins and the starch with an oily layer, cutting down on the production of gluten. Gluten is what is responsible for giving the cupcake its thicker texture. Leaving out margarine produces thick, heavy cupcakes. The cupcake without baking powder was flat and dense because baking powder acts as a raising agent. Leave out the baking powder and you have a hockey puck, not a cupcake. The short video effectively demonstrated the importance of each ingredient. Leaving out just one produces some less than desirable cupcakes. Cupcakes lacking certain ingredients are ill-prepared. They are lacking in the essential components they require.

An important influence in my life growing up was my friend Dave. Dave and his wife Shirley serve as missionaries to the small communities of Northern Ontario that dot the shores of Lake Huron. During the summer they work as kitchen coordinators at a Bible camp. It was at that camp that I met Dave. Alongside their missionary endeavors, they also operate a small catering service with a great reputation for providing excellent food at a great price. Weddings, funerals, graduations, anniversary dinners, you name it, Dave and Shirley have catered it. But everything hasn't always gone perfectly. For instance, once they were making a chocolate cake for dessert but forgot to add the baking powder. As you would expect, the cake didn't rise, but Shirley saved the day by serving the cake as brownies, and no one knew the difference! Sometimes, leaving an ingredient out of a recipe doesn't mean disaster, but it won't likely produce the desired result. In the case of Dave and Shirley, it produced an ill-prepared chocolate cake disguised as a brownie.

As you might have guessed by now, I think that Christians, not just cupcakes, can be ill-prepared. Ill-prepared Christians, like cupcakes or chocolate cakes, can lack something important. For cupcakes, and Dave and Shirley's chocolate cake, it was a key ingredient that was left out. For Christians, it is crucial theological concepts that are missing. When key elements are missing in how Christians think about crucial scriptural concepts, those concepts will not sufficiently map on to reality. Having inadequate conceptions of God and the Bible may not doom a believer's faith, but inaccurate conceptions about God and the nature of the Bible are two of the most prominent misconceptions that stories of former believers display. Somewhere along the way they picked up notions about God and the Bible that lacked important elements necessary to being balanced and healthy. Armed with incomplete notions of God and the Bible, such Christians are ill-prepared to face reality because their concepts set them up to have expectations about what God would do for them and how the Bible should look. When those expectations are unmet, a crisis of faith is often the result. Consider once again Derek and Richard.

Derek and Richard have a number of similarities in their stories. Each came from a home that was either nominally Christian or nonreligious. Each had his own interest in religion that led to them becoming followers of Jesus independently of their families. They both came to know Christ in high school, and both fit the deconversion profile. At the same time, there are also many differences between Richard and Derek. Each of these differences plays a role in why Derek maintained his faith while Richard did not. Two differences that stand out between Derek and Richard are the concept of God and the concept of the Bible that each holds. While it is too much to claim that the way Richard was discipled is what caused him to lose his faith, there is no doubt that he serves as a prime example of what deconversion narratives often reveal. Somewhere along the way Richard came to the conclusion that the Bible should look a certain way and God should act in a certain way. When each of these expectations was unmet, his crisis of faith ensued. The question is, where did Richard get his conceptions and expectations?

Derek describes his faith journey as beginning in high school, where he started dating a Christian girl who gave him an ultimatum; come to church with me or we have to break up. Derek went to church. Church and everything that went with it was foreign to him, given his upbringing. In hindsight, he describes the church as a semi-charismatic environment characterized by high-pressure evangelism, a simplistic handling of the Bible, and a prosperity gospel message. It was there that Derek made a shallow profession of faith. Soon after his "conversion," Derek's girlfriend's family moved, and as a result, they began attending a new church that he accompanied them to. It was this move to the new church that Derek identifies as being a major reason (humanly speaking) why he is still a Christian today. At the new church they presented the Bible in a way that was nuanced and interacted with its "easy" and "hard" sayings. It didn't focus on the wants of Christians but rather the worship of God as the greatest good. He came to realize that the pleasure of knowing God is what we were designed for, not getting things from God. Contrary to the old church, his new one taught him that although God does love people and wants the best for them, he is also sovereign and holy. God can and does allow evil and suffering to touch the lives of his people, but he also promises to redeem it. He was encouraged to read helpful books about Scripture that gave him a framework to understand its nature and how to interpret it. Today, Derek is a pastor in that very church that provided him with balanced, nuanced conceptions of God and the Bible. From a human perspective, Derek credits how he was discipled by his church as the major reason he has remained a Christian.

Like Derek, Richard became involved with a local church in his teens. In Richard's case, it wasn't a girl he was interested in that caused him to go to church, but music. He began playing drums in the church band. This led to becoming a member of the youth group, which in turn, like Derek, led to him making a profession of faith in Jesus. Here is where the differences in their journey begin to manifest themselves. The church that Richard was discipled in either did not provide him with the kind of theological instruction needed to either correct his inadequate and erroneous conceptions of God and the Bible or they instilled those in him.

It is clear that Richard's conception of the Bible and what the Bible actually is did not line up. He appears to have understood the Bible in a simplistic, overly literal, ahistorical manner. He gives no indication that his church community helped him think critically and engage with the complexity and difficulty of the Bible. His first serious interaction with the Bible led him to conclude that it was filled with clear contradictions, ridiculous stories, and, worst of all, a deity that was angry and violent, not loving, and gracious. As an example of his approach to handling the Bible, consider the following complaint:

> Why would it say in Psalm 21:7, God is going to keep us from harm, when clearly that's not the case? Atheists and Christians experience harm in the exact same statistical way. Why, if people are, in fact, biologically born gay, would they be immediately condemned to a life of never experiencing love? Or in Leviticus 20:13, be killed because of their actions in simply acting out of love? Why would a God of love condemn someone for feeling love when he's the one that made them that way? [2]

Richard's protest exhibits an overly literal reading of the text combined with the assumption that God actively creates people who are broken. He also assumes that the way a person is born justifies their desires. Other criticisms he has raised about the Bible is that Genesis can't be true because it is not a scientific account of the beginning of the universe; the Bible is filled with contradictions, such as God being a God of war and a God of peace; and Jesus being God, but God also being his father. More instances of how he viewed the Bible could be cited, but I trust these are sufficient to show that he did not have a well-balanced, healthy conception of the nature of Scripture.

He continued as a member of the youth group, participating in evangelistic outreaches and playing in the church band but began to wrestle with the concept of God, particularly harmonizing his conception of God with evil. He argued, "When we look at the problems in the world, when we look at starvation, tornados, hurricanes, leukemia striking children, earthquakes crumbling down, and they are trapping under these giant blocks, obviously they can't move. These terrific events in our lives are terrifying, and when we insert a God into the equation that adds thousands more questions."[3]

He added, "Why doesn't God cure the children from leukemia; it creates this cognitive dissonance that God is love, and yet he watches these horrific things happen and he does nothing to stop it. I would stop it if I could, and I'm just an atheist. Every Christian that I have ever met would stop these things. So, these types of things start to pop up for me. Why

2. Richard in discussion with the author, May 2013.

3. Richard in discussion with the author, May 2013.

would these happen, why would this happen, why would that happen?"[4] It all proved to be too much to endure. The incongruity between what he thought the Bible should look like and what he found, combined with his expectations of what God should do but doesn't, eventually extinguished his faith.

While it may not be *the* reason that Richard lost his faith, it is clear that his church ill-prepared him with conceptions about God and the Bible that were inadequate to reality. The Bible, in reality, isn't how Richard conceived of it, nor is God. The Bible is a messy book that is filled with hard sayings and difficult passages. God is good and loving, but he allows evil and suffering to afflict those who believe in him and those who do not, sometimes horrible evil. It's not that Richard was completely wrong in his beliefs about God and the Bible. The problem is that those conceptions were only *Half-Baked.*

Half-Baked

Ill-prepared believers suffer from a philosophical condition I refer to as being *Half-Baked. Half-Baked* believers are individuals whose Christian community failed to provide them with balanced or accurate theological concepts. This is a philosophical problem because the formation of conceptual models is a philosophical endeavor. Conceptual analysis is at the heart of what it means to think philosophically. Conceptual analysis seeks to discover what it is we are referring to when we use terms like "goodness" or "justice." The ancient philosopher Socrates was an expert at revealing the importance of conceptual analysis. He was also famous for demonstrating that although civic leaders made many claims, they really didn't know what they were talking about. In the book *Euthyphro,* Plato, Socrates's pupil, recounts a conversation that Socrates has on the matter of conceptual analysis. While standing outside of the court of the magistrate king, Socrates encounters Euthyphro, whom he engages in conversation. Euthyphro, it turns out, is there to prosecute his father for murder. Incredulous that he could charge and prosecute his own father, Socrates flatters him, affirming that he must be an expert in moral and religious matters such as piety, since he is doing something so counterintuitive as prosecuting his own father. Euthyphro, supremely confident, agrees with Socrates; he knows what piety is. With the trap set, Socrates asks Euthyphro that if he knows what piety is, would he mind telling Socrates what it is. Euthyphro gladly provides Socrates an answer, however, it soon becomes apparent that Euthyphro does not know what piety is. At best, he can provide examples of pious behavior.

4. Richard in discussion with the author, May 2013.

But Socrates points out that unless he knows what piety is, how does he know the behavior he identifies as pious really is pious. After several rounds of Euthyphro offering answers and Socrates showing how the answers are insufficient, it becomes clear that Euthyphro, for all his confidence, doesn't know what piety is. Instead of Euthyphro teaching Socrates what piety is, Socrates taught Euthyphro that he had no idea what he was talking about. What, then, is piety?

Plato sought an answer to this vexing question. His answer was to propose that piety actually is a thing, existing outside of space and time, that somehow enters into events, states of affairs, substances and artifacts, giving them the property of being "pious." Plato's theory is one of the most important ideas in the history of philosophy. There have been other attempts to account for the nature of abstract nouns, like goodness, justice, piety, etc. But, all of them have one thing in common. They each engage in what is called conceptual analysis. Conceptual analysis is the discipline of examining our concepts to discern the necessary and sufficient properties that comprise something like piety itself. This can be helpful, because in doing so we may discover that what we think about piety (our concept of it) is not essential to piety itself. In such instances we may realize that because of our faulty assumption about the nature of piety, we have inappropriately applied the concept to things that were not, in fact, pious. An example may prove helpful.

My neighbor has a young child, a boy who is learning to identify objects in the world and label them correctly. Presently he refers to both cats and dogs as "dogs." His concept of "dog" is broad and unrefined. It appears to include all things that are furry, have four legs, and are kept as pets. It's not that he can't see a difference between cats and dogs, he just hasn't realized that they are not the same kind of thing. Given enough time, he will begin to realize that his concept "dog" is inaccurate and that there are two four-legged furry kinds of house pets that he is identifying as one kind of thing. Somehow, he will form the concept "cat," and that category will exclude the things he puts in the category "dog." In his own childlike way, he will have, if only at a subconscious level, engaged in conceptual analysis. In doing so he will have discovered that his original concept of "dog" was inadequate.

So how does the above discussion on conceptual analysis relate to being ill-prepared or, as I am calling, it being *Half-Baked*? When Christian communities provide believers with theological concepts that are false—or more commonly—inadequate, believers develop erroneous assumptions that in turn lead to expectations that will never be met. Unmet expectations lead to spiritual crisis that can in turn lead to a loss of faith. Being *Half-Baked* is a result of:

- Having an inadequate conception of the Bible.
- Having an incomplete conception of God.

In the first instance, former believers appear to have a concept of the Bible that was partly correct but lacking important aspects that ultimately contributed to their loss of faith. The conception they had was lopsided. On the one hand, they understood the Bible to be a divine book, a revelation from God that was authoritative. On the other hand, they seemed largely unaware of the human element of the Bible, specifically the process of its transmission and canonization. When they discovered challenges to the divine aspect of the Bible, along with the role of humans in the composition and production of the Bible, it hit them hard. A significant number, perhaps even a majority, of deconverts trace their loss of faith to problems they had with the Bible. Digging deeper into these stories reveals that inadequate conceptions about the Bible was the birthplace of unrealistic expectations about the Bible. These unmet expectations contributed significantly to a crisis of faith.

In the second instance, former believers possessed an incomplete conception of God. Like their conception of the Bible, their understanding of God was not completely wrong, but only *Half-Baked*. Former believers are not rejecting a concept of God made from whole cloth. To be sure, there are many things deconverts once believed that are true of God. He is loving, good, and merciful. But at the same time, their conception of God appears to lack aspects of God's character that are also equally true of God. God is not only loving, good, and merciful but also sovereign, holy, and just. Lacking a well-balanced conception of God ultimately led to unmet expectations and disillusionment. What I find interesting about the above is that so few former believers ever choose to question those concepts. Most assuredly, some do. There are lots of testimonies of former believers who have re-evaluated their fundamental conception of the Bible, God, and Christianity only to find they could not find a suitable or more accurate conception. But there are many more whose testimonies belie the fact that they never thought to do so. In faith, they took what they were taught about the Bible and God by their Christian communities and accepted it as an accurate representation of reality. When those teachings did not pan out as they expected, they were quick to relinquish them.

Inerrancy: Make No Mistake About it

The message of the Bible is at the heart of Christianity. Christianity stands or falls with the Bible. Discredit the Bible, and much of the warrant for being a Christian is lost. Which is why it is so important to have correct assumptions about the Bible. Incorrect assumptions lead to expectations that will likely be unmet, which in turn will create a sense of disillusionment with Christianity. In the literature on deconversion, the following three assumptions about the Bible regularly appear as contributing factors in the loss of faith. The first is that former Christians have a conception of the Bible that includes the assumption that the Bible *must* be inerrant or it *cannot* be the word of God. In my opinion, this assumption underlies the number one reason offered by deconverts for their loss of faith. They were told the Bible had to be inerrant or else it wasn't the word of God. They then became convinced the Bible contained at least one error. I can't emphasize enough how central this assumption is in the loss of faith. Deconverts had bought into this "either/or" mentality as a bedrock assumption about the nature of the Bible and simply took for granted that it didn't have any errors. But then something happened; they picked up their Bible and began reading it for themselves. Upon doing so they encountered what they perceived were clear and irreconcilable contradictions.

Given that over forty authors wrote the Bible over 1,500 years, in diverse geographic areas, and under radically different circumstances, one might expect to find inconsistent statements. That is, unless you assume that for the Bible to be the word of God, it must be inerrant. There is a certain logic to such an assumption, and it does reveal a high view of Scripture. Ironically, however, for many it was this high view of Scripture, along with a rigid and simplistic understanding of inerrancy that proved to be a lethal combination for their faith. Based on their operating assumptions, finding what they took to be errors in the Bible was definitive proof it could not be the word of God.

Their Christian communities had taught them that since God inspired the Bible, it means that the Bible must be without error of any kind. Accepting the teaching that "if there is even one mistake in the Bible it cannot be the word of God," they had a choice to make when they encountered what they believed were clear errors. They could either ignore the error or have the intellectual integrity to accept the conclusion that the Bible is not the word of God. As one former believer remarked, "The only two choices (as

I saw them) were fundamentalism [or] total disbelief in the Bible as a holy text."[5] Another recalled his experience this way:

> I recall a sermon in which the lead pastor of my church referred to a Scripture having to do with getting tattoos and how it was against the word of God. I recall him saying specifically, "Do you believe the Bible is correct and is the infallible instruction of God or not? There is no middle ground." . . . For whatever reason, that was the first time I finally realized that he was actually right, the Bible either is, or is not the infallible word of God. After reading a bit more, I realized there were so many fairy tales and inaccuracies in the Bible, and that there is no way it could be the product of some all-knowing God.[6]

One woman shared with me that, "When you come up fundamentalist, there are no contradictions in the Bible. It's the perfect word of God. And if you see a contradiction, it's because you read it wrong."[7] Steve, the son of a prominent evangelical leader, was powerfully impacted by his discovery of what he "knew to be a contradiction" in the Bible. He estimated that, growing up, he had "read the Bible twenty times, cover to cover," but while at a Christian liberal arts college, he came across "the contradiction," as he called it. As he read through the Bible, he encountered what, for him, was an irresolvable problem, and he was floored. He decided to turn a critical eye back to the Bible and began to reread it. He "took three months and went through it again," and by the time he had finished, he estimated that he "had forty pages of notebook filled" with contradictions and difficulties.[8]

Whether Steve found forty pages of genuinely difficult Bible problems can be debated. One thing is certain; in his mind they were difficulties that could not be overcome and that disqualified the Bible from being the word of God. But might it just be the case that a large number of those difficulties rested on questionable assumptions Steve had about the Bible that set him up for a crisis of faith? Might it also be true that given what he was taught about the Bible, he could have come to no other conclusion? Steve is not alone in feeling a sense of disillusionment with the Bible. Rodney Wilson, author of *Killing God: Christian Fundamentalism and the Rise of Atheism*, surveyed over 1500 former conservative Christians concerning the reasons they lost their faith. He discovered that perceived problems with the Bible is the number one reason Christians begin to have doubts. Nearly all of the

5. Wilson, *Killing God,* 34.
6. Wilson, *Killing God,* 167.
7. Anonymous in discussion with the author, May 2013.
8. Steve in discussion with the author, June 2013.

perceived problems are grounded in the assumption that the Bible must be inerrant or it is not the word of God. According to Wilson, "No other issue in the FCNA Survey elicited as much input as the open-ended question on the role of loss of belief in Bible inerrancy on the deconversion process of the respondents. . . . No other question fueled as extensive an outpouring of thoughts, which is indicative of the primary importance of the rejection of biblical inerrancy in the deconversion process."[9]

I agree with Wilson's assessment. After listening to and reading many deconversion stories, it became apparent that one of the expectations many deconverts had of the Bible—and which in their eyes it could not meet—was that it was inerrant. This isn't at all surprising given the fact that many deconverts leave churches that are situated somewhere on the continuum between fundamentalist and conservative evangelical. In the environments in which their faith was shaped, belief in inerrancy was a fundamental of the faith. In fact, many deconverts report that they were taught that if they were to have any confidence in the doctrine of the Trinity and the resurrection of Christ, the Bible had to be inerrant. If the Bible was wrong about a single fact of geography, then what confidence could they have it wasn't wrong on doctrinal matters as well? The reasoning behind this conclusion is as follows:

1. God inspired the Bible.
2. God cannot make a mistake.
3. Therefore, the Bible is totally without error of any kind.

It follows then, if there is even one single error in the Bible, it cannot be inspired by God; and if God did not inspire the Bible then it is not the word of God, and if it is not the word of God it is unworthy of basing one's life on. Let's call this argument "The Single Error Argument."

It doesn't take long for the reflective reader to begin to feel the tension between the Single Error Argument and how they think the Bible presents itself. The Bible is a complex, messy book that comes to us from the ancient past. It has, on the surface at least, passages that do not cohere well with each other. For example, multiple passages in the synoptic gospels or the resurrection accounts are difficult to harmonize with each other. Add to this the fact that there are copyist errors that have crept into the copies of the Bibles we read from every Sunday. These issues combine to raise a significant challenge to the Single Error Argument. A further mistake is made when we make inerrancy an apologetic for why it is reasonable to

9. Wilson, *Killing God*, 32.

believe the Bible is the word of God. I have heard some apologists argue that one of the reasons that we know the Bible is the word of God is because it contains no errors, and no other human book can make such a claim. The best explanation why it has no errors is because God inspired it. But such a claim puts one in the difficult position of having to refute all claims of error in order to not only maintain that the Bible is inspired, but that it is God's word in the first place. Scottish theologian James Orr argued, "It is urged . . . that unless we can demonstrate what is called inerrancy of the biblical record down to even the minutest details, the whole edifice of belief in revealed religion falls to the ground. This, on the face of it, is the most suicidal position for any defender of religion to take up."[10] Orr is correct. In the words of one former believer, "If you are to believe that the Bible is the inerrant word of God or even that it was written under divine inspiration, then it only takes one mistake for that belief to crumble."[11]

The doctrine of the inerrancy of Scripture is complex and requires time and a fair bit of theological savvy to gain an understanding of what the doctrine actually is. If one does investigate the doctrine, it becomes apparent that what inerrancy means is so nuanced that it is in danger of dying the death of 1,000 qualifications. The Chicago Statement on Biblical Inerrancy—the definitive statement on the doctrine—has nineteen articles explaining what inerrancy means. The combined force of the nineteen articles is such that actually proving an error is nearly impossible. When all is said and done, inerrancy only applies to the originals, which we don't have.

What we do have are reliable copies of the original manuscripts but which do have discrepancies and contradictions in them. Even the most conservative and ardent inerrantist evangelical scholars like Gleason Archer and Norman Geisler recognize that the text we have today includes, at the very least, scribal errors. For instance, 1 Kings 4:26 says that Solomon had 40,000 stalls for his horses, but 2 Chronicles 9:25 says he had only 4,000. Geisler's solution is to confidently assert, "This is undoubtedly a copyist error."[12] This is likely true, but for those who have an inadequate understanding of inerrancy and subscribe to the simplistic Single Error Argument, it's still a contradiction in the Bible—the inerrant, no-mistakes Bible.

When people who have assumed the Single Error Argument of inerrancy come across what appears to be an error, they can experience major theological vertigo. A new Single Error Argument may replace the old Single Error Argument. The new one is:

10. Orr, *Revelation and Inspiration*, 198.

11. Wilson, *Killing God*, 36.

12. Geisler and Howe, *When Critics Ask*, 181.

1. If the Bible has even one error, it can't be the word of God.
2. The Bible does have at least one error.
3. Therefore, the Bible can't be the word of God.

One of the most popular deconversion video narratives on the Internet belongs to Christopher Redford. In his "Why I am No Longer a Christian" series, Redford recounts in eight episodes—with a total of over one million views—how he went from conservative Christian to active atheist. In an episode dedicated to the Bible, he explains the role the assumption that the Bible *had to be* inerrant played in his loss of faith. In the video, he dramatically describes the moment he discovered that the Bible has two different accounts of Judas's death and how it was devastating to his faith in the Bible.

> My tongue caught in the back of my throat. My chest seized up, adrenaline rushed through my body. My heart pounded. It felt as if the very fabric of reality itself was tearing apart. It felt as if the paint on the walls around me would tear apart revealing an empty darkness. Everything I believed lay vulnerable on an altar, waiting to be pierced, waiting to be sacrificed to this horrifying moment of realization . . . I braced myself to face the consequence that my entire religion was a mistake.[13]

Redford's description seems a bit over the top. But I have no doubt that discovering what he took to be an error in the Bible produced in him a sense of cognitive dissonance. Given that he accepted the Single Error Argument, if his faith was to survive he would have to find a way to harmonize the two passages in such a way that his intellectual integrity would allow. In the end, he could not do so. Convinced the Bible had errors in it, he was left with little choice but to conclude it could not be the word of God.

Where former believers experience the problem of inerrancy most acutely is as it relates to science. It is common for former believers to point out that for a book that is supposedly inerrant, it is repeatedly in conflict with what we know to be true about the world from science. There are at least three sub-assumptions operating under the radar that give this objection its force. The first usually has to do with an overly strict understanding of what it means for the Bible to speak truthfully. Former believers tend to be under the impression that if the Bible is going to speak truthfully, it must speak literally.

> I believed it fully and with a passion until my crisis of faith a little over two years ago that eventually led me to becoming an

13. Redford, "Why I am No Longer."

> agnostic. But before my crisis I didn't question my faith. I was one of those people who agreed fully with the Bible and thought it should be taken literally in all circumstances *unless the passage clearly stated or implied that it was figurative.* Looking back at that now, it's kind of embarrassing, I mean, have you really taken a look at Genesis lately?[14]

The second sub-assumption many deconverts who have a problem with the Bible exhibit is a very strong tendency toward scientism or, at the very least, they assume that empirical evidence is the primary criterion by which truth claims are evaluated. "Evidence," for such individuals, is almost always construed in terms of scientific evidence. One former believer put it this way:

> I remember thinking religion is the only subject where my teachers don't have to prove their answers. In math class I could take two pairs of apples and make four, in science you could look at the planets/stars in the sky, in history you could see real documentary footage but religion, well that was all based on word of mouth and instead of empirical truth they revered faith. Faith? Faith is not tangible, faith cannot be measured, faith is . . . blind. In grade six I chose to never accept knowledge that was based on blind faith and could not be proven.[15]

Another commented that,

> Religion is a thing of the past, something we used to explain the unexplainable, something we used before the age of science. Such primitive beliefs that divide us and cause so much suffering should not exist in the modern world; we should all be using science to find out the truth. Science sets us free from the bondage of religion. It allows you to question it as much as you like and, although it is not perfect, it is always correcting itself. Science will lead us to the truth, it sets our mind free, and satisfies our curiosity.[16]

A third remarked, "As I came to understand not only the claims of science but the process, I came to believe that this is really the singular reliable way to examine reality. Since science does not show that any gods exist, I do not accept their existence."[17]

14. Cooper, "From Christian Fundamentalist," lines 12–16.
15. Delms, "What Made You," lines 32–42.
16. Karen in discussion with the author, October 2017.
17. Anonymous in discussion with the author, September 2017.

The third sub-assumption is that believing in evolution is irreconcilable with believing in the Bible. One former believer lamented, "I took an anthropology course where I learned a great deal, and it was during that course I became convinced that evolution was true and then all of my beliefs in the Bible and God came crashing down like a house of cards."[18] A second said, "My belief was based on an understanding that the Bible was completely true. As that belief clashed with actual facts and evidence, it became clear that the truth wasn't found in the Bible, but in science."[19] A third reported, "I took a geology class and finally realized that the Earth and the Universe is older than what is described in the Bible. I thought, if they were wrong about something as important as that, what else could they be wrong about?" [20] Another credited evolution with their faith demise by arguing, "It was my study of biology and especially evolution that caused me to doubt and finally leave the faith."[21] Finally, this former believer confessed that:

> I adamantly rejected/mocked the idea of evolution. I avoided science classes because I did not want to be confronted or have to confront evolution any more than necessary. During my twelve- to eighteen-month deconversion process, I began to allow myself to consider the details of evolution and found it a very compelling and fascinating idea. Once the Bible wasn't true, it was not too hard to understand the ideas that had previously seemed ridiculous and impossible."[22]

Once convinced of the reality of evolution, they no longer could maintain their belief in God. The combination of their assumptions about inerrancy, the need to read literally, and the authority of science made believing in the biblical account of reality impossible.

Holding any one of these sub-assumptions can generate serious doubt about the Bible's veracity. Holding all three of them leads to disaster. When believers assume that for the Bible to be true it must speak literally, they not only make a wrong assumption about the nature of truth, but the essence of communication itself. Given that the Bible is the product of the divine and human, we should expect that the Bible is a product of its time and culture and therefore it should display evidence of that. When this basic fact is ignored, it can lead to seeing errors in the text that are, in fact, not errors at all. The best example of this is the continuing debate about the first two

18. Wilson, *Killing God,* 178.
19. Wilson, *Killing God,* 182.
20. Wilson, *Killing God,* 153
21. Wilson, *Killing God,* 179.
22. Wilson, *Killing God,* 180.

chapters of Genesis. Are the creation accounts in Genesis chapters 1 and 2 true? It all depends on what you assume "true" means. The creation account of Genesis was not written to contemporary readers. Nor was it intended to be a scientific account of how God created. Instead it was written to an ancient people group who were immersed in a culture that acted, for them, as the boundary conditions for what was conceivable. God communicated to them in terms that they were familiar with to tell them important theological truths. That is why the creation account in Genesis looks so similar to that of the Egyptians, Mesopotamians, and the Canaanites at the time. God used a common story template to teach the Israelites theological truths about who he is, who they are, and where the world came from. So, is the creation account "true"? If you mean, is it literally true from a scientific perspective then the answer is clearly no. But if you mean, does it achieve its purpose to communicate accurate theological information, the answer is yes. Unfortunately, for many deconverts, they were convinced that if the Bible is to be inerrant it must be literal, and being literal means lining up with contemporary science. Naturally, then, given these assumptions, former believers could not ignore the massive discrepancies they saw between the Bible and their science textbooks.

What they assumed the Bible had to be played a major role in the loss of faith of many former believers. Their assumptions about the doctrine of inerrancy and what the doctrine holds, combined with what they discovered in the pages of the Bible, generated serious doubts about the Bible's divine status. Whether the apparent errors were historical or scientific, they were enough, in conjunction with their assumptions, to sink their faith.

The Immaculate Conception

Former believers frequently hold a second inadequate conception about the Bible, and that is what I call the *Immaculate Conception*. Although not explicit, the testimonies of former believers demonstrate that, like most Christians, they never gave much thought to the origin and preservation of the Bible. For the most part, before they lost their faith, the stories of former Christians reveal they held assumptions about the Bible very similar to those Christians who remain in the faith. They believed that that Bible was the divinely inspired word of God, the book that Christians everywhere have trusted to be a sacred communication from God to humans. This assumption is true, as far as it goes. However, it does not go far enough. Although the Bible is a divine book, it is not *merely* a divine book. The Bible is also a human book; in fact, it is a collection of books, with a long and complex history. And though it is divine, it has human fingerprints all over it. From the original authors, to the editors, to the copyists, to the process of canonization and then translation, the Bible is a book that in some sense is as much human as it is divine. But the unstated—and unthought—elements of what I am calling the *Immaculate Conception* of the Bible are that: a) because the Bible is from God it is divine to such a high degree that it practically excludes the role of humans in its composition, and b) because it is the word of God it somehow stands outside of the normal course of human history, untainted by human frailty. Like the physical conception of Jesus, the Bible stands unblemished by any negative human input.

For believers raised in Christian homes, the Bible was a normal part of their life, an ever-present, unchanging book that told the story of God and his people. It was a book about history but without a history of its own. The Bible, for most Christians, is like Melchizedek, king of Salem, who, according to Hebrews, was "without father or mother or genealogy, having neither beginning of days or end of life." (Heb 7:3 ESV) If it does have a history, it doesn't dawn on many believers to ask what it is. No doubt, the fact that their Christian community assumed that the Bible was sacred Scripture is why former believers adopted the same assumption. Or, perhaps, it had been part of their life for so long that it never dawned on them to question it. In the same way that most people never think about the fact that their parents had sex to create them—they just know that they are here now with parents—most Christians don't think to ask about how the Bible came to be. It is just part of their life, like the air we breathe.

It needs to be said that former believers rarely state they conceived of the Bible as described above, but from their testimonies it is clear that they did. Consider how Valerie Tarico, psychologist, author, and former believer frames her experience:

> When I was a child, the Bible was as timeless as my parents. Along with the foundations of the Earth and the valleys of the sea, it had always existed in its present, unchanging form. As a teenager, I spent hours weekly studying its passages under the guidance of others, wiser and more experienced than I. The contents of the Bible opened up to me. I learned the basics of "biblical exegesis," the methods by which Evangelicals analyze Scriptures phrase by phrase, word by word, even turning to the original Greek or Hebrew to better mine the depths of meaning layered into each perfect word of God. It never occurred

> to me to ask the book's history, because it had no history. Like God, it simply was.[23]

She goes on to say that "even through college, when I took one course called Old Testament as Literature and another called New Testament Theology it never occurred to me to ask about the histories of the Bible rather than the histories in the Bible."[24]

Tarico, like many Christians, former and faithful, had assumptions about the Bible. And, given her early experience, there was nothing that would cause her to question those assumptions. The Bible had always just been the word of God, a taken-for-granted part of her life and the life of her community. But, as she encountered others who didn't operate according to the assumptions of her community, it generated questions about the Bible. Why, she wondered, if God wanted to communicate with humanity did he do so in such a limited way? She asks, "If we step back from debates about higher criticism and inerrancy, a larger question looms: suppose God really wanted to make a perfect revelation of himself to humankind. Does it not seem likely that he would show himself in some form equally accessible to all rather than in a specific, corruptible literary tradition?"[25]

Tarico's objection is one that former believers frequently raise. Essentially, it says if the Bible is really God's word, then why does it look the way it does? Surely a book from God would look more Godlike. But when believers do begin to ask questions about the nature of the Bible, they get a big surprise. The word of God starts to look very human. While I suspect that, if pressed, many would not be able to give a clear accounting of what they think a Godlike book should look like, they definitely know how it shouldn't. For starters, it should look a lot less human than it does. One individual commented that, "The obvious flaws in the Bible helped lead to my loss of faith. I remember thinking that with all the competing religious texts, that if one were actually the word of God, it would stand above the others in some clear way, which the Bible did not seem to do.[26]

Far from criticizing former believers' problems with the Bible, I can appreciate the disillusionment they felt at discovering the Bible has a very human history. For years, I read, studied, memorized, and applied the Bible to the best of my ability without ever asking any questions about it. Like Valerie Tarico, the Bible acted as a foundation for my life. It was the bedrock of my worldview. Questioning the nature of the Bible never occurred to me

23. Tarico, *Trusting Doubt*, 23.
24. Tarico, *Trusting Doubt*, 23.
25. Tarico, *Trusting Doubt*, 32.
26. Wilson, *Killing God*, 168.

any more than questioning the laws of logic or if the universe would continue to act in a uniform manner in the future. And, as long as I was content in my Christian community, it acted as a sturdy plausibility structure that reaffirmed the divine nature of the Bible. Maybe it was my exposure to other faiths, or maybe it was my own insecurities, or maybe a combination of both, but one day it occurred to me that I had committed myself to this book without having any idea where it came from. Of course, I knew the Bible didn't drop out of Heaven as one complete volume, but in hindsight I might as well have thought that. When I began looking into the history of the Bible, I was quite disturbed at what I found. Like many former Christians, I wasn't quite sure just what I thought the history of a divine book should look like, but I knew what it shouldn't. And everything I discovered made the Bible look less divine and more human. I discovered that we are not sure who wrote many of the books of the Bible. We have some good reasons to believe they were authored by those individuals whose names they bear, but not certainty. Which made me wonder, if a book has its origination in God, shouldn't we know with certainty who it was that he chose to write on his behalf? I found out that the Bible is a copy of ancient original manuscripts that we do not possess. Which caused me to ask how, if God took the time and care to inspire a collection of manuscripts, could they get lost? I learned that despite not having the originals we have copies of them. But those copies are mostly fragmentary and the best ones are, for the most, part dated to a couple hundred years after the originals were written.[27] Furthermore, no two manuscripts are identical. In fact, there are more textual variants among the manuscripts than there are words in the New Testament itself. This caused me to question the trustworthiness of the copy on my nightstand. You can only imagine how I felt when I discovered the textual support of the Old Testament is worse. I then began to notice that various authors of the Bible had their own writing style and way of expressing themselves. Why, if God inspired the Bible, was there so much of the humanity of the authors in it, I wondered? I studied the process of canonization and was shocked by what I found out. The exact process of how the Old Testament came to be a single volume consisting of thirty-nine books is a bit unclear. We are fairly certain that the Jews recognized a canon of sacred Scripture prior to the birth of Jesus. The clearest and earliest evidence we have of the existence of an Old Testament canon comes from the Jewish historian Josephus. In

27. I am aware that the manuscript evidence for the New Testament is quite impressive compared to all other ancient texts. However, the Bible is the word of God, so accuracy in preservation matters much more than it does for the words of Plato. It would be nice if we had more complete manuscripts that are closer in time to the originals.

his work *Against Apion*, Josephus mentions that prior to the destruction of Jerusalem in 70 CE, the Jews kept a collection of books in the Temple that they considered to be a canon of sacred texts. He even listed the books, which are identical to the thirty-nine books in the Old Testament, except for Song of Solomon. The list of books that came to be known as the New Testament, although recognized and adopted by many Christians earlier, wasn't officially ratified until the Council of Carthage in 397 CE. The process of canonization in both cases wasn't smooth, and there were competing lists of books, debates, and dissenters. This is not what I expected from a book that was supposed to be a divine revelation. If God inspired the various books of Bible, then why did it take so long for people to recognize they were inspired and to put them into one volume? I then started to realize that much of the Bible looks like a cultural product of its time. For instance, the Old Testament authors clearly share a common worldview about cosmology with their pagan counterparts. Both believed that the Earth was a flat disc sitting on pillars surrounded by chaotic waters under a dome with Heaven located on the other side of the dome. If God inspired the Bible, then why did he inspire something like that? Why wouldn't he give them correct information? Likewise, as previously mentioned, the Genesis creation account is strikingly similar to the creation accounts of the Canaanites, the Egyptians, and the Mesopotamians. And the Noah story sounds so similar to the Gilgamesh epic and the story of Atrahasis, that it couldn't be a coincidence. What was I to make of this apparent plagiarism?

When I learned about the history of the Bible after so many years of holding the *Immaculate Conception* assumption, it was faith-shaking. Why, I wanted to know, did God's book look like a product of grubby human hands? At the time, I shared the feelings of a YouTube commentator, who, like me, discovered that the Bible was not quite what he assumed it was:

> I want to talk about this idea that the Bible is the complete inerrant word of God. The reason why I had to give up that idea was the way that the Bible came to be today is because of an event that happened in the fourth century. It was called the Council of Nicaea . . . What happened at the Council of Nicaea is that the canon was closed. The books that were to become part of standard Scripture were decided at that council once and for all. So, certain books were let into the canon, and other books were excluded. Whenever I learned about this, it was a rude awakening for me . . . I realized that the books of the Bible were written by ordinary people, and the books were assembled in a very human and ordinary manner, because it was put together by disagreements, largely for political purposes. I simply couldn't

> accept that counts as divine inspiration. How can you say that something is divinely inspired when it is assembled in a way that is so ordinarily human? If the Bible was divinely inspired, we should expect it to not appear of human origin. The fact that it has all these contradictions in there, the fact that it was put together by a council, the fact that it was all written by people, shows me there is nothing divinely inspired about it.[28]

Spoiler alert: I found answers to my questions and continue to believe the Bible is the word of God. But my conception of the Bible had to change in order to do so. I had to recognize the *Immaculate Conception* of the Bible that I assumed was wrong and that the problem wasn't with the Bible, but what I thought the Bible had to look like. I don't blame my church community for instilling in me the *Immaculate Conception* assumption. I tend to think that it is a much bigger problem than local churches not providing an adequate understanding of the Bible. It is a problem of the evangelical/fundamentalist community at large not realizing they need to provide a more accurate and complete conception of the Bible in light of the readily available data that exists online challenging the Bible as the word of God. Until we do a better job of educating believers in the nature of the Bible as a divine and human book, we will set them up for a crisis of faith.

The Greatest Story Ever Told?

The third assumption that deconverts hold about the Bible is that it's a nice story about God's love for the world. The basic storyline is well known by deconverts; God created the world, humans rebelled against God resulting in their separation from him, some famous Old Testament figures did some interesting things like killing a giant and spending the night with lions and being swallowed by a whale, then God sent Jesus into the world to die on the cross as our punishment so that if we believe in him we can go to Heaven when we die. I'm not being facetious or mocking the biblical knowledge of former believers. Ask many Christians what the storyline of the Bible is, and that's about what you'll get. At some point, former Christians desired to learn more about the story, decided to pick up the Bible, and read it from cover to cover. What they read shocked and disturbed them. To their surprise, the Bible is filled with horrific violence, bloodshed, and immoral behavior. What's worse is that much of the really detestable stuff is done at the command of God. Practices, which are completely at odds with contemporary moral sensibilities, including (but not limited to) slaughtering entire people

28. Drosera, "Reasons to Deconvert."

groups, slavery, and gender inequality are done at God's behest by direct commandment or legislation. One former believer put it this way:

> The more I read about the Abrahamic religions, the more I got sure that there could not exist an insecure, hateful, cruel, and a vengeful "God." A "God" that "commanded" his followers to believe that he was the only "True God," demanded worship to himself (and only him in a prescribed manner), to kill the "unbelievers" (women, children et al.), and to wipe out entire cities and civilizations. He was an absolute dictator, he did not like to be questioned, and any deviation from his "command" would entail death in this life and condemnation for all eternity. Further, it established that not all people "he" created were equal—God peddled the mistreatment of women and promoted misogyny as religious diktat.[29]

A second deconvert recalled, "As a teenager, I began to have difficulty with the violence of the Old Testament and the problem of homosexuality . . . I decided to read through the entire Bible. This time, the Old Testament violence was absolutely too horrible to justify, and it kicked off the beginning of the end of my faith.[30] So, too, a third struggled with the same problem. "After no longer being brainwashed into believing the infallibility of the Bible, I further realized it also has so truly abhorrent things in it that Christians somehow must justify in order to believe in their religion. Horrible genocides, infanticide, rape, incest . . . but somehow you have to accept it as "good" because God sanctioned it despite the obvious realization that it really is filled with horror.[31]

If one has inherited a particular view of God, one that focuses only on his kindness and love, then when one encounters such troubling stories, this can cause a sense of disequilibrium. How could the good and loving God of the Bible command such heinous acts like slaughtering all of the inhabitants of the Promised Land? Martin, a former believer, shared with me his experience at encountering the stories of "genocide" in the Old Testament. The dissonance was so great between the view of the Bible he was taught (a nice story about God's love) and what the Old Testament recorded that he expressed he "felt lied to about the Bible." He elaborated by pointing out, "There are things that aren't so nice in the Bible," specifically "the stories of genocide." It was difficult for him "to reconcile the God of the Old

29. Anonymous in discussion with the author, April 2017.

30. Wilson, *Killing God,* 161.

31. Wilson, *Killing God,* 163.

[Testament] and the God of the New Testament,"[32] whom he saw as warlike on one hand and loving and gracious on the other.

Martin, like other deconverts, feels that when it comes to the Bible he was only ever given one side of the story. The Bible was portrayed to them as the story of a loving God who entered the world to save his people. What they discovered is that, in the Bible, redemption often comes through violence. Some violence might be tolerable, but the amount of violence in the Bible ordered by God himself stands in stark contrast to the concept of the Bible they had received from their Christian communities. Reading the Bible opened their eyes to the darker aspects of Scripture. Although Martin and others were familiar with a number of shocking events in the Bible, those stories were typically whitewashed of the horrible reality of what actually happened. I can recall being in Sunday school as a child joyfully singing, "Joshua fought the battle of Jericho, Jericho, Jericho. Joshua fought the battle of Jericho and the walls came a tumblin' down." It was a fun song about how God helped Joshua and the Israelites so they could settle the Promised Land. What the song leaves out is that after the walls fell, Joshua and the Israelites slaughtered everything in the city that lived.

> 16 The seventh time around, when the priests sounded the trumpet blast, Joshua commanded the army, "Shout! For the Lord has given you the city! 17 The city and all that is in it are to be devoted[a] to the Lord. Only Rahab the prostitute and all who are with her in her house shall be spared, because she hid the spies we sent. 18 But keep away from the devoted things, so that you will not bring about your own destruction by taking any of them. (Josh 6:16–18a NIV)

> They devoted the city to the Lord and destroyed with the sword every living thing in it—men and women, young and old, cattle, sheep, and donkeys. (Josh 6:21 NIV)

Imagine what that looked like. The carnage and bloodshed from killing every living person, young and old, plus all of the livestock is troubling. No wonder the song ends with the walls coming down and not with what followed. Who would ever want to sing about that?

Or consider the Noahic flood. The story of Noah and his floating zoo is one of the most beloved stories in the Bible. And for good reason; who wouldn't want to be on that ship with all those cute cuddly animals, knowing that God was taking care of you through the storm? A casual Internet search for "Noah's ark toys" brings up dozens, if not hundreds, of items for

32. Martin in discussion with the author, July 2013.

children to play with. Nurseries in churches throughout North America are decorated with images of a Santa Claus-like Noah, smiling from the ark surrounded by cartoon animals, all seemingly having a great time. In fact, on the wall in my own children's bedroom is a mural that I painted of such a scene! Overlooking my son's bed is a grandfatherly cartoon depiction of Noah waving, surrounded by the happy animals on the ark and a rainbow overhead. I also recall singing about it in Sunday school.

> The Lord said to Noah: there's gonna be a floody, floody
>
> The Lord said to Noah: there's gonna be a floody, floody
>
> Get those children out of the muddy, muddy,
>
> Children of the Lord
>
> So, rise and shine, and give God the glory, glory
>
> Rise and shine, and give God the glory, glory
>
> Rise and shine, and give God the glory, glory
>
> Children of the Lord

After several stanzas recounting how the animals arrived, the rain fell, and that Noah sent out a dovey-dovey, the song ends with the following stanza:

> Now, this is the end of, the end of my story, story
>
> This is the end of, the end of my story, story
>
> Everything is hunky dory, dory
>
> Children of the Lord.

Everything was hunky dory? Really? Maybe for Noah and those on the ark things were hunky dory. But for everyone else it sure wasn't. God had destroyed them in a cataclysm so violent and terrifying that it reshaped the entire planet. If the story recorded in Genesis chapters 9 through 11 is a literal account of the life of Noah and not something else, it tells not only of God's faithfulness, but also of his wrath.

> The LORD saw how great the wickedness of the human race had become on the Earth, and that every inclination of the thoughts of the human heart was only evil all the time. The LORD regretted that he had made human beings on the Earth, and his heart was deeply troubled. So the LORD said, "I will wipe from the face of the Earth the human race I have created—and with them

> the animals, the birds, and the creatures that move along the ground—for I regret that I have made them." (Gen 6:5–7 NIV)

Clearly, the story of Noah and the ark is not just a reassuring story of how God delivered Noah, but also of a terrifying story of how God drowned the population of the entire world. Imagine the terror as the water climbed higher and higher. Imagine mothers and fathers as they tried to help their children reach ever higher ground, only to be swept away and drowned. Noah and Joshua are but two of the many violent and difficult passages in the Bible. I assume there are good reasons for such passages. I am not passing judgment on God's commands to Joshua or his decision to flood the Earth. That judgment is far above my pay grade. What I am trying to point out is that for former believers, discovering these darker stories was a shock to the system. They had a conception of the Bible that failed to correspond to what it is. The Bible, in their experience, was for all intents and purposes cashed out in terms of a story of God's loving goodness in rescuing a wayward humanity. When stories such as the conquering of the Promised Land, or the Noahic flood were taught, only one side of the story was emphasized, the part you sang about was God's goodness. No one sings:

> The Lord said to Noah: I killed everybody, body
>
> The Lord said to Noah: I killed everybody, body
>
> I did it with water so it wouldn't be bloody, bloody
>
> Children of the Lord.

And for good reason—that would be horrible. But when former believers picked up the Bible and read it for themselves, they encountered parts of it they never knew existed. Stories of God commanding the wholesale slaughter of people groups, disturbing penalties for violating the Mosaic law, God condoning slavery and the lower status of women, God's jealousy, God's apparent capriciousness, his acceptance of human sacrifice,[33] and his anger are either ignored, or, as in the cases of Joshua and Noah, cashed out in only the most positive of terms.

Assumptions about the Bible are at the heart of many deconversion narratives. The faith of former believers was undermined by inadequate assumptions about the nature of the Bible. The first is the assumption that the Bible cannot contain a single mistake and still be the word of God. When

33. A reoccurring criticism of Yahweh in deconversion narratives is that he allowed Jepthath to sacrifice his daughter to him in return for a victory in war. The text does not say that God wanted such a sacrifice. Furthermore, Deuteronomy 12:31 and Jeremiah 19:4–5 make it clear that God never commanded such a thing, and he finds it detestable.

believers encounter apparent errors or contradictions in the text of Scripture (and there are many examples), it can be devastating. The second assumption is that the Bible is a divine book, to the near exclusion of the human element. A lack of knowledge about the human role in the production of the Bible is problematic when believers encounter that information, especially if it is from hostile sources. The third assumption is that the Bible is a nice story of God's love for people. While the Bible is a story of God's love for people, it is much more. It contains violence and judgment in the form of floods, harsh penalties, and eternal separation from God. Coming face to face with these darker passages of Scripture has caused numerous former believers to harbor serious doubts about the Bible being the word of God. In the next chapter, we take a look at the second area where deconverts exhibit erroneous assumptions. In the same way that unbalanced conceptions of the Bible underwrite false assumptions and create unmet expectations, so too do incomplete conceptions of God.

Chapter 7

Ill-prepared Part 2

In all matters, before beginning,
a diligent preparation should be made.

Cicero

God Complex

In the previous chapter we saw how an inadequate conception of the Bible can have dire consequences because it creates in Christians expectations for the Bible that go unmet. In this chapter we will continue to look at how Christians can be philosophically ill-prepared or, as I like to call it, *Half-Baked,* by their Christian communities when it comes to how they conceive of God.

A.W. Tozer once claimed that "what comes into our minds when we think about God is the most important thing about us . . . For this reason, the gravest question before the church is always God himself, and the most portentous fact about any man is not what he at a given time may say or do, but what he in his deep heart conceives God to be like."[1] I think Tozer is correct, and deconversion narratives lend support to his claim. God, or more accurately the concept of God, held by many former believers appears to play a major role in their loss of faith. When God did not live up to their expectations, it generated within them a sense of betrayal that led to doubting God's existence.

Being let down by an acquaintance, coworker, or distant relative can be discouraging. But being let down by the ones closest to you can be deeply painful. Unfaithful spouses, siblings that don't keep their word, parents who

1. Tozer, *Knowledge,* 1.

don't fulfill their responsibilities all have the capacity to wound us at a much deeper level. Spouses, siblings, and parents should be those who we can always count on and who always have our best interest in mind. I know that my parents will always look out for my interests and always be there when I call. I know that my brother will always have my back and will do almost anything for me in a time of need. Likewise, I would do the same for him. And that's the way it should be; we should be able to count on those closest to us to be there in our time of need. They shouldn't let us down. Theologically speaking, no one is closer to and cares more about people than God, ergo he is the last person that Christians should ever feel let down by. But that is exactly what large numbers of former believers feel that God has done to them; he let them down when they needed him most. The question is, did God let them down or was it that their conception of God was inadequate to who God actually is that set them up to have unrealistic assumptions and unmet expectations? I am convinced that it is the latter. Just as difficulties with the Bible arise when believers have an inadequate view of Scripture, so too do they arise when they have an incomplete view of God. And, as with the inadequate conception of Scripture, the incomplete conception of God is not totally in error. It is not so much that deconverts have erroneous conceptions of God, but that they have incomplete conceptions of him. In short, their idea of God is missing important ingredients.

The conception of God that emerges from deconversion narratives bears similarities to what Christian Smith has labeled Moralistic Therapeutic Deism.[2] Between 2001 and 2005, the National Study of Youth and Religion surveyed 3,370 teenagers and parents throughout the United States and then followed that up with 267 in-person interviews. The goal of the project was to discover the religious and spiritual lives of American adolescents. What they discovered is that American teenagers have a view of God and religion that can be summarized as follows:

1. A God exists who created and orders the world and watches over human life on Earth.
2. God wants people to be good, nice, and fair to each other as taught in the Bible and most world religions.
3. The central goal of life is to be happy and to feel good about oneself.
4. God does not need to be involved in one's life except when God is needed to resolve a problem.
5. Good people go to Heaven when they die.

2. Smith and Lundquist, *Soul Searching.*

Moralistic Therapeutic Deism holds that God exists, (deism) he wants us to be happy (therapeutic), and we should treat others in ways that maximizes their happiness by being good, nice, and fair to each other (moral). If that is how we make others happy, it is reasonable to conclude that is how God makes us happy, by being good, nice, and fair. According to Smith, for American teenagers "God is something like a combination Divine Butler and Cosmic Therapist: he is always on call, takes care of any problems that arise, [and] professionally helps his people feel better about themselves."[3] It should come as no surprise, given what Smith has discovered about the beliefs of American teenagers, that the three inadequate conceptions of God appearing in deconversion narratives map closely to the three attributes that American adolescents believe make up God's character: Since God wants us to be good to each other, we can expect him to be good to us and intervene, preventing misfortune and evil. Since God wants us to be nice, we can expect that he will be nice by being experientially present in our lives by answering prayers in ways we think he should. Since God wants us to be fair, we can expect he will be fair and so we can anticipate a predictable amount of reciprocity in our relationship with him. While there is some truth in these assumptions, they are not the whole story about who God is or how he acts. When Christian communities provide believers with *Half-Baked*, one-sided conceptions of God, disaster ensues.

Although being disappointed with God is at the heart of countless deconversion narratives, it's possible to discern three variations on this theme. The first is, if God is good, why doesn't he intervene in the face of suffering? The second is, if God is nice (as in kind), why does he remain silent in response to the pleas of his people? The third is, if God is just, why does he treat the faithful so poorly? Not just former believers, but probably most believers hold these three *Half-Baked* and inadequate conceptions of God, as well.

Good Grief: Why Doesn't God Intervene?

Once again, former believer, psychologist, and author Valerie Tarico provides us with a good example of the problem of unmet expectations. In her book *Trusting Doubt*, she explains why she rejects apologetic arguments seeking to exonerate God's lack of intervention in the midst of suffering. Tarico maintains, "Orthodox Christianity insists that God cares about human suffering and intervenes in a myriad of ways to relieve it." Yet, in the midst of the vast majority of human suffering, God is conspicuously absent,

3. Smith and Lundquist, *Soul Searching*. 164.

leaving the arguments made by apologists for human suffering unsatisfying "in part because they contradict those foundational beliefs and images." Quoting Psalm 23 and pointing out its declaration of God's tender care for his people, Tarico wonders if the psalm isn't to be the universal experience of all Christians. If it isn't, she asks,

> Then why does this psalm hang, illustrated by soft-hued portraits of the good Shepherd cradling a lamb, in bedrooms around the world . . . What does it say that he watches over little children if it doesn't mean he protects them from horrors like molesters and spinal cord tumors and napalm? Ask an evangelical child what it means. Ask her parent. Ask her pastor. Ask a hundred. Without exception, they will tell you Jesus watches over his beloved to protect them from earthly harm, not just spiritual harm.[4]

No doubt Tarico's complaint expresses a number of erroneous assumptions, which we will address in due time, but it is not without force. Don't we expect a good and loving God to care for, at the very least, innocent children?

The problem of God's lack of intervention in light of his supposed goodness is perhaps the most mystifying thing about him. It is a vexing problem that resists easy explanations, maybe all explanations this side of eternity. I don't want to minimize the problem of suffering and God's apparent lack of concern. Valerie Tarico isn't wrong to claim that God cares about human suffering and that some of the most cherished images of God are as a caring father that desires the best for his children. She is also not wrong to feel a sense of confusion and frustration at God's lack of intervention to alleviate the problem. Jewish and Christian Scriptures wrestle with God's apparent indifference to suffering. Some of the Bible's most admired and faithful individuals expressed the same frustration as Tarico. At times, God's ways were as opaque to them as they are to us.

One of the most poignant expressions of disillusionment with God in the face of suffering comes from the pen of Holocaust survivor and Nobel Peace Prize winner Elie Wiesel. From the time he was a child, Wiesel was a devout Jew. Growing up in a Hasidic family in Romania, Wiesel regularly spent hours a day for ten to eleven months of the year studying the Torah, Talmud, and Kabbalah. His study and piety were so intense throughout his youth that he was chronically ill due to his habitual fasting.[5] At fifteen years of age, he and his family were deported to Auschwitz, and then he and his father to Buchenwald, where he endured mental, emotional, and physi-

4. Tarico, *Trusting Doubt*, 78.

5. Henry, "The Life and Work."

cal torment. He described his experience the first night in the camp and the toll it took on his faith in God.

> Never shall I forget that night, the first night in camp, that turned my life into one long night seven times sealed. Never shall I forget that smoke. Never shall I forget the small faces of the children whose bodies I saw transformed into smoke under a silent sky. Never shall I forget those flames that consumed my faith forever. Never shall I forget the nocturnal silence that deprived me for all eternity of the desire to live. Never shall I forget those moments that murdered my God and my soul and turned my dreams to ashes.[6]

Of all the horrific experiences he endured in the camps, one proved too much for his faith to bear. A young boy, accused of being party to a planned uprising, was hanged before the entire camp. Wiesel had witnessed other public executions before, but this one was different. That the Nazis could kill an innocent child with, as Wiesel described him, the face of a "sad angel" without intervention from a good covenantal God was more than he could take. The chair was kicked out from under the boy's feet and he dropped until the rope tightened around his neck. But because of his light weight, the rope neither broke his neck nor sufficiently cut off the blood flow to his brain. This resulted in him writhing in anguish, dangling between Heaven and Earth, life and death. Forced to walk past the boy and look at him in the face, Wiesel recounted:

> And so he remained for more than half an hour, lingering between life and death, writhing before our eyes. And we were forced to look at him at close range. He was still alive when I passed him. His tongue was still red, his eyes not yet extinguished. Behind me, I heard the same man asking: "For God's sake, where is God?" And from within me, I heard a voice answer: "Where He is? This is where—hanging here from this gallows . . ."[7]

The God whom Elie Wiesel had committed himself to learning about and serving could not survive in the face of such abject depravity and evil. Like the sad angel, Wiesel's conception of God died that day. Later he would describe a Rosh Hashanah service conducted in the camp that he took part in. As the leader of the makeshift congregation prayed, he cried out, "Blessed

6. Wiesel and Wiesel, *Night*, 34.
7. Wiesel and Wiesel, *Night*, 64.

be your name." The absurdity of blessing God's name in the midst of such horror struck Wiesel as bizarre. He thought to himself:

> Blessed be God's name? Why, but why, would I bless him? Every fiber in me rebelled. Because he caused thousands of children to burn in his mass graves? Because he kept six crematoria working day and night, including Sabbath and the Holy Days? Because in his great might, he had created Auschwitz, Birkenau, Buna, and so many other factories of death? How could I say to him: Blessed be Thou, Almighty, Master of the Universe, who chose us among all nations to be tortured day and night, to watch as our fathers, our mothers, our brothers end up in the furnaces? Praised be Thy Holy Name, for having chosen us to be slaughtered on Thine altar?[8]

Despite everything he experienced in the camps, Elie Wiesel's belief in God survived, but not unscathed. The God he believed in when he entered the camp and the God he believed in when he left were not the same. The latter was more complex, paradoxical, and harder to understand.

But it doesn't take living in a concentration camp to cause one to question God's love and care. All it takes is for God not to respond how you think he should in the face of evil. Although not experiencing the kind or amount of suffering as Wiesel, Ian, a former evangelical believer, nevertheless pointed to God's lack of intervention as a significant piece in his loss of faith. Reflecting on his Christian experience, Ian described himself as a former believer "who took it too seriously and ended up crushed when it failed to deliver." Born into a conservative Christian family, Ian came of age in the 1970s in a religious environment "wherein nothing but God mattered," and he "wholeheartedly embraced Christianity." Ian's family gave him the freedom to think through his beliefs but within the confines of one axiom, which was that the Bible was true and meant what it said. Until, in his eyes, it didn't.

> So where and why did this "bullet-proof" system fail me? Quite simply, it failed me because it made so much sense that I felt I could actually lean on it. I feel the situation is best summed up by the very ironic quotation from the Bible itself "Lo, thou trustest in the staff of this broken reed, on Egypt; whereon if a man lean, it will go into his hand, and pierce it: so is Pharaoh king of Egypt to all that trust in him." Ironically, the God described in

8. Wiesel and Wiesel, *Night*, 66.

> the New Testament is just such an unreliable staff: Christianity is great until you count on it.[9]

Ian married at twenty-four; sadly, his wife has suffered from depression and has been suicidal for as long as she could remember (back to at least the age of seven). She clung to Ian because he gave her hope. In hindsight, Ian lamented:

> As it turns out, the hope I so confidently gave her was an empty illusion, and I now feel as though I have let her down. I spent about seven years earnestly trying everything. At first, I was confident that the solution lied in giving her a happy, stable, fulfilling life. Things did not improve at all, but, of course, I accepted that it's a long, slow process and that she had many wounds to heal from. After six or seven years of this, I started to get worn thin. I was coming apart at the seams, and my confidence started to be shaken.

His waning confidence in his faith coincided with a growing sense of skepticism toward God. He wondered,

> If God is all-powerful, how can he be so cruel as to allow anyone to go through such mental anguish for so many years, despite undeniable and extreme adherence to his precepts? What did she do to deserve that? And why, oh why, does Jesus, my long lost friend, insult me by saying that if I ask I shall receive and that if I knock he'll open to me when, in reality, he stays deathly silent in the face of our anguish? Whatever happened to the joy of the Lord? What sin would justify depression so deep that every morning you wish you hadn't made it through the night?

He added:

> My wife and I have recently concluded that if the almighty God truly does exist, he is a cruel and evil bastard whom we want nothing to do with. So it's much less painful to consider that he doesn't exist. Because, you see, I still love Jesus, in spite of it all. So I'd rather think I was deluding myself with an imaginary friend than consider that he would actually have betrayed me. What did I do to deserve that?[10]

Who can read Ian's lament and not feel moved? If I were in his shoes I might feel the same way he does. His complaint and those of Valerie Tarico

9. Ian in discussion with the author, May 2017.

10. Ian in discussion with the author, May 2017.

and Elie Wiesel reveal that we all harbor deep expectations that God, if he is good and if he is loving, will intervene and do something to mitigate, if not abolish, evil and suffering. I think that expectation is correct, as far as it goes. God should, if he is indeed good, mitigate and abolish evil and suffering. The problem, of course, is that God doesn't always act in accordance with our conception of goodness. In such cases, we are left with three options; our concept of God, our concept of goodness, or our conceptions of both are inadequate. And by inadequate I do not mean fundamentally wrong. We can't be totally wrong about our conception of God being the paradigm of goodness. By definition God is the greatest conceivable being, so if he exists he has to be completely good. At the same time, we can't be completely wrong about what goodness looks like. If we are, then the Bible is useless to us because if our conception of goodness is so radically different from what goodness is, then when the Bible tells us that God is good, it fails to communicate anything at all. So there must be overlap between our conception of God and goodness and the reality of God and goodness. But overlap is not the same as identity. Our concept of God is always inadequate to who he is in himself. And our understanding of goodness is analogous to God's understanding, not univocal with it. We are fallen and finite creatures and, as such, we should expect to be perplexed at God's dealings. The question is, does the awareness of our fallenness and finitude create enough space for suspending judgment on God's nature in the midst of our suffering and his apparent indifference? Or does the amount of suffering make such a suspension and giving him the benefit of the doubt irrational?

Nice Try: Why Doesn't God Respond?

For others, it wasn't God's goodness that troubled them but his apparent lack of kindness. His silence in the face of their repeated entreaties made him seem uncaring and distant. Why, if God is supposed to be kind, doesn't he answer our prayers more often? What kind of parent sits silently as their child repeatedly begs for help? What kind of God does the same thing? Maybe one that doesn't exist or isn't worth following. One of the most powerful novels about the loss of faith due to God's silence is Shusaku Endo's *Silence*. The story takes place in the seventeenth century and focuses on Roman Catholic Priest, Fr. Sebastian Rodrigues and his companion and fellow priest Francisco Garrpe who travel to Japan seeking their mentor and colleague Fr. Ferreria, who, it has been reported, has apostatized after being captured and tortured. Upon arrival, the two priests discover the terrifying persecution that fellow Japanese Christians are suffering. Suspected Christians are forced to trample on a carving of Christ by security officials; those who refuse are imprisoned and brutally executed. Security officials raid the village that Rodrigues and Garrpe are staying in because of a rumor that it is harboring priests. Although Rodrigues and Garrpe are not discovered, the officials demand that three villagers be offered up as hostages to be taken away and imprisoned. Three men are chosen: Mokichi, Ichizo, and Kichiljio. Prior to their departure, one of the hostages, Kichijiro, asks the priests "Why has Deus Sarna imposed this suffering on us, what evil have we done?"[11] After the three men were taken away, Rodrigues writes in his journal:

> We multiplied our prayers to Heaven that they, together with the Jiisama, might be restored to us in safety. Night after night the people of the village offered up their prayers for this intention . . . as I write these words I feel the oppressive weight in my heart of those last stammering words of Kichijiro on the morning of his departure: "Why has Deus Sarna imposed this suffering upon us?" And then the resentment in those eyes that he turned upon me. "Father," he had said, "what evil have we done?" I suppose I should simply cast from my mind these meaningless words of the coward; yet why does his plaintive voice pierce my breast with all the pain of a sharp needle? Why has Our Lord imposed this torture and this persecution on poor Japanese peasants? No, Kichijiro was trying to express something different, something even more sickening. The silence of God.[12]

Upon arrival at the prison, the hostages are forced to renounce their faith by spitting on a carved image of Christ. Kichijiro does so, but Mokichi and Ichizo are unable to bring themselves to commit such a dastardly act. In response, they are taken to the shoreline of the ocean near their village and fastened to crosses. For several days, they are suspended in the frigid waters of the ocean as the tide rises and falls. Eventually, they each succumb to the elements and sheer exhaustion. During their torture, a peasant woman is allowed to venture out in a boat to give them something to eat. Along with the physical nourishment she provides them, she offers them spiritual sustenance as well by telling them that even though they "are suffering terribly; but be patient. Padre and all of us are praying. You will both go to Paradise."[13] Watching their martyrdom from the safety of

11. Endo, *Silence*, 84.
12. Endo, *Silence*, 84.
13. Endo, *Silence*, 89.

his hideout overlooking the village, Fr. Rodrigues begins to have doubts about his faith. He says:

> They were martyred. But what a martyrdom! I had long read about martyrdom in the lives of the saints—how the souls of the martyrs had gone home to Heaven, how they had been filled with the glory . . . but the martyrdom of these Japanese Christians I now describe to you was no such thing. What a miserable and painful business it all was! The rain falls unceasingly on the sea. And the sea which killed them surges on uncannily—in silence . . . I cannot bear the monotonous sound of the dark sea gnawing at the shore. Behind the depressing silence of the sea, the silence of God . . . the feeling that while men raise their voices in anguish God remains with folded arms, silent.[14]

Fr. Rodrigues is eventually captured but refuses to renounce his faith despite an ominous warning that his refusal will result in the suffering of other Christians. True to their word, the Japanese officials force Rodrigues to watch as Japanese believers are bound, thrown onto a boat, and rowed out to sea, where they are then thrown overboard to drown. Rodrigues is then told that those who he has just watched drown had not died because they refused to renounce their faith, but because his companion, Fr. Garrpe, refused to renounce his. By now, Rodrigues is suffering a crisis of faith due to God's silence amidst all of the tragedy that is directly a result of Christ's command to go into the entire world and preach the gospel. Near his breaking point, Rodrigues is taken to see the man for whom he had come to Japan, Fr. Ferreira. Shocked to see him dressed as Buddhist monk, Rodrigues rebukes his mentor. Undaunted, Fr. Ferreira explains that it wasn't being tortured by the Japanese that lead him to renounce his faith. Rather, it was the suffering being experienced by the Japanese because he refused to renounce his faith that brought him to apostatize. He himself had endured days of torture hanging upside down over a pit, but he could no longer endure the fact that his recalcitrance was causing the Japanese to suffer.

> The reason I apostatized . . . are you ready? Listen! I was put in here and heard the voices of those people for whom God did nothing. God did not do a single thing. I prayed with all my strength; but God did nothing.[15]

Unable to bear the words of his mentor, Rodrigues demands that Ferreira stop speaking such blasphemy. Ferreira, undaunted, mocks Rodrigues,

14. Endo, *Silence*, 93.

15. Endo, *Silence*, 253.

"Alright. Pray! But those Christians are partaking of a terrible suffering such as you cannot even understand. From yesterday—in the future—now at this very moment. Why must they suffer like this? And while this goes on, you do nothing for them. And God—he does nothing either."[16]

Rodrigues can handle it no more, shaking his head wildly and putting both fingers in his ears, he tries to drown out Ferreira's charges. But he could not. Ferreira's voice, along with the moans of the tortured Christians, was incessant. Distraught and broken, Rodrigues cries out, "Stop! Stop! Lord, it is now that you should break the silence. You must not remain silent. Prove that you are justice, that you are goodness, that you are love. You must say something to show the world that you are the august one."[17]

Shusaku Endo poignantly described what happened next:

> A great shadow passed over his soul like that of the wings of a bird flying over the mast of a ship. The wings of the bird now brought to his mind the memory of the various ways in which the Christians had died. At that time, too, God had been silent. When the misty rain floated over the sea, he was silent. When the one-eyed man had been killed beneath the blazing rays of the sun, he had said nothing. But at that time, the priest had been able to stand it; or, rather than stand it, he had been able to thrust the terrible doubt far from the threshold of his mind. But now it was different. Why is God continually silent while those groaning voices go on?[18]

Rodrigues then turns to Ferreira and cries, "And you . . . The priest spoke through his tears. You should have prayed."[19] Ferreira responds by describing to Rodrigues the torture the Japanese Christians are experiencing as they are suspended upside down over a pit:

> I did pray. I kept on praying. But prayer did nothing to alleviate their suffering. Behind their ears a small incision has been made; the blood drips slowly through this incision and through the nose and mouth. I know it well, because I have experienced that same suffering in my own body. Prayer does nothing to alleviate suffering.[20]

16. Endo, *Silence*, 254.
17. Endo, *Silence*.
18. Endo, *Silence*, 254–255.
19. Endo, *Silence*, 255.
20. Endo, *Silence*.

Shattered and in despair, Rodrigues can take it no longer. He gives in to the voices of Ferreira and the groaning of his fellow believers, suffering because of him. Rodrigues, steps on the carved image of Christ and apostatizes.

Unable to reconcile his conception of God with God's silence and refusal to answer prayer in the face of such great suffering proved ultimately too much. Why, if God is omnipotent, omniscient, and omnibenevolent, didn't he respond to the cries of his people? Why, if he loved the Japanese Christians, did he not communicate that love to them in the form of answered prayer? Why was his presence so conspicuously absent? These questions are not just the questions of a fictional character but of many former Christians who feel that God has been silent in the midst of their suffering as well.

In the book *Faith No More,* Phil Zuckerman, professor of sociology and secular studies at Pitzer College, notes that the failure of prayer is a significant reason given by deconverts for their loss of faith. One of those is Penny, a 29-year-old young woman from Pasadena, California. Penny attended a Four-Square Gospel church growing up and also a Christian elementary school. She gave evidence of being a committed believer and even spoke (or believed she spoke) in tongues. According to her testimony, she appeared to be a sincere follower of Jesus who believed that "any sort of problem I had in life I needed to pray or read the Bible."[21] The first experience Penny had with God letting her down came when she was nine years old. Her cat Theo ran away, and she prayed to God to bring Theo home. God did not bring her cat back home.

> I prayed so diligently that God would return my cat—that Theo would come home. I looked through my Bible and I found this verse about if you have as much faith the size of a mustard seed, you can move mountains. I highlighted it and prayed over it and I just believed that even if she had died that God would bring her back because God can do anything, right? And the cat never came back, and I got increasingly upset about it and just cry and cry and cry. I'm getting emotional right now talking about it . . . I was just so . . . I guess disappointed . . . I'm going to cry, but [has to take a moment to regain composure] . . . because I was so sure God would answer my prayers and he didn't.[22]

It's hard not to feel sorry for Penny. Anyone with a young child whose pet has died or ran away knows how heartbreaking it can be for them. And in her moment of despair, she in childlike faith turned to God for help. Penny

21. Zuckerman, *Faith No More,* 46.

22. Zuckerman, *Faith No More,* 46.

claimed a promise from God's word that if she had even the smallest faith that God would answer her prayer. She did. He didn't. And that was the beginning of the end for Penny. In her mind, God had betrayed her by not answering her prayer for something that was near and dear to her heart.

Believers pray for and about many things. Sometimes it is for protection or blessing for one self, other times it is for the well-being of another person. A Christian husband might pray for his wife's employment or that she would maintain her health. A parent may pray for a child's safety, protection, and salvation. Sometimes, however, we rise above the mundane elements of life and seek the transcendent itself. Nothing is more noble in prayer than to know God. When Moses had a chance to ask God for a favor, he asked that he would be able to see him in his glory. This pleased God, and he allowed Moses to behold only his back as he passed by. God, we are told, wants people to seek him. He is seeking worshipers and he rewards those who seek him. Given that is the case, it's easy to see how discouraged an individual would be if they earnestly prayed to God for a sign of his existence but God remained silent. That is what happened to Carl, a young man from a Pentecostal background, who shared, "There were many nights while in bed I would ask God to show me the truth or give me some type of sign to show that he or she existed. These prayers would never be answered. So I would just go on with my life having doubts."[23]

Kim, a middle-aged Canadian friend, recounted to me that she used to lay in bed night after night seeking God's reassurance that she was saved, but he never comforted her despite her prayerful appeals. He stayed silent.

> I can't actually recall accepting Jesus into my heart, but I always knew it was something I'd done around the age of three or four. While this should have brought me peace, it caused great angst because I never felt certain of my salvation. I was all too aware of the fact that I was born sinful and that I was worthless without Jesus, but if I couldn't remember the act, how could I really be saved? I remember many nights, as a young child, lying awake in the dark and crying out to God. I regularly begged Jesus to forgive me of my sins and come into my heart but I never felt anything happen. I also spent a great deal of time contemplating eternity. The thought of living forever, whether in Heaven or Hell, terrified me. I'd eventually fall asleep, exhausted, only to

23. Wright, "Why Do Christians Leave," lines 57–62. In the article the man's name is Dave. To avoid confusion with the other Daves referred to in the book I have renamed him Carl.

> awake the next morning, still unsure of my salvation and dreading everlasting life.[24]

It saddens me to imagine Kim, as a child, lying in bed literally begging God to forgive her of her sins and expecting God to confirm her request with a sign of some kind. That a child would feel terror of being unsure of her salvation when God could alleviate such feelings by simply giving her a small sign makes me wonder why he wouldn't. Especially since he knew that his refusal to answer her prayer for confirmation would produce doubts in her that would lead to her loss of faith.

Likewise, Steven, a former Baptist missionary, wrote: "I've begged God to show himself to me and put an end to my inner torture. So far it hasn't happened, and the only thing I know for sure is that I have unanswered questions."[25] Even C.S. Lewis, the great defender of the faith, was shaken by God's silence. In *A Grief Observed*, Lewis recounts what it was like for him to go through the process of losing his wife Joy Davidman to cancer. Lewis's complaint is a scathing critique of God's silence just when Lewis needed to hear from him the most.

> When you are happy, so happy you have no sense of needing him, so happy that you are tempted to feel his claims upon you as an interruption, if you remember yourself and turn to him with gratitude and praise, you will be—or so it feels—welcomed with open arms. But go to him when your need is desperate, when all other help is vain, and what do you find? A door slammed in your face, and a sound of bolting and double bolting on the inside. After that, silence.[26]

I sympathize with those who have lost faith over a sense of disillusionment with God due to unanswered prayer. I too wonder why God doesn't answer our prayers the way we think he should. God should be kind; the Bible says so. But that's not all it says about him. God's is also inscrutable. His ways are not only above our ways but also, at times, his actions will seem baffling and contrary to good sense. But this should not be surprising, given what we read in the Bible. It provides ample precedent for us to expect that alongside God's kindness there will be aspects of our experience that will be inexplicable and at odds with our understanding of what kindness looks like. The Bible does not hide the fact that God's people experienced times when they felt God was silent, absent, lacking in concern and unjust. The

24. Kim in discussion with the author, August 2013.

25. Wright, "Why Do Christians Leave," lines 63–66.

26. Lewis, *A Grief Observed*, 5–6.

psalms and prophets regularly express disillusionment with God and his apparent absence, silence, and injustice. Psalm 88 is so bleak and depressing it has been called the Black Psalm. Whereas other psalms express their frustration with God but end with an expression of trust in his wisdom and goodness, Psalm 88 never does. It stands as an expression of anger and bitter resentment toward a God who has not acted the way the psalmist expected. And yet, God saw fit to include it in his word. Likewise, David, Job, Gideon, Jeremiah, Ezekiel, the people of Israel in Babylon, and Habakkuk wrestled with God's silence and inactivity in the midst of their darkest moments. Being frustrated with God is neither new nor necessarily wrong. Former believers may have a reason to be frustrated with God's silence in the midst of the calamity they find themselves in. God is supposed to be caring and kind. But seeing him in only those terms, to the exclusion of him being incomprehensible and infinitely wise, is an incomplete conception of God. Somewhere along the way, the kindness of God was clearly communicated but at the expense of his wisdom, inscrutability, and omniscience, setting believers up to have expectations of God that he did not fulfill, which lead to feeling betrayed by him. Betrayal led to bitterness, which in turn caused them to wonder if God existed at all.

Fair Play: Why Doesn't God Treat Us Better?

Bradley Wright, a sociologist at University of Connecticut, surveyed a number of online deconversion narratives to discover what it was that contributed to the loss of faith. His research uncovered four prominent themes: intellectual and theological difficulties, interactions with Christians, interactions with non-Christians, and God's failures. Nearly half (44 percent) of the deconversion narratives studied by Wright and his colleagues complained that God had, in various ways, let them down.[27] Specifically, he failed to do what they felt he was obligated to do. He did not reciprocate. A former elder at a charismatic church complained, "In my own life, no matter how much I submitted to 'God' and prayed in faith, 'sin' never seemed to leave me. Well, what's the point of being 'saved' if you aren't delivered from 'sin'?"[28] Similarly, Paul, a 31-year-old former Southern Baptist, contended that:

> God promises me a lot in the Bible and he's not come through. Ask and it shall be given. Follow me and I will bless you. I promise you life and promise abundance. Man should not be alone. I

27. Wright et al., "Explaining Deconversion."
28. Wright et al., "Explaining Deconversion." 8.

> have a plan for you. Give tithe and I will reward you. All broken promises. This God lacks clarification. This God lacks faith in me. He wants my faith. I want his, too.[29]

Consider Lydia, a former worship and youth group leader. She came to Christ in her late teens and quickly was asked to lead worship on Sunday morning. Happy to help out, she threw herself into the role. Over time, Lydia realized that although she enjoyed her work in ministry, she felt something was missing. That thing was a husband. Lydia wanted to be married and not just to any man, but one man in particular, Kevin, a church staff member. Unfortunately for Lydia, Kevin had eyes for another woman in the church named Sara. Kevin and Sara eventually married, which caused tension in her relationship with Lydia and Lydia's relationship with God. When Sara and Kevin wed, and Lydia remained single, Lydia felt hurt, and she perceived that God had ignored her earnest petitions. She complained "Things [were] cracking with my relationship with Sara, and . . . when she married Kevin, I felt so let down. I prayed for my husband. I had prayed for that man, a godly man, for so long. I ended up dating someone in the internship that year who was gay, who was trying to be straight that year. But God wasn't bringing me my godly man."[30] Lydia had dedicated her life to God, was serving full-time in ministry, and yet God not only wasn't answering her prayers, he seemed to go out of his way to hurt her. The one man she wanted and prayed for ended up marrying her best friend. To add insult to injury, the man that she thought God had brought into her life turned out to be gay. God let her down by not appropriately responding to her devotion.

At the heart of the above examples is a deeply held belief that God should rewards us according to how we live. If we live for him, he ought to return the favor and bless us in ways that are meaningful to us. Whether that is by taking away besetting sins, giving us an abundant life, or the husband we want. The idea that God owes us something in return for our devotion is known as the rule of reciprocity. The rule of reciprocity is the social norm that holds that we pay back benefits that we receive from others, and others pay back benefits they receive from us. The rule of reciprocity runs deep in all of us. In fact, as a social norm, it is universally acknowledged. We are hardwired, so it seems, to expect that if someone does something nice for us we ought to return the favor, and we profoundly expect the same from them. When others do not respond how we think they should, depending on who they are, we feel slighted, put out, or even betrayed. We can usually tolerate an acquaintance that forgets to repay a small favor. The less

29. Wright et al., "Explaining Deconversion." 8.

30. Lydia in discussion with the author, November 2014.

doing something for another costs us, the less slighted we feel if they do not return the favor. But when we make big sacrifices for the sake of others and they don't acknowledge or reciprocate in a meaningful way, things are much different. When that happens, we are likely feeling more than just irked at their refusal to fulfill the social norm, we likely feel angry at their self-centeredness and ingratitude. When we sacrifice for another's benefit, who is near and dear to us and with whom we share multiple social bonds, such as a family member or close friend, we feel not just irked and angry but quite possibly betrayed. How, we wonder, could my sister refuse to come and pick me up, after all, I gave her my kidney?! The closer the relationship and the greater the sacrifice, the greater the feeling of betrayal will be when the one who has benefited at our expense does not reciprocate. The frustration of former believers with how God "treated" them is deeply rooted in the rule of reciprocity and how it applies to our relationship with God. Ultimately, they had expectations of God that he did not meet, and when that happened former believers felt not just let down, but betrayed.

In his helpful book *When God Doesn't Make Sense,* psychologist James Dobson refers to this aspect of being let down by God as the "betrayal barrier." The barrier is that into our life come negative experiences that cause us to wonder, why, if I am following God, is he treating me this way? Dobson is convinced that all Christians eventually must get past the betrayal barrier if they are to progress in their relationship with God, otherwise the result is a shattered faith. For example, "The new convert loses his job, or his child becomes ill, or business reverses occur. Or maybe after serving him faithfully for many years, life suddenly starts to unravel. It makes no sense. It seems so unfair. The natural reaction is to say, 'Lord, is *this* the way you treat your own? I thought you cared for me, but I was wrong.' I can't love a God like that."[31]

Reciprocity is nearly synonymous with fairness and, more broadly, with justice. Justice may look different across cultures, but one thing is certain; we all desire justice. The belief that people should get what they deserve is part of our very constitution as humans. That belief, combined with the equally powerful presupposition that love means doing what is best for another, can be a powerful cocktail in bringing about disillusionment with God. God, above everyone else, should be just. But squaring God's justice with his actions can be very challenging. The problem of God not treating us in a way that seems just to us is a subset of the much bigger problem of evil and suffering. Why, we wonder, if God exists and is good, does he allow so much evil and suffering in the world to exist? And only when we experience

31. Dobson, *When God Doesn't*, 26–27.

disappointment with God do we realize how deep the belief goes that there should be reciprocity between ourselves and God.

In 2 Corinthians, the apostle Paul engages in what he calls folly. The Corinthians had come to question Paul's apostleship and were disregarding his instructions. Instead, they were following other teachers who besmirched Paul and cast doubt on the legitimacy of his calling. In addressing this problem, Paul lowered himself to the level of the Corinthians who were impressed with the resumes of the false teachers. Paul, against his better judgment, in effect says, "All right, if you insist on listening to only those with whom you are impressed and consider only those with impressive resumes apostles, let me engage in a bit of folly and list my accomplishments." He then goes on to summarize his ethnicity, education, and experiences that leave little doubt he is qualified to be an apostle. As such, they should treat him as one. In the same way, I want to indulge in my own bit of folly. Not to convince you that I am saint, but to give you insight into my own struggle when I went through a very dark time and felt that I had received the short end of the stick from God.

For nearly my entire life I have attempted to follow Jesus to the best of my ability. I have often failed to do so. But the general direction of my life, with all of its moral failings, spiritual dryness, and doubts, was set when I was 14 years old at camp Aush-Bik-Koong, a Bible camp in Northern Ontario. It was there I made a decision that I would be a committed follower of Jesus. Since then, all of my major decisions have been passed through the grid of the Lordship of Christ. I have sought to please the Lord in my vocation, my marriage, my finances, my concern for the marginalized, my commitment to the church, and how I raise my children. I have been in pastoral ministry for six years, Christian education for ten years, and para-church ministry for even longer. As a teenager I sacrificed being a member of the Canadian Junior Track and Field team to serve the Lord at a Bible camp. In my twenties, I sacrificed the opportunity to try out for the Canadian Olympic Track and Field team to preach at a church event that was the same day as the Olympic trials. I have worked with the homeless, sleeping in my car with them, donated money to missions when I couldn't afford to do so, preached in Times Square as part of an open air evangelism team, and spent hours in prisons and nursing homes ministering to inmates and shut-ins. I have organized and led mission trips, preached to thousands across the country at churches, Bible camps, and conferences, and "suffered" being ridiculed for my faith from coworkers and acquaintances. Three years ago, I quit my job teaching at a Christian high school to establish the Center for Christian Study, a nonprofit institute similar to a Christian junior college. It was to be located just off the campus of the University of California at

Irvine, in Orange County, California. It was my dream job. I secured a facility, recruited and interviewed professors, created a board of directors, and arranged to offer thirty units of general education credits, the equivalent of a full freshman year of courses. The average price for one year at any of the five big Christian colleges in Southern California is over $35,000. I was able to offer thirty units of credits for only $11,000. That was not only cheaper than all of the Christian colleges in the area, but also cheaper than any of the colleges in the University of California system or the California State University system. I spent two years marketing the program to over one hundred churches and Christian schools in Southern California. I personally emailed over 700 high school seniors three times each to let them know about the study center. And I went to numerous homeschool conferences and college fairs promoting the study center. I had every reason to believe that it would be a success, not the least of which was my faithfulness to the Lord over the last twenty-five years of my life. I was sure he would come through for me; he owed it to me. I had been faithful to him and now, in return, I expected him to be faithful to me and bless me with what I deeply wanted. But the study center never opened. Even though I really believed the Lord had led me to start the study center and I had discerned his providential hand in opening numerous doors, I couldn't manage to recruit enough students. The study center was a bust and so was my dream. The failure of the study center to launch was very disappointing, but worse was that I had no prospective income. We had put all of our eggs in one basket. I had raised enough money for us to pay the bills for one year leading up to the launch of the center. We were counting on the Lord to meet our future needs through the income generated through the study center. When it became clear that the center wasn't going to happen, we realized that in a few short months we would run out of money. If that happened, we would have to sell our vehicles to pay the mortgage on our home. If a job did not materialize, we would eventually have to sell our home, pull our kids out of school, and move in with my in-laws in Florida. All of our friends would be left behind. We would have to step out of the church and para-church ministries we were involved in and start over in a new state where we knew no one except Nancy's family. The thought of taking my kids and wife away from their friends and community made me angry and sad. Why did God let this happen? He knew from the beginning that it would fail. He could have saved me nearly three years of planning and pouring my life into an endeavor that was doomed to fail. But he didn't. My depression turned into bitterness, and I expressed to my wife my frustration. "My whole life has been committed to following the Lord, I risked our financial security and future on the study center, and this is what I get?"

"This is what I get?" In hindsight I'm embarrassed that I responded that way. But what it taught me is that I had certain expectations about God that I wasn't aware of. If you had asked me two years prior if I thought God owed me anything, I would have been quick to say, "No, God doesn't owe me anything. But he has graciously given me many things." And yet, when life started to go sideways, my good theology was overwhelmed by what I really believed deep down in my heart. I, like everyone else, am deeply committed to the reciprocity principle when it comes to how I expect other people to treat me, but especially when it comes to how I expect God to treat me. The problem, however, wasn't with God but with me. My expectations of what God ought to do for me were the result of a *Half-Baked* understanding of God and what he has promised I could expect from him. I expected God to repay me for my "faithfulness" by giving me what I wanted. I had forgotten that while God is just, he is also omniscient and sovereign, and he's working out his plan in the world. He is under no obligation to give me what I want. He is only required to treat me according to what he has promised me. What he has promised me is a covenantal relationship with himself, that he has a good end in store for me, and, according to the author of Hebrews, that he "is not unjust, he will not forget your work and the love you have shown him as you have helped his people and continue to help them." (Heb 6:10 NIV) That should be enough for me to trust him even when it doesn't seem to me that he is being fair.

The Curious Case of Bart Ehrman

One of, if not the most well known critics of Christianity in the United States is historian Bart Ehrman. Ehrman, an agnostic atheist, is the Chair of the Department of Religious Studies and the James A. Grey Distinguished Professor at the University of North Carolina at Chapel Hill. He is widely regarded as an expert on the New Testament and early Christianity, having authored over thirty books, five of which ended up on the *New York Times* Best Sellers list. All five of those books challenge the traditional Christian understanding of God, the Bible, or Jesus, in one way or another. When he is not teaching classes or working on his writing projects, he can often be found debating evangelicals about the nature of the Bible, the state of early Christianity, or the historicity of the resurrection of Jesus. He is perhaps the most effective voice on the scene today arguing against an orthodox understanding of the Bible and Jesus. Ehrman is a gifted writer with the ability to switch between academic and popular levels, an engaging personality, and a prolific scholar. And once he was a committed Christian. However, he came to realize that he could "no longer reconcile the claims of faith with the facts of life."[32] Specifically, he found himself wrestling with the subjects of this and the previous chapter. He could not reconcile his conception of the Bible with what he came to see the Bible as being, and he could not reconcile his conception of God with the existence of suffering and evil.

For most of his early life, Ehrman identified as a devout and committed Christian.[33] He was baptized in a congregational church and later raised Episcopalian, where he served as an altar boy until his teens. In high school he began attending a Youth for Christ Club and had a born-again experience. As a result, he became, in his words, "an extremely zealous, righteous, pious (self-righteous), studious, committed evangelical Christian with firm notions about right and wrong and truth and error."[34] That passion was a contributing factor in his decision to attend Moody Bible Institute to train for ministry. Bart worked diligently to master the Bible at Moody, committing several books of the New Testament to memory. From Moody, Ehrman moved on to Wheaton College, where he learned Greek so he could read the New Testament in its original language. It was at Wheaton that he decided to commit his life to studying the Greek manuscripts of the New Testament. In order to do so, he chose to go to Princeton Theological Seminary and study with Bruce Metzger, regarded as the foremost expert in New Testament manuscripts. Metzger was also a conservative Christian, which was a bonus for Ehrman who, at the time, had a high view of the text of Scripture. While at Princeton, he completed a Master of Divinity degree and a PhD in New Testament Studies.

During his time in college and seminary, he was actively involved in a number of churches, including a Plymouth Brethren church, an Evangelical Covenant church (where he served as a youth pastor), a conservative Presbyterian congregation, and an American Baptist church. Upon graduation from seminary, he became the pastor of the Princeton Baptist Church, preaching every Sunday morning, visiting the sick, holding prayer meetings, etc. Bart Ehrman was a dyed in the wool, card-carrying evangelical. But deep inside something was stirring in him that would eventually lead to his loss of faith.

By his own admission, Bart Ehrman describes himself as a former fundamentalist, someone who believed "the very words of the Bible had been given by God." He had a passion for the Bible and studied it "assiduously,

32. Ehrman, *God's Problem*, 3.

33. Ehrman, *God's Problem*, 1.

34. Ehrman, *Forged*, 3.

intensely and minutely."[35] The more he studied, the more he realized the existence of "an enormous problem," which is that "we don't have the original copies of any of these [New Testament] books. All we have is thousands of manuscripts from centuries later. This realization that we didn't have the originals and that some places we didn't know what the original said, that had a profound effect on my faith, that these words had been given by God."[36] Why the lack of original manuscripts was so difficult for Ehrman to come to terms with was because he was well aware that the copies from which our current Bibles are reconstructed contain thousands of discrepancies between them. He wondered how we could ever know what God said if the originals are lost and the manuscripts disagree with each other.

> How does it help us to say that the Bible is the inerrant word of God if in fact we don't have the words that God inerrantly inspired, but only the words copied by the scribes—sometimes correctly but sometimes (many times!) incorrectly? What good is it to say that the autographs (i.e., the originals) were inspired? We don't *have* the originals! We have only error-ridden copies, and the vast majority of these are centuries removed from the originals and different from them, evidently, in thousands of ways.[37]

But it wasn't long before he began to realize that even if the manuscripts were sufficient to reconstruct the original text, there was another problem. During his second semester at Princeton, Bart wrote a paper attempting to harmonize an apparent contradiction between Mark 2:26 and 1 Samuel 21:1–6 concerning the identity of the high priest. In the Markan passage, Jesus identifies the high priest as Abiathar, but Samuel identified him as Ahimelech, Abiathar's father. Upon getting his paper back, Bart read a comment by his professor that would have a major impact on how he looked at the Bible.

> At the end of my paper, [the professor] wrote a simple one-line comment that for some reason went straight through me. He wrote: "Maybe Mark just made a mistake." I started thinking about it, considering all the work I had put into the paper, realizing that I had to do some pretty fancy exegetical footwork to get around the problem, and that my solution was in fact a bit of a stretch. I finally concluded, "hmm . . . maybe Mark did make a mistake." Once I made that admission, the floodgates opened.

35. Ehrman, *Forged*, 5.
36. Ehrman, Interview with Jon Stewart, *The Daily Show,* March 14, 2006.
37. Ehrman, *Misquoting Jesus*, 7.

> For if there could be one little, picayune mistake in Mark 2, maybe there could be mistakes in other places as well.[38]

In time he came to the conclusion that the "Bible was a very human book with all the marks of having come from human hands" comprised of "discrepancies, contradictions, errors, and different perspectives of different authors."[39]

It has been pointed out by no small number of observers that in spite of his claim to have shifted from an evangelical fundamentalist view of Scripture to a more "mature adult liberal phase,"[40] underlying his current view is the same set of assumptions about what the Bible *has* to be if it is the word of God that he held in his more fundamentalist days. Certainly, he no longer has the same beliefs about the Bible as he once did as a student at Moody. That has radically changed. But what hasn't is his assumption of what the Bible must be if it is the inspired word of God. In other words, he has questioned the Bible but not his assumptions about the nature of Bible. One biblical scholar who has publicly debated Ehrman shared with me that he believes part of Bart's problem is that he retains the very same wooden and overly literalistic conception of the Bible that he received from his fundamentalist socialization. Unable to reconcile his assumptions about the nature of the Bible with what he discovered about the Bible left Ehrman in a state of theological limbo. He remained a Christian, but not for long.

Ehrman's unmet expectations of the Bible did not immediately cause him to lose his faith. What did, he says, is a lingering problem that had troubled him for a long time, and that was the inability to reconcile the existence of a good and loving God with vast amounts of evil and suffering.

> If there is an all-powerful and loving God in this world, why is there so much excruciating pain and unspeakable suffering? The problem of suffering has haunted me for a very long time. It was what made me think about religion when I was young, and it was what led me to question my faith when I was older. Ultimately, it was the reason I lost my faith.[41]

He added:

> I came to a point where I could no longer explain how there could be a good and all-powerful God actively involved with this world, given the state of things. For many people who

38. Ehrman, *Misquoting Jesus*, 9–10.
39. Ehrman, *God's Problem*, 3.
40. Ehrman, "Leaving the Faith," line 10.
41. Ehrman, *God's Problem*, 1.

> inhabit this planet, life is a cesspool of misery and suffering. I came to a point where I could not believe there was a good and kindly disposed Ruler who is in charge of it.[42]

During a Christmas Eve service he attended with his wife, who is a Christian, a man prayed, thanking Jesus for coming into this dark world and intervening on our behalf. To which Ehrman thought to himself:

> Why doesn't he enter into the darkness once again? Where is the presence of God in this world of pain and misery? Why is the darkness so overwhelming? . . . Where is this God now? If he came into the darkness and made a difference, why is there still no difference? Why are the sick still wracked with unspeakable pain? Why are babies still born with birth defects? Why are young children kidnapped, raped, and murdered? Why are there droughts that leave millions starving, suffering horrible, excruciating deaths? If God intervened to deliver the armies of Israel from its enemies, why doesn't he intervene now when the armies of sadistic tyrants savagely attack and destroy entire villages, towns, and even countries? If God is at work in the darkness, feeding the hungry with miraculous multiplication of loaves, why is it that one child—a mere child!—dies every five seconds of hunger? Every five seconds.[43]

God's unwillingness to intervene on behalf of his people, or any people, for that matter, proved to be a bridge too far for Ehrman. His faith had managed to survive the blow that his studies landed on his concept of the Bible, but it could not withstand the blow that the fact of evil landed on his concept of God. It's difficult, if not impossible, to determine if things would have turned out differently for Bart Ehrman had he had a more balanced understanding of the Bible. It seems that even when he managed to come to terms with the nature of the text he could not shake his assumptions about what the word of God needed to look like. Where did he get those assumptions? It's not clear. Perhaps his fundamentalist church background implanted them in him. Or perhaps they are the product of his own mind. Either way, his assumptions concerning the Bible were a stumbling block that started him down a road from which his faith never recovered. What about his belief that there is too much evil in the world for there to be a good God? What are the assumptions he has about God and goodness that are at odds with the state of the world, such that he must conclude God doesn't exist? One is that if God exists and is good he would intervene more often:

42. Ehrman, *God's Problem*, 3.

43. Ehrman, *God's Problem*, 5–6.

> The God I once believed in was a God who was active in this world. He saved the Israelites from slavery; he sent Jesus for the salvation of the world; he answered prayer; he intervened on behalf of his people when they were in desperate need; he was actively involved in my life. But I can't believe in that God anymore, because from what I now see around the world, he doesn't intervene.[44]

Where did Ehrman get the idea that if God is good he would intervene more often? I suspect it is a combination of two things. First, he points to the Bible as evidence of how God intervened on behalf of his people in the past and argues that if that God exists he should act in a similar manner in the present. Since he does not intervene, he likely does not exist. The second source is his own intuitive understanding of what goodness amounts to, which in turn boils down to the assumption that goodness is the removal of evil and suffering. Since God does not intervene to stop or even mitigate the vast majority of human suffering, it is strong evidence that he does not exist. Perhaps. I say "perhaps" because on the surface Ehrman's complaint has both logical and emotional force. The existence of evil and suffering does seem to count against the existence of God, or shall I say, a conception of God. But if God does in fact exist, then the problem is not with him and his goodness but with our conception of him and his goodness. It's not that Bart's conception of God is entirely wrong; part of being good does mean intervening to stop or mitigate suffering. The problem is Bart's conception of God is inadequate to the overall picture of God as revealed in the Bible. God is not only good but also sovereign and omniscient. Just because Bart Ehrman or anyone else cannot discern a good reason why suffering and evil persist in the world does not mean that God doesn't have one. Obviously, if God exists, he does have such a reason. An important reminder that needs to be said is that if we do not know what the reason is, then we are in no position to pass judgment on whether it is a good reason. The question is, are we willing to give God the benefit of the doubt that he does? Bart is not.

Teach Your Children Well

Over and over again, the narratives of ex-Christians reveal that they had been given an inadequate conception of the Bible, which led to them having wrong assumptions and unmet expectations. I have yet to read a deconversion story that attributed the loss of faith to the Bible looking too divine, too scientifically accurate, or too loving. On the contrary, the criticism of

44. Ehrman, *God's Problem*, 16.

the Bible is that it failed to live up to expectations by being in error, too human, scientifically inaccurate, and too violent and immoral. I maintain that is because they were provided a perspective on the Bible that was true as far as it went, but that it did not go far enough. The Bible is a divine book, a book that speaks truthfully, a book that is the story of God's love for his people. But it is also a book covered with human fingerprints from start to finish, a book that is scientifically inaccurate, and a book filled with violence and morally challenging practices. The church doesn't do believers any favors by presenting them with an inadequate concept of the Bible. An inadequate concept of the Bible is one that emphasizes the divine nature of Scripture to the exclusion of the human. It is one that simply takes for granted the current state of the text and ignores its complex history. It is one that presents the text as acultural as opposed to a product of multiple cultures. In doing so, believers form assumptions about Scripture that give them expectations that, when unmet, result in devastating consequences for faith. Likewise, those very same deconversion narratives also often express ideas and conceptions about God that are inadequate to who he is. God is loving, good, and kind but he is also holy and sovereign. He does not promise to answer all prayers, intervene in all circumstances, or always act in accordance with our idea of fairness. He is often silent, inactive, and apparently unjust. But he is always good. By not exposing believers to these contrasting truths and helping them to see how they can be held in tension, we run the risk of setting believers up for a crisis of faith resulting from unjustified and therefore unmet expectations.

Chapter 8

Painfully Prepared

What's wrong with you? We're a family!

Walter White, *Breaking Bad*

The Pastor and the Porn Star

James is working on a Master of Divinity degree with an emphasis in pastoral care and counseling because he wants to come alongside people in the church and lovingly lead them into a deeper faith. And that's just what he had been doing throughout his undergrad years as a leader with the high school group in his church. However, given what we know about deconversion, the fact that James still identifies as a believer and is still a member of his local church says a lot about him and the leadership at the church. That's because James endured an experience that deconversion narratives reveal is a primary catalyst for a spiritual crisis, which in turn has led to the loss of faith for no small number of individuals.

During his time as a volunteer with the youth he came to take on a important role as a leader in the group. Loved by all the kids in the group, it was obvious to everyone that he was in his element. It came as no surprise to anyone, therefore, when the youth pastor stepped down, that James was asked to step in as the interim leader for the youth group. Happily, he did so and everyone—the pastoral staff, the parents, and the kids—were thrilled with the job he was doing. Over time it became obvious to everyone that he would be a great person to lead the youth group as the new youth pastor. When the church began the hiring process for the new youth pastor, James threw his hat into the ring. Right from the beginning he was the favorite for the position. He already had established a relationship with the kids, and the kids loved him, the parents were pleased with him, and he shared the church's philosophy of youth ministry. It seemed like he was a shoo-in for the job. But James didn't get the job. What looked to be the beginnings of a ministry career ended up with him being placed under church discipline. Why did it all fall apart? During the hiring process—to his credit—James revealed to the leadership that he had recently solicited a prostitute. As a result, the pastoral staff felt that they could not put him in a position of spiritual leadership. Not getting the position was hard for James, especially because he lost it due to his own honesty. He could have just as easily kept quiet about his sin, but wanting to be honest with the leadership, he took the high road. As you can imagine, James was hurt. He was told by the leadership he was not qualified for the role of youth pastor, and then, to compound the problem, he had to endure the embarrassment of going through a process of discipline/restoration.

If I didn't know James and you were to ask me how I thought the story ended, I would venture to guess that James probably left the church and maybe even left the faith because of the hurt he experienced at the hands of the leadership. And that would be a reasonable prediction given that one of the most significant reasons deconverts cite for their loss of faith is being hurt by the church. Yet, that is not how the story ends. Today, James still identifies as a Christian and still attends the same church. He continues to pursue a career in ministry despite his difficult experience. Why? What is it about his experience that didn't lead to him having a crisis of faith and walking away?

One of the people who I admire is an individual I came to meet doing research for my doctoral dissertation. Her name is Devyn. At the time she was completing her PhD in sociology at a major university in the southwest. What makes her so admirable is that, given her history, she is one of the last people that you would expect to be a PhD candidate, published author, conference speaker and university adjunct professor. Devyn grew up in New York in a broken home and was sexually abused by her stepfather for eight years. She left home in her mid-teens and moved to the Pacific Northwest. Needing work, she began dancing in strip clubs. This brought with it all of the things that you might expect; drugs, shady characters, and a longing for something more. She thought she had found it when she met a man who gave her attention. She became pregnant, and they had a little girl. But being in a relationship didn't make her life better; instead it only made things worse. Her boyfriend turned out to be violently abusive, beating her so badly that he put her in the hospital. Devyn finally managed to free herself and her daughter by way of a harrowing escape that saw her driving across the country with no money and no destination. Although she was free from her abusive boyfriend, Devyn, like all of us, desired to be in a meaningful romantic relationship. Unfortunately, her desire outran her discernment, and she wound up married to a man who deceived her about who he was only to get her down the aisle. As it turned out, he was not only a deceiver but also a lousy bookkeeper. His financial mismanagement nearly cost them their home. Devastated by his deception and their impending financial doom, she felt that to keep a roof over her daughter's head she needed to do something. But with no education and no marketable skills, her options were limited. So, she returned to the one thing she knew, dancing in strip clubs. As you might suspect, her marriage broke up, and now she was alone with her daughter. Unable to care for her, she did the hardest thing she had ever done and gave her up to be raised by a family she trusted. Life continued to get worse for Devyn; stripping, in turn, led into the adult film industry, where she performed in over 200 hardcore pornographic films. But that was then, and this is now. Somehow, despite all of her hardships and trials, she has put her life back together piece by piece. She found her way out of the porn industry, enrolled in university, then graduate school, and soon she will soon be Dr. Devyn PhD. She has published articles in peer-reviewed journals and regularly speaks at conferences. I trust you can see why I say that she is someone I admire.

I forget to mention that she is also a former worship leader and youth pastor. That's right, after she moved to the Pacific Northwest in her midteens she became a Christian and was involved in fulltime ministry at two churches for several years. She basically went from the pulpit to porn—from teaching young men the Bible to being the images they looked at in secret on the Internet. She was once a minister of the gospel but now is a voice for secularism. How, you may ask, could such a thing happen? If you ask Devyn, she will emphatically tell you the catalyst for her deconversion was how leadership of her church and her fellow Christians mistreated her.

Boiling Mad

A debate is currently raging over whether lobsters feel pain. Why does this matter, you ask? It matters because of the way that lobsters are cooked. Recently, I took my family to a restaurant that had live lobsters in a tank in the restaurant's lobby. My children, along with the other children waiting to be seated, enjoyed looking at all of the large crustaceans crawling around in the tank. Occasionally, a person accompanied by a restaurant employee would walk over to the tank, point at a particular lobster, and the employee would reach in and remove the lobster from the tank. When my seven-year-old daughter asked me where they were taking the lobsters I didn't have the heart to tell her that they were being taken to the kitchen to be cooked and served as a meal. My nine-year-old son, on the other hand, was keenly aware of why they were being taken out of the tank. He knew they were heading to their own version of the Last Supper. What he didn't know was how they were going to be cooked, and I didn't have the heart to tell him that. As you probably already know, lobsters, like other crustaceans, are cooked by submerging them into boiling pots of water while they are still alive. Boiling lobsters alive sounds pretty terrifying; I can't imagine a much worse manner of death for a human to experience. But maybe boiling lobsters to death sounds so bad to us because we have a tendency to anthropomorphize the lobster. We attribute the feeling of pain and traumatic emotions that we would experience if we were in the lobster's place to the lobster. But what if the lobster doesn't experience physical pain or emotional trauma from being boiled alive? What if it doesn't consciously experience anything because its brain and nervous system are not capable of doing so? Would that make a difference in how we viewed lobsters being boiled alive? Probably it would. However, the jury is out on what the fact of the matter is. There is a live debate on whether lobsters feel pain, and eminently qualified biologists take opposing positions. On one side is Robert Elwood, professor emeritus of animal behavior at Queen's University in Belfast, Northern Ireland, who believes lobsters can feel pain. On the other side is Joseph Ayers, a professor of marine and environmental sciences at Northeastern University in Boston, who believes they do not feel pain. The Swiss aren't taking any chances. Recently they passed a law forbidding dropping live lobsters into boiling water. Now, before the lobster is dropped into the water, its brain must be rendered inoperative by electric shock. I fail to see how that is much better!

It might be stretching the analogy to say there is a similarity to the way lobsters are prepared for dinner—perhaps quite painfully—and the way that numbers of deconverts feel they were prepared. However, a common refrain among former believers is that what set them off on their deconversion journey is how they were treated by their church leadership or other Christians. Feeling let down, wounded, mistreated, and abused caused former believers to re-evaluate what they believed. It made them ask questions like, "If these people are really followers of Jesus, then where is the love, grace, and mercy he spoke so much about?" and, "If Christianity is true, why do I get more acceptance from my non-Christian friends than my Christian ones?" It's clear that was the case for Devyn. She felt that her deconversion was less an experience of falling away from the faith and more a case of being pushed. Let me fill in some of the missing elements in her story.

Recall that Devyn found herself in a marriage to a man who lied to her to get her down the aisle and financially bankrupt due to her husband's mismanagement. Desperate to feed her daughter, she chose to return to stripping. On her way to her club, she was involved in an accident that left her car totaled. With no income, no transportation, and bills piling up, Devyn and her husband felt they had nowhere to turn. So, they did what many people do in times of need, they contacted the church. They reached out to the church that Devyn had previously been involved with as a youth leader. They told them everything: the marital problems, the mistakes they had made, the financial woes, the car accident, and, yes, even the stripping. Devyn expected that her old church would show her the compassion they had always preached during her time there. But how they responded devastated her. The pastor, instead of expressing sympathy, told her that she was "nothing but a whore" and that if she ever showed up at the church again they would have her charged with child endangerment. The pastor then called all of her friends and shared with them what she was doing and instructed them not to help her if she contacted them. Devyn was distraught and humiliated. She had looked up to the pastor, and even though she knew she was living a life that was outside the moral framework of the Bible, she counted on him to show her compassion. When he didn't and instead belittled her and violated her privacy, she noted, "Is this what I should have expected from an institution that establishes its principles on the love of God and loving your neighbor like you love yourself? I had known most of these people for over ten years."[1] Her friends ignoring her pleas for help was equally shattering, "For these people to have turned on me, like that, because I just wanted to make sure that my daughter wasn't homeless. Because I wanted to make sure that my daughter didn't know how it felt to be really, really poor growing up, I was going to take my clothes off on stage. And for them to turn me out like that was horrible."[2] She added:

> I was like, "You people suck. You are horrible people." That actually pushed me into [losing my faith] that [fellow Christians] would do that! That actually pushed me into [a crisis of faith]. I struggled for a while because I just couldn't believe that these were God's people. You know, I couldn't believe. It's just not, like these are not Jesus's works, you know. Jesus walked with the sinners, Jesus said to turn the other cheek. Although these people

1. Devine, *Born Again*, 167.
2. Devyn in discussion with the author, February 2013.

didn't really negate the existence of God for me, eventually that started to chip away.[3]

James, if you recall, also went through a difficult experience with the church because of sexual sin. Like Devyn, he admitted to the leadership that he had committed sexual sin. But his story ends very differently than Devyn's, and that's because of the way the leadership at the church handled his situation. Instead of responding to James's confession with a knee-jerk reaction, they created a plan that would address the situation in a redemptive manner. First, they communicated to James their love for him. They did so by expressing their commitment to him as a member of their church family. What that meant was they accepted him as a brother and were willing to walk with him through a process of restoration. Second, they also identified with him by acknowledging that they too were sinners, and even though no one is expected to be without sin, some sins have greater consequence. Third, they shared with him that his sin of soliciting prostitution combined with the fact he was applying for a leadership position at the church required they discipline him. He would no longer be allowed to work with the youth group or lead a home group. Fourth, they clearly communicated to him that they believed there was a place in ministry for him in the future depending on how he responded to the plan they had put in place. Finally, they shared with James their plan, which included having an accountability partner, attending counseling, and installing accountability software on his computer. Because James was a person in leadership—and in the eyes of everyone at the church the next youth pastor—the church leadership had to publicly address James's situation. They did so by telling the congregation that James had committed a sexual sin that prohibited him from being in leadership. They did not fill in the details. They told the congregation that as a result of his behavior he was no longer in any positions of leadership. The leadership reminded the congregation they were his family and they should treat him as such. They emphasized that he had demonstrated genuine repentance and it would be wrong to treat him as a pariah. Instead, they should pray for and encourage him. The leadership also informed the church that there was a plan in place with the goal of seeing James restored to full fellowship and hopefully one day in the future, and, if appropriate, a place of leadership.

Is there any question that how their churches handled their unfortunate circumstances played a role in why Devyn left the faith and James remained? James was confronted with his sin in a loving and restorative manner. Devyn was shamed and ostracized from her church community when she needed them most. James was treated as a family member in need

3. Devyn in discussion with the author, February 2013.

of help. Devyn was treated as an enemy to be fought against. She was struck by what I call *Friendly Fire.*

Friendly Fire

The three previous stumbling blocks or problematic methods of preparing/socializing believers into the Christian faith that we looked at: the *Tyranny of the Necessary* (theological), *Spiritual Cultural Shock* (sociological), and *Half-Baked* (philosophical), have all been cognitive in nature. The *Tyranny of the Necessary* had to do with the need to affirm too many beliefs. *Spiritual Cultural Shock* had to do with the difficulty of affirming countercultural beliefs. *Half-Baked* had to do with having beliefs that were inadequate or imbalanced. In each instance, believers struggled with different intellectual elements of the faith. When we come to the fourth stumbling block or method of preparation, what I refer to as *Friendly Fire,* the problem moves from the cognitive to the existential. Over and over again, those who have lost their faith tell stories of being hit by *Friendly Fire* in the form of judgment and condemnation from fellow believers. Harsh words spoken from self-righteous lips, by those who identify as Christians, can leave deep wounds. Truly, as Proverbs says, "the tongue has the power of life and death." (Prov 18:21 NIV) Christians can sometimes have fairly sharp tongues. When they use them to cut other believers, the results can be tragic.

There are two kinds of hurts that consistently show up in deconversion narratives where *Friendly Fire* played a role in the loss of faith:

- The hurts inflicted by church leaders.
- The hurts inflicted by rank-and-file believers.

Twist of Faith

Several individuals personally shared with me their experiences of disappointment with church leadership or those who were in positions of leadership in para-church ministries. They attributed what they perceived as harsh treatment or hypocritical behavior from their spiritual leaders as playing significant roles in their deconversions. Instead of finding support in times of personal crisis, they noted that the leadership they looked to for guidance had let them down. For Andrew, a former member of a United Pentecostal church, it was the moral failings of leadership. He maintained that what impacted him was "the stealing, fraud, [and] sexual promiscuity running rampant among UPC pastors."[4] The blatant hypocrisy of the spiritual leadership in which he trusted played a role in undermining his faith. For others, it was not so much the moral failings of leadership that negatively impacted their faith but more the way the leadership in question exercised its authority.

In the case of Sherry, she felt that the heavy-handed approach by the elders of her church played a major role in her deconversion. In her situation, the elders refused to endorse her as a cabin leader for a preteen girls' Bible camp because, at the time, she was dating a non-Christian. Instead, they encouraged her to consider serving in another capacity, one that did not entail being an example to young, impressionable girls:

> While the rest of my Christian friends went off to teach at Bible camp that summer, I was required to stay in town. Looking back, I realize that was a real turning point for me. I'd signed up to be a counselor at the camp and, although I had already proven myself to be a capable teen and a good teacher, Bill [the pastor] was sent to talk to me in my home. He explained that the elders just couldn't let me counsel unless I broke up with Ken. While the elders of our church possibly protected some preteen girls from possibly hearing that their counselor had a possibly (Who were they to judge?) non-Christian boyfriend, they pushed me down a path from which I never returned. Clearly, everyone already assumed I was sinning, so I might just as well begin! I hung out with the church crowd less and less and became more and more involved with Ken and his friends.[5]

Being hurt by church leadership ranks pretty high on the list of reasons people cite for why they leave the faith. It's easy to pick on the church and point out its flaws and shortcomings. Laying the blame on church leadership for deconversion is one of the easiest ways of doing that. In fact, it is too easy. Sometimes good church leaders do bad things, and sometimes bad church leaders do bad things, and that is on them. They will answer to the Lord for their sin and the lives they negatively impacted.

But in some cases, it's not clear that the fault rests solely on the shoulders of the leadership. Just as churches can exhibit closed-mindedness and rigidity in how they interpret and apply the Bible, individuals can be obstinate and become easily offended by leadership exercising their authority in a healthy manner. So, who is to blame when deconverts point to the church hurting them as the reason for their deconversion? Is it overbearing church

4. Andrew in discussion with the author, May 2014.

5. Sherry in discussion with the author, June 2015.

leaders who legalistically and harshly apply the Bible or individuals who took offense too easily? Sometimes it's hard to tell.

Church leaders are responsible to make many decisions, all of which are open to scrutiny and to misunderstanding. Even when decisions are made and actions taken with the best of intentions, church leaders cannot control how others will perceive their actions and decisions. People can be hurt and offended by leadership not so much because the leadership has done anything wrong but because churches are filled with people, and people can get offended over just about anything. What makes discussing the role of leadership in deconversion so difficult—and Sherry's story illustrates this well—is that church leaders are responsible before God to shepherd their flock according to what they believe the Bible teaches. Church leadership has to take positions on issues and doctrines that are going to make some people upset, no matter how graciously they do so. Clearly, church leaders can't compromise what they believe to avoid offending everyone.

In the case of Sherry, the leadership committed no sinful actions or moral failure in asking Sherry to work at the Bible camp in a support role instead of as a cabin leader because of her relationship with her non-Christian boyfriend. Some readers will agree with the decision of the elders and argue that, given what they knew about her relationship with her boyfriend, it gave them just cause to not endorse her as a cabin leader. Perhaps others might disagree with the elders and maintain that prohibiting Sherry from being a cabin leader was a bit drastic. Regardless of who you agree with, I think most people would agree the great offense she took at their decision and the subsequent choices she made to turn from her faith can't really be laid at the feet of the church leadership. Sherry, of course, would disagree. To her, it was a big deal. I don't want to trivialize Sherry's perspective, for her the church leadership played a contributing factor in her deconversion. Maybe it was the straw that broke the camel's back.

The fact that it is not always clear who is to blame when former believers claim they were mistreated by the church—the church for being abusive or them for being too sensitive—does not take away from the fact that there are many cases where church leadership is culpable. The moral failings and hypocrisy of church leaders that are repeatedly mentioned in deconversion narratives bears this out. Failing to not only live up to what they preach but actually living in opposition to it proves to be intolerable for former believers. So, too, the heavy-handed tactics such as public shaming disguised as discipline and abusive control in the name of holiness are unquestionably failures on the part of the leadership.

You're Killing me, Bro!

Criticism and harsh judgment are not only short fallings of leadership. Fellow believers who are not serving in leadership positions can also be quick to hit their fellow believers with *Friendly Fire*. Criticism from other believers that he perceived as unjust or petty caused Sam to question just what Christianity was all about. Because he liked to listen to pop music and watch television, he was told, "You are obviously not a good Christian or obviously a bad one because, if you're a Christian, you wouldn't be doing all those kinds of things." Instead of challenging him to a deeper Christian commitment, it made him say, "Wait a minute! What does pop music have to do with Christianity?" The answer, in his mind, was that it had very little to do with being a Christian. This hurt was further compounded by comments that he received upon sharing with the church that he had been diagnosed with cancer. Instead of rallying around him, they said, "The reason you have cancer is because you are getting a divorce." Understandably, he was offended by such reasoning and responded by pointing out that, if the accusation is valid, then, "Why doesn't everybody else have cancer, because there's a lot bigger problems than divorce?" Moreover, he raised telling indictments of certain members of the church by pointing out, "There's a lot of people's lives around me that, if that is the case, everyone should be walking around with cancer."[6] Eventually, he perceived that through his divorce and battle with cancer, "the church abandoned"[7] him. Today he no longer identifies as a Christian and points back to the treatment he received from other Christians as the spark that started him doubting his beliefs.

Tammy also was going through a divorce while she was a Christian. She commented, "When people heard that there was going to be a divorce, all of a sudden I started losing connection with people." Although she recognized that getting a divorce while being a member of the church counsel created an awkward situation between her and other members of the church, the treatment by church members during that period led her to ask herself hard questions about her faith. She wondered, "What am I doing, and what is this group that I'm involved with? Do I still want to be part of it?" She concluded that, because of the negative treatment she experienced at the hands of her fellow believers, she did not "want to be part of [the church]." In the end, she felt like she "was abandoned"[8] by fellow Christians. Subsequently, she left the church and, ultimately, her faith.

6. Sam in discussion with the author, February 2013.
7. Sam in discussion with the author, February 2013.
8. Tammy in discussion with the author, March 2013.

When Martin was serving as a pastor he questioned traditional positions on various social issues. This resulted in his own congregation attacking him personally and with great hostility. Martin described his church upbringing as a place where, "questioning was looked upon really negatively . . . and doubt was something you just push aside." Nevertheless, he chose to teach an adult Sunday school class to "talk about stigmatized topics" such as "the death penalty, gay rights, and stuff like that," he said. Consequently, he found himself on the wrong end of some pointed criticism: "We had this class, and it turned out that a lot of people were in it. We just got hammered by the churchgoers. . . . After that, everything changed. Everybody looked at my wife and myself completely differently. We were Christians, and we happened to be anti-death penalty and pro-gay rights." The response from the angry congregants was strategic, "Get personal and attack!" he said. The apparent desire was to get Martin and his wife fired from the church. The church no longer wanted him "to teach their kids" because they thought he "was wrong." He described the hurt and disappointment from his congregants' reactions as "a pretty horrible experience."[9] Shortly thereafter, he left the church. It was not long after that he left the faith altogether. What are we to think about claims of former believers that the way they were treated played an important role in losing their faith? I think there are two important factors to take into consideration when addressing this issue.

Perception Is(n't) Reality But it Sure Looks Like it.

The first is that interpersonal conflict takes at least two parties. Sometimes it's clear which party is in the wrong but in most interpersonal conflicts there is more than enough blame to go around. So, I am not saying that it is always church leadership or fellow Christians who are responsible for the mistreatment that deconverts often point to as the beginning of their deconversion process. In all instances of disagreement, each side has their own perspective. In the case of some former believers, they appear to be the ones quick to take offense. But there is little doubt that many former believers have been hurt by the careless words and actions of fellow believers. Self-righteousness is a sin that Christians seem especially prone to and one that can have devastating consequences. There is a reason why Paul says, "knowledge puffs up." (1 Cor 8:1 NIV) The more we know of the truth, the more inclined we become to look down on others who we take to be ignorant of it. We can be tempted to feel a sense of superiority at the

9. Martin in discussion with the author, March 2013.

knowledge we believe we possess that others don't. The classic example of this is the Pharisees. Their self-righteousness was ugly and hurtful. Jesus saved his most scorching words of judgment on the Pharisees for their hypocrisy and pride. He went so far as to say that the attitude and practices of the Pharisees was responsible for prohibiting individuals from entering the kingdom of heaven (Matt 23:13).

(Not So) Great Expectations

The second important point to note when considering the complaint that mistreatment by other Christians leads to the loss of faith is the role played by expectations. As we have previously seen, expectations are unavoidable and incredibly powerful. Unrealistic expectations set an individual up for disillusionment. That is exactly what happened to Devyn.

> I was dating a guy named Jeff who was four years my senior. Jeff was a Christian and wanted me to become one, also. He would talk to me about God's love and what it meant to give your heart to Jesus. I started to believe that Christians were the best people on Earth. The sales pitch always sounds convincing, and eventually I bought into it. My views were very black and white. God is the ultimate judge, so Christians won't judge. Christ died for our sins, so Christians will always forgive. God loves us like Christ loved the church, so Christians will always want to be our friend.[10]

The assumption at work in the background of Devyn's expectation was that, "If Christianity is true, Christians should be like Jesus." That's not a completely unfair assumption. Christians should increasingly reflect the image of Jesus. Regrettably, that is not always the case. While Christians should look more and more like Jesus as they grow in their faith, it is also true that Christians are broken, fallen people who are just as capable of being thoughtless and offensive as anyone else. Sanctification is a long process whereby the Spirit of God slowly but surely conforms us into the image of Jesus. Forgetting that, and expecting Christians to always act practically in accordance with what they are positionally in Christ, can lead to unmet expectations. Devyn found that out the hard way:

> Christians are people, and people, by nature, will judge. They will become offended, making forgiveness difficult, if not impossible, to freely give. People will find friendship with whomever

10. Devine, *Born Again*, 60–64.

> they have the most in common with. The bottom line is this: the notion that, in church, everyone loves unconditionally and that all good things come to those who believe in God, is fiction. The broader truth is that if you don't have the same convictions as them, many Christians will cast you aside. If an action doesn't cause you to sin but can offend your best friend, then you lose a best friend. It is better to protect the body as a whole instead of helping the one who is lost, holding on only to her faith and good intentions. Of course, my comments are generalized and not everyone may have had these experiences, but these stories are a representation of what I have experienced.[11]

In the end, it's unclear where the blame lies in deconversion narratives. As author Drew Dyck points out, "Some personalities are more susceptible to hurt than others. It's entirely possible for two people to grow up in the same church, and even the same family, and for one to be hurt and for another to emerge with their faith relatively unscathed."[12]

I have seen instances of exactly what Dyck is referring to. Dominic and his sister Jessica grew up in the same evangelical home, went to the same church, the same Christian private school, went on the same missions trips, and to all appearances were deeply committed to their faith. Today, Jessica is a missionary, while Dominic is an atheist who has no time for religion in general or Christianity specifically. Listening to Dominic, it became clear to me that even though they had many similar experiences, they had two different perspectives. According to Dyck, that's what really matters: "What's important is the perception of abuse. If someone feels they've been victimized and associates that hurt with God, it's more likely that they will experience struggles with their faith."[13] Studies show that when individuals feel the church or other Christians have victimized them, it manifested in two specific ways: judgmental attitudes and hypocritical behavior.

You be the Judge

It shouldn't give us any consolation that unrealistic expectations and individual perspectives of former believers can be contributing factors in deconversion. It might be tempting to blame former believers' criticisms of the church on their warped perceptions of reality. But we must resist the temptation to believe that for at least two reasons. One, because it would be

11. Devine, *Born Again*, 65–67.
12. Dyck, *Generation Ex-Christian*, 683.
13. Dyck, *Generation Ex-Christian*, 682–84.

foolish to think it's only former believers who have a wrong perception of reality. As Christians, we have good reason to believe that our perception is capable of being distorted as much as the next person's due to our fallenness and finitude. Scripture and our own experience testify to the fact that we are more than capable of being the offending party in a relationship. Two, because being judgmental and hypocritical is what characterizes Christians in the eyes of a large segment of the population, and we would be foolish to think that such views are baseless. In a groundbreaking and revealing study from the Barna Group, lead researchers David Kinnaman and Gabe Lyons surveyed outsiders (their term for non-Christians) between sixteen and nineteen years old. Eighty-seven percent of those surveyed said that being judgmental is characteristic of Christians, and 85 percent see Christians as hypocritical.[14] Moreover, 53 percent of Christians in that same age demographic feel the same way. Kinnaman and Lyons point out that two out of every five outsiders have a bad impression of present-day Christianity, and one-third of young outsiders say they view Christianity negatively and would not want to be associated with it. Furthermore, one out of six have a "very bad" perception of Christianity. Only 3 percent, or about half a million young outsiders out of a total of roughly 24 million, have a positive view of evangelicals. Kinnaman and Lyons note that it is not evangelical theology that bothers young outsiders so much as our attitude and that the growing hostility toward evangelicals is "very much a reflection of what outsiders feel they receive from believers."[15] After studying thousands of outsiders, a dominant theme emerged from the data. "Christians have become famous for what we oppose, rather than who we are for."[16] Admittedly, some of the negative perception of Christians comes from the fact that we have a radically different worldview than the surrounding culture. A biblical worldview will always stand in stark contrast to, and in condemnation of, the sin and ungodliness that is endemic to our broken world and the human structures that inhabit it. As our culture becomes progressively secular and relativistic in terms of truth, goodness, and beauty, Christians will stand out more and more as judgmental and intolerant. At the same time, Kinnaman and Lyons force us to ask an important question; what if young outsiders are right about us? Indeed, "If we have been poor representatives of a holy and a loving God then, absolutely, what they think about us matters. If we have been un-Christian, then we bear responsibility for the problem—and the solution."[17]

14. Kinnaman and Lyons, *UnChristian,* 34.
15. Kinnaman and Lyons, *UnChristian,* 26.
16. Kinnaman and Lyons, *UnChristian,* 26.
17. Kinnaman and Lyons, *UnChristian,* 37.

That so many young people outside the church, a large percentage of those within, and many former believers perceive Christians as judgmental and hypocritical, we would be unwise to think that the problem lies primarily with the misperception of disgruntled former Christians.

People in Glass Houses . . .

The Bible records a number of sins that the Lord hates. One of those is hypocrisy. Jesus spoke his harshest words of condemnation to those he identified as hypocrites. In Matthew 23 he excoriates the Pharisees and the teachers of the law for being two-faced. Seven times, Jesus pronounces judgment on the Pharisees and the teachers of the law for appearing righteous on the outside but being inwardly wicked. The difference in who we are and how we present ourselves is the essence of hypocrisy. When we, like the Pharisees, condemn others for their behavior and yet engage in it ourselves, we are guilty of being hypocrites. But not all inconsistency is hypocrisy. There exists a gap in the lives of everyone between what we believe and how we behave. The problem is when we put forward a public persona that is at odds with our inner character.[18] There are not many sins uglier than hypocrisy and, sadly, there is hard data demonstrating that Christians are guilty of it on a wide scale. Kinnaman and Lyons make the case that when it comes to living what we profess to believe, Christians fall short.

> In virtually every study we conduct, representing thousands of interviews every year, born-again Christians fail to display much attitudinal or behavioral evidence of transformed lives . . . we found that most of the lifestyle activities of born-again Christians were statistically equivalent to these of non-born-agains . . . believers were just as likely to bet or gamble, to visit a pornographic website, to take something that did not belong to them, to consult a medium or a psychic, to physically fight or abuse someone, to have consumed enough alcohol to be considered legally drunk, to have used an illegal, nonprescription drug, to have said something to someone that was not true, to have gotten back at someone for something he or she did, and to have said mean things behind another's back.[19]

It's not just Christian sociologists who notice the gap between our walk and our talk. In 2013, Mars Hill Church in Seattle conducted a study of the objections and perceptions of the un-churched and the de-churched toward

18. Challies, "God Hates Hypocrisy."

19. Kinnaman and Lyons, *Unchristian*, 47.

Christianity.[20] Un-churched were those who had never attended a Catholic or Protestant church and the de-churched were those who at one time did attend a Catholic or Protestant church but no longer do. The study was conducted in two parts. The first consisted of focus groups in four major U.S. markets—Austin, San Francisco, Phoenix, and Boston—comprised of the un-churched and the de-churched. The second was a telephone survey of 1,000 adults throughout the United States. For the telephone survey, respondents were given a list of twenty-three objections to Christianity and asked which they found applicable. Both the focus groups and the telephone survey revealed similar findings. A key finding of the phone survey is that the un-churched and the de-churched perceive Christians as hypocritical. The perception that Christians do not practice what they preach ranked in the top five objections for the un-churched and the de-churched at 44 percent and 45 percent, respectively. Likewise, hypocrisy was a dominant theme emerging from the focus groups. A male participant noted, "People react to hypocrisy among Christians because they seem to be the ones shouting loudest"[21] but not living up to their own claims. A second male participant concurred and added that what he finds distasteful about Christianity is that Christians are always "saying one thing and doing another and then also trying to impose their judgment or will upon you."[22] A third male said, "One of the central teachings [of Christianity] is to be nonjudgmental. But what I find is, and this is a hypocrisy of Christians more so than [other] religions . . . is some of the most judgmental people I have ever known have been Christians.[23] The claim Christians are hypocritical is subjective and is open to debate. But there is no debating that we are viewed by outsiders as hypocrites. Therefore, it shouldn't be surprising that when deconverts offer reasons they are no longer Christians, hypocrisy comes up again and again.

Returning again to the work of sociologist Bradley Wright, who studied online narratives of former Christians to better understand why deconversion occurs, a similar theme emerges. Forty-two of the fifty narratives (84 percent) expressed frustrations with Christians. One of the main areas of frustration of former believers was the hypocrisy of Christians they had experienced. A former Pentecostal Christian spoke about her relationship with a fundamentalist Christian who lied to her, saying one thing but being another:

20. Mars Hill Church, *The Resurgence Report,* 2013.
21. Mars Hill Church, *The Resurgence Report,* 2013.
22. Mars Hill Church, *The Resurgence Report,* 2013, Austin, Texas, 21.
23. Mars Hill Church, *The Resurgence Report,* 2013, Austin, Texas, 17.

> I also found out that he was an addict, and had lied about it . . . After being with this person, I felt spiritually raped. It has taken a *very* long time to get over the emotional and spiritual devastation the whole thing left behind. It was kind of surprising to me, how deeply it impacted me, but it makes sense in light of how willingly vulnerable I made myself to this person, based on how he initially presented himself. My experience with this person was what sealed the deconversion: after him, I was *definitely* not Xian. After him, I realized that if being Xian meant I had to be like him, I'd rather go to Hell.[24]

Like Bradley Wright, social scientist Julie Krueger's research identified hypocrisy as an important factor in deconversion. She notes that, "Christians are often seen as hypocrites, incapable of loving their neighbor."[25] For example, Kelly, a former Christian and participant in Krueger's study, believes many "use it [religion] to demean people or treat people horribly."[26] Another participant, Kayla, said, "They say they're Christians, and say they follow the path of Christ or whatever, but they're so . . . they're so mean."[27] My own research into deconversion supports the findings of Wright and Krueger.[28]

Hypocrisy can lead to deconversion because it presents a dilemma of loyalty because it forces one to ask: How can I continue to identify with Christianity when the actions of Christians are indefensible? How can this way of life be what it claims to be if it forces me to choose between my conscience and what the group believes? If loyalty is only deserved of worthy objects and individuals, hypocrisy and corruption in the church gives me a moral obligation to abandon my loyalty to Christianity for my own integrity.[29]

In God We Trust?

The twin problems of judgmentalism and hypocrisy can have a chilling effect on faith. Karen Ross, a Canadian researcher with interests in deconversion, provides valuable insights into the nature of saving faith and how being hurt by fellow believers can play a role in the deconversion process.[30] A common

24. Wright et al., "Explaining Deconversion," 10.
25. Krueger, "The Road to Disbelief," 5.
26. Krueger, "The Road to Disbelief," 5.
27. Krueger, "The Road to Disbelief," 5.
28. Marriott, *The Cost of Freedom*.
29. Schulz, "Hypocrisy as Challenge," 11.
30. Ross, "Losing Faith."

pattern that emerges in deconversion stories is that an emotional/experiential shift occurs that paves the way for an intellectual reappraisal of beliefs. By that, Ross means that when an individual is hurt by a fellow believer it often has the effect of allowing them to consider latent doubts and questions. When relationships are strong and individuals are happy with their faith communities, it is easy for individuals to ignore many of the intellectual challenges to their beliefs. But if an emotional factor comes into play—such as being hurt or deeply offended by other Christians or church leadership—they are more likely to reconsider information that was threatening to their faith. Prior to their negative emotional or existential experience, the individuals in Ross's study were not receptive to faith-threatening knowledge and generally happy to ignore their own skeptical questions. They turned their attention to the troubling cognitive aspects of their faith only after they had reached a high level of frustration or emotional disconnect resulting from negative experiences. Many of those experiences came at the hands of other believers. Being wounded by the church resulted in former believers having not only a beef with the Christians that wounded them, but also God, whom they could not distance from the behavior of his people. Once an initial emotional shift occurred, it established doubt or disillusionment. It was then deconverts began to think in new ways about their beliefs. Many of those beliefs became open for debate.

In her work, Ross makes an important distinction between the concepts of belief and faith that are crucial for any discussion of deconversion. When Christians find out that my area of research focuses on deconversion, I am asked the same two questions; why does it happen, and do you think they were ever really saved in the first place? The answer to the first question is never so simple as to be stated in a sound bite, and so I suspect my response leaves my interlocutors a bit disappointed. I usually tell them, "it's complicated" and then say something about intellectual, emotional, and experiential factors combining with personality traits, social environment, and spiritual influences. The answer to the second question is equally complex. It is my experience that Christians are quick to account for deconversion by claiming that deconverts where never Christians in the first place. There are a number of reasons why this strategy is the first to be employed by Christians to explain why someone would leave the faith. The first is theological. The doctrine of eternal security affirms that everyone truly born-again will endure in the faith, kept by the power of God. According to this way of thinking, salvation is not something that can be lost because of the work of Christ and the Holy Spirit. Christ, as the sinner's substitute, has paid the price for all sins and reconciled believers to God. Moreover, Christ is not only a substitute for sinners but also their representative before God. Theologically, this is expressed in terms of "being in Christ." All believers are "in Christ," and it is Christ who represents them before God. As such, a believer's salvation is secure as long as Christ does not falter in his role as their mediator. Furthermore, the Holy Spirit has regenerated and sealed Christians "for the day of redemption." (Eph 4:30 NIV) For these reasons and more, many Christians are quick to judge deconverts as those who never really were saved; because if they were, they would still be Christians.

The second reason why Christians are quick to challenge the genuineness of the faith of former believers is fear. If genuine believers can lose their salvation as a result of a crisis of faith, then what is to stop them from losing theirs? It is a great sense of comfort believing that one's salvation is secure based on the work of Christ. In order to retain that comfort, an explanation has to be given to refute what looks like clear counterexamples. The existence of those who once professed belief in Christ, only later to renounce that belief, is problematic for the doctrine of eternal security and the emotional comfort it provides. To salvage both, a counterargument of sorts needs to be offered. The most common approach is to deny that former believers ever "truly" believed. Rather than authentic, salvific belief, former believers possessed a substandard kind of faith that was lacking in some essential property, making it ineffectual for obtaining salvation. Therefore, according to the argument, when individuals apostatize it does not furnish evidence that the doctrine of eternal security is false, but reveals that apostates were never really saved in the first place.

Whether one finds the above argument explaining why deconverts were never believers in the first place persuasive, it does contain a truth about the relationship between being wounded by the church and the loss of faith. That truth is that there is a difference between a loss of faith and a loss of belief. Ross argues that the loss of *faith* is associated with emotional shifts, whereas the loss of *belief* is the result of being undermined by the evaluation of contradictory evidence. Crucially for Ross, faith is understood as trust in and loyalty to God, and belief is giving mental assent to a proposition, such as "God exists." Being hurt or offended by the church tends to weaken trust in the church and, by extension, trust in God. When trust in the goodness of God and the church wane, it tends to create space to consider the doubts and questions that were easy to ignore when Christianity met emotional needs. In other words, the loss of faith (trust) often leads to the loss of belief (mental assent). Why is this observation important? It's important because it is trust in Christ that is at the heart of what it means to be a Christian. Although the New Testament repeatedly speaks of salvation in terms of "belief," a better translation would be to substitute the word belief with the word trust. The contemporary usage of the word belief connotes for us the idea of affirming a proposition or sets of propositions. But it is clear from the New Testament that an individual can affirm all of the right propositional claims and still not be saved (James 2:14–17). Salvation is trust in a person not giving mental assent to a list of doctrines. Biblical scholar Peter Enns argues that faith "is not so much defined by what we believe but in whom we trust. In fact . . . I argue that we have misunderstood faith as a *what* word rather than a *who* word—as primarily beliefs about, rather than primarily as trust in."[31]

This is partly because in the New Testament one Greek word (*pistis*) is translated as both "belief " and "faith." Even though in English we see two different words, in Greek they are one and the same word with the same meaning; faithfulness or trustworthiness. Unfortunately, the decision of translators to use the English words "belief" and "believe" to translate *pistis* gives the impression that what is important is the affirmation of a set of truth claims. It implies that faith is essentially right thinking about propositions. This makes salvation dependent on being convinced of the informational content of the gospel. Admittedly, to be saved an individual does need to be persuaded of a number of truth claims. But that is only one aspect of what the Bible means when it uses the word belief. In philosophical lingo, intellectual assent is necessary for salvation, but it is not sufficient. More is required than just affirming that Jesus died on the cross for our sins. Mental assent must be combined with a trust or reliance on Jesus and his work. This is sometimes illustrated by pointing out the difference between believing a chair will support one's weight and actually sitting in the chair. In the first instance, one believes certain truths about the chair. In the second instance, one places their faith in the chair. The same is true with salvation in Christ; belief *that* what the Bible says about him is necessary but not sufficient. It must be combined with trust *in* him. How does all of this relate to deconversion and the role played by interpersonal conflict?

Propositional content is foundational to the gospel. To be a Christian, an individual first needs to know and also have a positive doxastic attitude toward the claims of the Bible about who Jesus was and what he has done. But that is not enough; belief must be followed by trust. The purpose of propositional truth is to lead to trust in Christ. As Ediger notes, "belief in the veracity of propositions that prove Jesus's identity do not, in and of themselves, result in salvation. The moment of transition from condemnation to eternal life occurs when trust is placed in Jesus for one's eternal destiny."[32] The first step in becoming a Christian is being persuaded that what the Bible

31. Enns, *The Sin of Certainty*, 22.

32. Ediger, *Faith in Jesus*, 24.

says is true. The second is trusting Jesus. However, just the opposite order occurs in the case of a high number of deconversions. In such cases, trust is lost in God either by perceiving God as being absent or apathetic or by God's people hitting their own with *Friendly Fire*. Being hurt and losing faith/trust in God because of the church in turn gives people the space and freedom to allow themselves permission to consider the intellectual doubts that they could easily ignore when things were going well and their emotional needs were being met by their Christian community.

In short, many former believers trace the beginning of their loss of faith not to doubts about the truth of Christianity but to negative experiences they suffered at the hands of other Christians. Those negative experiences are what caused them to reconsider and reevaluate the evidence for Christianity. The belief that led to trust in Christ was reversed by a loss of trust that ended in unbelief. A clear example of this can be seen in Chris's story, a former believer who lost his faith in large measure due to *Friendly Fire.* "I've certainly had people assume I deconverted because of bad people. The truth is, yes, certain morally repugnant Christians did move me along the path to deconversion—but not in the way you might think. Their actions gave me the social distance from my beliefs that I needed to think clearly,"[33] he claimed. In his deconversion narrative, Chris shared two instances of *Friendly Fire* and the impact they had on his faith. To his credit, Chris recognized that just because a person is hurt by Christians it does not follow that Christianity is false. "Deconverting after having gone through two such incidents may come as no surprise, but people don't seem to understand that it's not simply a matter of not liking Christianity because of what happened to me. The bad actions of some should not influence whether you accept an idea as being true; we should evaluate ideas on their own terms, not on how those ideas are presented." And yet he acknowledges that *Friendly Fire* did play a significant part in his loss of faith because the damage done to the social bonds between him and the church opened the door for him to re-examine the truth claims of Christianity.

> What that means for someone in my situation is that the dissolution of my social connections to Christianity showed me my true beliefs. Once I no longer had to perform for the approval of others by inventing reasoning to justify foregone conclusions, I was free to accept my most natural conclusions on a variety of subjects. Thus, it was not that my negative experience caused my deconversion; rather, it was my prior social connections that caused my belief in the first place.[34]

33. Attaway, "Deconversion After Religious Abuse," 6–10.
34. Attaway, "Deconversion After Religious Abuse," 68–74.

The Times, They Are A-Changin'

By his own admission, *Los Angeles Times* reporter William Lobdell's life was a mess. He was twenty-eight, a new father, and had nearly ruined his marriage. He had grave doubts about being a father and felt intensely lost. A friend suggested what was missing in his life was God. Lobdell accepted his friend's invitation and soon found himself at one of Southern California's biggest mega-churches. The pastor's messages connected with him and fed the hunger in his soul. Desiring to learn more about what he was hearing in church, Lobdell enrolled in a Bible class, resulting in not only new knowledge of the Bible but new Christian friends. Some of those friends invited him to a weekend men's retreat in the mountains for a time of worship, fellowship, and teaching. William decided to attend, and while there he heard the Gospel and accepted Jesus Christ as his savior. The change was immediate. He recalled, "I began praying each morning and night. During those times, I mostly listened for God's voice. And I thought I sensed a plan he had for me: To write about religion for the *Times* and bring light into the newsroom, if only by my stories and example. I didn't just pray for a religion writing job, I lobbied hard for it."[35] In 1998, the *Times* relented and gave Lobdell what he wanted, a weekly column about faith in Orange County. He was thrilled and believed God had answered his prayers. He thrived in his new role and felt as though his life had fallen into place. His marriage had turned around, he had two great kids, and he "couldn't wait to get to work each day or, on Sunday, to church."[36]

In 2001, the Catholic sex abuse scandal involving large numbers of priests who had assaulted mostly young boys with impunity was about to break nationwide. Six months before it did, the dioceses of Los Angeles and Orange found themselves in the midst of their own scandal. Five point two million dollars was paid to a law student who claimed a priest, who was the principle of a local Catholic high school, had molested him as a high school student. As a result of the investigation, it came to light that both dioceses had many known molesters still working in parishes along with two convicted child pedophiles still working as priests. In the case of the priest named in the lawsuit, the church had long known about his proclivity for adolescent boys. In 1994, he quietly resigned from being the principal at another high school due to an allegation of another male student that the priest had molested him. The church did not inform parents or students of the reason he quit. That same year, another student came forward, this time

35. Lobdell, "He Had Faith," line 25.
36. Lobdell, "He Had Faith," line 39.

publicly, and filed a lawsuit alleging the priest abused him as well. Although the church possessed a psychological report conducted by Catholic psychiatrists that diagnosed him as being attracted to adolescents and concluded that it was likely he molested multiple boys, the diocese said he was an icon of the priesthood. To add to their shame, they also remained silent as the priest's lawyers publicly attacked and slandered the accusers who they knew were, in all likelihood, telling the truth. Upon his departure from the dioceses, some of the most senior priests threw him a going away party. To say the least, Lobdell was troubled by the church's handling of the whole affair but thought perhaps it was an aberration. "At the time, I never imagined Catholic leaders would engage in a widespread practice that protected alleged child molesters and belittled the victims. I latched onto the explanation that was least damaging to my belief in the Catholic Church—that this was an isolated case of a morally corrupt administration."[37]

In 2002, he began reporting on the nationwide sex scandal involving numbers of Catholic priests. What he discovered deeply troubled him. It became clear that priests, with a history of abusing, abused many children. The response of the church to the allegations was to move the priests to another parish and pay off the victims or bully them into silence. Unbelievably, in some cases the bishops encouraged priests to flee the country to avoid being charged. Lobdell was becoming increasingly disillusioned. He recollected, "I understood that I was witnessing the failure of humans, not God. But in a way, that was the point. I didn't see these institutions drenched in God's spirit. Shouldn't religious organizations, if they were God-inspired and -driven, reflect higher standards than government, corporations, and other groups in society?"[38]

But it wasn't just the scandals of the Roman Catholic Church that troubled him. Evangelicals had their own issues. In 2002, he spent several years investigating the Trinity Broadcasting Network and the cast of characters associated with it. TBN began broadcasting in 1973 and has since gone on to become the largest Christian television network in the world, reaching millions of people daily with its popular programs. The network, however, is controversial for its prosperity gospel message, which Lobdell saw as a scheme by which believers could cajole God into giving them what they want, even if it was financially irresponsible for them to do so. He described what he referred to as the TBN creed as follows: "If viewers send money to the network, God

37. Lobdell, "He Had Faith," lines 58–59.

38. Lobdell, "He Had Faith," lines 101–02.

will repay them with great riches and good health. Even people deeply in debt are encouraged to put donations on credit cards."[39]

The opposite is true as well. Lobdell once heard Paul Crouch, co-founder of TBN, tell viewers. "If you have been healed or saved or blessed through TBN and have not contributed . . . you are robbing God and will lose your reward in heaven."[40] Lobdell began investigating the claims of Crouch and others, and what he found was disturbing. Many people who had given money to the network in the hopes of receiving more money from God in return were sorely disappointed. People were giving their hard-earned money and large amounts of their savings and getting nothing in return; meanwhile the Crouches were living like royalty. Via TBN they owned thirty houses across the country, a 21-million-dollar jet, and two mansions in Newport Beach, just to name some of the perks of being the head of the "ministry."

It wasn't just the leaders of the network who were fleecing the flock, it was also some of the high-profile Christian personalities who had programs on the network. One of these was self-proclaimed faith healer Benny Hinn. Hinn packed out large stadiums with promises that God will heal people if they have enough faith, all the while raking in millions of dollars from the desperate and credulous. Lobdell attended Hinn healing services and reported that his "heart broke for the hundreds of people around me in wheelchairs or in the final stages of terminal diseases, believing that if God deemed their faith strong enough, they would be healed that night."[41] It was obvious to Lobdell that Hinn, like the Crouches, was a fraud and a huckster who preyed on the hopes and fears of fellow Christians for the love of money.

To counteract what he saw as corruption and spiritual abuse, he tried to get several prominent pastors to comment on the error of the prosperity gospel, condemn Hinn's faith healing and expose the Crouches' lifestyle, but they would not. In their failure to speak up, he saw a parallel to the Catholic bishops "who didn't want to risk what they had."[42] His experience reporting on the Catholic sex scandals and the corruption and spiritual abuse taking place among high-profile evangelicals began to undermine his faith. The effect of observing such callous cases of *Friendly Fire* resulted in him having intellectual questions. "The questions that I thought I had come to peace with started to bubble up again. Why do bad things happen to good people? Why does God get credit for answered prayers but no

39. Lobdell, "He Had Faith," lines 107–08.

40. Lobdell, "He Had Faith," line 109.

41. Lobdell, "He Had Faith," line 120.

42. Lobdell, "He Had Faith," line 142.

blame for unanswered ones? Why do we believe in the miraculous healing power of God when he's never been able to regenerate a limb or heal a severed spinal cord?" he wondered.[43]

He sought help from a pastor whom he respected, hoping that he could provide satisfying answers to his intellectual objections. But in the end, the reality of what he experienced outweighed the rationality of the arguments offered by his pastor. "I had tried to push away doubts and reconcile an all-powerful and infinitely-loving God with what I saw, but I was losing ground. I wondered if my born-again experience at the mountain retreat was more about fatigue, spiritual longing, and emotional vulnerability than being touched by Jesus. And I considered another possibility: Maybe God didn't exist."[44]

By 2005, he had seen enough. Reporting on religion had left him feeling "used up and numb."[45] The *Friendly Fire* he witnessed that, in his experience, so often characterized the Roman Catholic and evangelical leadership eroded his confidence in the message they proclaimed. Today, William Lobdell identifies as an unbeliever.

Practice What You Preach

The quantitative and qualitative data are clear; Christians behaving badly toward other Christians—what I have called *Friendly Fire*—increases the likelihood of believers suffering a crisis of faith that may end in the loss of faith. When Christians don't reflect the unity and love that Jesus spoke of as the identifying markers of his followers, it casts doubt on the truth of the gospel. If Jesus says that the world will know we are Christians by our love for one another and that a primary apologetic for the veracity of his claims is our unity, then we shouldn't be surprised that our *Friendly Fire* in terms of judgmentalism and hypocrisy lead people out of the church. We might ask ourselves, what else are they supposed to conclude, given Jesus's own words? It is imperative that the Church teaches and practices love and unity, not only because they are virtues, but because the lack of them can have such dire consequences in the formation of believers. Brennan Manning's well known quote seems appropriate to end this chapter.

> The greatest single cause of atheism in the world today is Christians who acknowledge Jesus with their lips and walk out the

43. Lobdell, "He Had Faith," lines 148–50.
44. Lobdell, "He Had Faith," lines 158–60.
45. Lobdell, "He Had Faith," line 194.

> door and deny Him by their lifestyle. That is what an unbelieving world simply finds unbelievable.[46]

And, I might add, painfully prepared deconverts tell us that some in the "believing" world find it unbelievable as well.

46. Manning, *Free At Last* Audio Recording.

Chapter 9

A Recipe for Success Part 1

I think baking is very rewarding, and if you follow a good recipe, you will get success.

Mary Berry

Alternative Preparation

In the previous chapters, I have tried to make the case that despite the best of intentions, the church can inadvertently prepare believers for a crisis of faith that may lead to deconversion. The combination of a specific constellation of personality traits, inadequate socialization into the Christian faith, and our increasingly secular culture constitute the ingredients, preparation, and cooking environment of the *Recipe for Disaster*. In these final two chapters I offer an alternative approach to each of the inadequate methods of preparation. These alternative approaches at socializing believers into the faith don't guarantee that believers will maintain their faith. However, I am convinced they do two positive things: one, they avoid putting the common and unnecessary stumbling blocks in front of believers; two, they provide believers with a foundation that sets them up for a flourishing Christian faith.

The Tyranny of the Necessary vs. the Tranquility of the Sufficient

The first way that the church poorly socializes or prepares believers is by over-preparing them. Over-preparation occurs when believers are required to affirm and defend an excessive number of theological beliefs that are held, either implicitly or explicitly, as necessary to be a biblical Christian. I labeled this state of affairs the *Tyranny of the Necessary* because it places a heavy burden on believers that many cannot carry. All it takes is for one belief to be disproven and the entire house of cards comes crashing down. Three assumptions underwrite the *Tyranny of the Necessary.* The first concerns the nature and role of the Bible, where the Bible is understood to be an inerrant, supremely authoritative standard of truth, which serves as the foundation of an individual or community's meaning making system. The second is that God's intention in giving us the Bible is so we can have correct theological truths. The third is assuming that one's interpretation of the Bible is identical to Christianity itself.

In contrast to the *Tyranny of the Necessary,* I propose what I am calling the *Tranquility of the Sufficient.* The *Tyranny of the Necessary* tends to produce a fragile, inflexible faith that is ripe for a crisis. The *Tranquility of the Sufficient* provides believers with a stable, flexible faith that sets them up to flourish. Just as the *Tyranny of the Necessary* is driven by three assumptions, so too is the *Tranquility of the Sufficient.* We will get to those in a moment, but first a few words about tyranny and tranquility, necessary and sufficient.

The word tyranny is used to describe a style of leadership that is oppressive and controlling. Jesus was aware of the tyranny his listeners experienced at the hand of the Pharisees, the teachers of the law, and the occupying Romans. The Pharisees were religiously oppressive according to Jesus because they "tie up heavy, cumbersome loads and put them on other people's shoulders, but they themselves are not willing to lift a finger to move them." (Matt 23:4 NIV) The Romans were politically oppressive and controlling, forcing the Jews to submit to their rule or risk death. Jesus acknowledged the oppressive nature of their rule when he commented on what appears to have been a common occurrence in that time, a Jew being commanded to serve a Roman soldier, "If anyone forces you to go one mile, go with them two." (Matt 5:41 NIV) To all who found themselves bending under the weight of their religious and political oppressors, Jesus said, "Come to me, all you who are weary and burdened." And in contrast to the tyranny of those regimes, Jesus offered them tranquility: "and I will give you rest. Take my yoke upon you and learn from me, for I am gentle and humble in heart and you will find rest for your souls. For my yoke is easy and my burden is light." (Matt 11: 28-30 NIV) To those who would submit to his Lordship, he promised a different way of life characterized by peace, serenity, and rest. The way of Jesus is not the tyranny of burdensome religion but the tranquility of being in humble submission to a master who seeks our flourishing.

The way of Jesus is tranquil, not tyrannical, because it is concerned not with the necessary but the sufficient. Here it is important that I am clear about what I am trying to communicate, lest I be misunderstood. The word *necessary* means essential or required, while the word *sufficient* means adequate or enough. It is necessary for water to emerge that two hydrogen molecules and one oxygen molecule form a bond. The presence of only one hydrogen molecule is not enough for water to emerge, two are necessary. Having two hydrogen molecules and one oxygen molecule is sufficient for water to emerge. When I say that the way of Jesus is concerned with the sufficient over the necessary, I do not want to be heard as claiming that doctrine is unimportant; quite the opposite is the case, as I will argue below. Indeed, there are essential beliefs and attitudes that one must possess to be a follower of Jesus and a member of his kingdom. But those beliefs and attitudes are relatively small in relation to what are considered necessary by some to be a "biblical" Christian. Many of those "necessary" beliefs and attitudes turn out to be not only unnecessary to be a "biblical" Christian but burdens that are difficult to carry. It seems to me that Jesus is not so much concerned with his followers working hard to maintain and defend a system of beliefs as much as he is in them sitting at his feet and growing in a relationship with him. We see this in the story of Mary and Martha. As Jesus traveled preaching the message of the kingdom, he went through Bethany and there was invited to the home of Martha and her sister Mary. Jesus accepted Martha's invitation and entered the home as their special guest. While Martha prepared a meal, Mary sat and listened to Jesus teach. Frustrated that her sister did not help her with the meal she was preparing, Martha complained to Jesus, "Lord, don't you not care that my sister has left me to do the work by myself? Tell her to help me!" To which Jesus responded, "Martha, Martha," the Lord answered, "you are worried and upset about many things, but few things are needed—or indeed only one. Mary has chosen what is better, and it will not be taken away from her." (Luke 10:40b–42 NIV) Martha was burdened by her inability to prepare an extravagant meal for Jesus all by herself. But Jesus gently corrected her faulty assumptions about what she needed to do. Rather than an extravagant meal, all that was needed was a simple, single dish to supply their needs. Chuck Swindoll's comments on this passage are instructive:

> When Jesus told Martha that only "one thing" was necessary, he was helping her see the importance of keeping everything in balance. There was nothing wrong with her wanting to prepare and serve something—she just didn't need to go overboard. It would have been much better to prepare something simple

> and easy. That would have allowed Martha time to sit and relax with them during Jesus's visit. She also would have stayed calm, rather than gotten "worried and bothered" about things.[1]

A bowl of soup would have been sufficient. It would have met the essential need of the moment and Martha could have spent time doing what was really important, being in the presence of Jesus and learning of him. Instead, she was burdened by a long list of essential duties she assumed she needed to perform to be a "good" host. Jesus's comments to Martha are helpful for us as well. Contrary to the assumptions behind the *Tyranny of the Necessary,* there are but "a few things that are needed" to be affirmed in terms of what it means to be a genuine follower of Christ. Just a few are sufficient. Does that mean that we shouldn't be concerned about developing in our doctrinal and theological positions? No, it simply means that our focus should be on those "few things that are needed" for an individual to enter into the kingdom. Once a person adopts those beliefs and attitudes, our focus should be on helping them become more like Christ through sitting at his feet, not burdening them with nonessentials they must maintain to be a "biblical" Christian according to our interpretation of the Scriptures. Let us now look at the three assumptions that drive the *Tyranny of the Necessary.*

Back to Nature

The first assumption driving the *Tyranny of the Necessary* concerns the nature and role of the Bible in the life of the Christian community. In chapter 4 I argued that an essential element of the *Tyranny of the Necessary* is that the Bible is viewed as the supremely authoritative repository of objective and absolute propositional truth. It is important to note that although that assumption is an essential element of the *Tyranny of the Necessary,* it is not sufficient to produce it. Christians should believe the Bible teaches propositional truth about the world and can do so without veering off into the *Tyranny of the Necessary.* The problem comes not from seeing the Bible as teaching truth but when it is seen as supremely authoritative. If you recall, back in chapter 4 I introduced the work of three psychologists of religion whose work focuses on fundamentalism. One of their main arguments is that essential to fundamentalism is seeing the text of the Bible as supremely authoritative to the point that "No other source of knowledge shall in any way alter the true meaning of the text."[2] As such, the Bible plays the role

1. Swindoll, "Keeping Your Balance," lines 34–39.
2. Hood et al., *Psychology of Religious Fundamentalism*, 37.

of final criterion on all matters, not just those of faith and practice. This becomes problematic when we: a) forget that the Bible is the final arbiter of truth and not our interpretation, and b) when we fail to allow the findings of other disciplines to influence our understanding of the Bible. I will address the former below, but for now I would like to address the latter. Not allowing any outside source of knowledge to alter our understanding of the meaning of the text has two problems. First, it presupposes that the disciplines of history, science, and critical scholarship are irrelevant to discovering the true meaning of the text. But what if those tools are necessary for discovering the true meaning of the text? Second, the intra-textual approach (one only need appeal to the text itself to gain knowledge) will inevitably bring one into cognitive conflict with widely accepted theories and philosophies of the modern world. When this happens, the intra-textual approach that sees the Bible as a supremely authoritative criterion that no other source of knowledge shall in any way alter, forces believers to reject out of hand any data that would cause them to re-evaluate what they believe the Bible teaches. They must ignore any theory that contradicts how they read the Bible because being a faithful, biblical Christian requires they do so. But maintaining one's faith utilizing this approach has proven much too difficult for many.

But shouldn't Christians take the Bible as the supremely authoritative and final criterion of knowledge? It all depends on what one means by "supremely authoritative." I want to affirm that when theories and philosophies that are widely accepted in the modern world are in *genuine conflict* with what one believes the Bible *actually teaches,* then, as a Christian, we are to side with the Bible. At the same time, we ought to be free to engage in conversation with other knowledge traditions such as history, science, and critical scholarship that appear to conflict with the Bible because they may help us understand the text better. In doing so, we may come to find what we thought was a conflict between the Bible and theories from other knowledge traditions was not a conflict in reality but only in appearance. Perhaps the conflict was a result of how we interpreted the Bible that can be resolved by reinterpreting it to bring it in line with what we believe we know from other disciplines. At other times, we may find that we cannot reinterpret the Bible to make it concord with contemporary theories because it would compromise a biblical claim in ways that impact the narrative of the Bible in a manner that is unacceptable. Regardless of what we conclude on any specific issue, we can remain faithful to the Bible as our ultimate criterion of truth without requiring that we burden believers with having them affirm one specific reading of the text by allowing them to bring insights gleaned from other knowledge traditions into dialogue with the biblical text.

How then do we go about determining when it is legitimate for us to reinterpret the text in light of the findings of an outside knowledge tradition such as science or history? The answer to that question is complex and deserves much more attention than I can give it here, however I think there are two principles that can provide us with guidance. The first is if the Bible itself opens the door to being better understood by bringing to bear findings of science, history, and critical studies. For example, there seems to be a conflict between the findings of archeology and the biblical account of the conquest of Canaan. Joshua records the account as a total annihilation of the Canaanites but archeology contradicts that account. According to the book of Joshua, "So Joshua subdued the whole region, including the hill country, the Negev, the western foothills, and the mountain slopes, together with all their kings. He left no survivors. He totally destroyed all who breathed, just as the LORD, the God of Israel, had commanded . . . As the LORD commanded his servant Moses, so Moses commanded Joshua, and Joshua did it; he left nothing undone of all that the LORD commanded Moses." (Josh 10:40; 11:15 NIV) But according to contemporary archeology, there is very little evidence that such a wholesale slaughter took place. On the surface, it seems like this is a straightforward case of a conflict between Scripture and science. Upon closer inspection, however, we find that Scripture itself lends some credibility to the findings of archeology. The book of Judges opens with a battle that takes place after Joshua's death. It says:

> After the death of Joshua, the Israelites asked the LORD, "Who of us is to go up first to fight against the Canaanites?" The LORD answered, "Judah shall go up; I have given the land into their hands." The men of Judah then said to the Simeonites, their fellow Israelites, "Come up with us into the territory allotted to us, to fight against the Canaanites. We in turn will go with you into yours." So, the Simeonites went with them. When Judah attacked, the LORD gave the Canaanites and Perizzites into their hands, and they struck down 10,000 men at Bezek. (Judg 1:1–4 NIV)

It appears that, according to Judges, Joshua did not annihilate all of the Canaanites. In the above passage we see that Scripture opens the door to being better understood in light of the findings of archeology. Perhaps the language of Joshua describing the annihilation of the Canaanites is better understood to be something less than literal. If so, it seems appropriate to resolve, or at least reduce, the tension between the claims that Joshua annihilated all the Canaanites and the record of the book of Judges and the findings of archaeology that he did not by reinterpreting the passage as an example of hyperbole that was typical of ancient descriptions of military battles.

A second principle that may help us determine when we may reinterpret a passage of Scripture in light of contemporary thought is how significant the specific passage under investigation is to the overall narrative of the Bible. When an apparent conflict occurs the question that needs to be asked is, does the conflict negatively impact an essential element of the biblical narrative such that the redemptive story of the Bible does not make sense without it. If so, the believer must side with the text of Scripture. An excellent example of this is the problem of the Exodus out of Egypt. Presently there exists no evidence for the Exodus of the Hebrews out of Egypt or their travel to the land of Canaan. Given the large numbers of people the Bible records and the length of time they wandered in the desert, it seems reasonable that if it happened archaeologists would have discovered some evidence of it. Even admitting that the absence of evidence is not evidence of absence, most students of archaeology in this case see a real conflict between science and Scripture. Given the theological importance of the Exodus in the history of Israel as the people of God and its soteriological relevance in the work of Christ, it would be illegitimate to reinterpret the Exodus based on the findings of archaeology. To do so would mean denying it ever occurred, and that is a price that is too high to pay.

Does this mean that the believer is being irrational in the face of contrary evidence? Not at all, rather it is to make a rational choice based on previous experience. Trusting that the Bible's account is true is rational, given that time and time again the biblical record has been vindicated despite being at odds with contemporary theories. Space permits me from listing the cutting edge, widely held academic theories that were at odds with the Bible that had to be discarded because further research ultimately vindicated the biblical account. King David was once thought to be a legend like King Arthur, until his existence was confirmed by the Tel Dan Stela that referenced "The House of David." Many other individuals and locations could be mentioned. In fact, fifty-three people mentioned in the Bible once thought to be fictitious by scholarship have been confirmed through archaeology.[3] Both science and history (to a lesser extent) advance by way of funeral. What is today's cutting-edge understanding may tomorrow be relegated to the academic ash heap. Those Christians who are quick to adopt theories that are at odds with the Bible because they are the most recent scientific and historical theories should heed the words widely attributed

3. Mykytiuk, "53 People in the Bible Confirmed."

to William Ralph Inge that, "whoever marries the spirit of this age will find himself a widower in the next."[4]

All truth is God's. The challenge comes in trying to discern whether our understanding of his word should be corrected by the understanding of his world provided by science, historical research, and critical studies or whether those understandings of his world should be corrected by our understanding of his word. Either way, we do well to remember that whatever our conclusions, they are always interpretations of the data and, as such, need to be held loosely in all but the most essential doctrines. This is true for our interpretations of Scripture *and* the reigning theories of science, history, and critical studies.

A Matter of Fact(s)

The second assumption the *Tyranny of the Necessary* holds is that the purpose of the Bible is to give us correct facts about God and the world. On this score, the goal of the Christian life in relation to the Bible is to use it to discover and hold correct beliefs about reality. I think this perspective is mistaken. The Bible is not a book of facts like the encyclopedia, nor is it a textbook divided into topical chapters, or a product manual that provides troubleshooting advice. It is, above everything, else a collection of books that tell a story about God reconciling the world to himself. I am convinced God gave us the Bible as story rather than a textbook of theological facts because story engages every part of our being, intellect, emotion, will, body, and spirit. Propositional facts engage only one part of us, our intellect. Anything that engages all of you is more effective in the long run than something that activates only part of you.[5] Stories also are the way we communicate with each other. We exchange stories with one another, not facts. We tell stories to others and invite them to tell them to us. It is how we get to know each other, and they form the basis of our relationships.[6] The same is true for God, which is why he chose to tell us about himself through the big story of the Bible, not through a textbook of theological truths. Does the story contain important theological truths? Yes! But even those bits of propositional truth get their meaning from the story. "God is love" is certainly a true proposition. But we only know what that means because of the story that tells us of God's willingness to humble himself unto death to rescue us. We can short circuit the *Tyranny of the Necessary* if we see the

4. This quote is attributed to Inge, but it cannot be found in print.

5. Taylor, *The Skeptical Believer*, 114.

6. Taylor, *The Skeptical Believer*, 115.

Bible first and foremost as a story to be indwelt rather than a repository of facts to be mastered.

To counter this assumption, I propose that we replace it with another assumption about why God gave us the Bible, one that places the emphasis not on what we know but who were are. Paul, in writing to Timothy, reminded him of the twin purposes of Scripture when he said, "from infancy you have known the Holy Scriptures, which are able to make you wise for salvation through faith in Christ Jesus. All Scripture is God-breathed and is useful for teaching, rebuking, correcting, and training in righteousness, so that the servant of God may be thoroughly equipped for every good work. (2 Tim 3:15–17 NIV) Salvation and good works are what Paul highlights as the chief ends of the Scriptures. Knowing the propositional and doctrinal content of Scripture is important but it is secondary in that knowledge is not the end in itself, but the means to an end, which is salvation and Christ likeness.

Reality Check

The third assumption constituting the *Tyranny of the Necessary* is that one's interpretation of the Bible is in fact Christianity itself. In this case, one is unaware of the role that interpretation plays in our encounter with the Scriptures. Being ignorant of the necessity of interpretation can lead to mistaking one's construal of Christianity with Christianity itself. When we do so, we elevate our limited and very human understanding into an idol that we insist others worship if they are to be truly Christian. To counteract this very human tendency to identify our interpretation of reality with reality itself, I offer the following suggestions. We need to always remember there is a difference between the map and the territory. By this I mean our apprehension of reality is always incomplete and partly a construction. As Paul said, "For now we see only a reflection as in a mirror." (1 Cor 13:12 NIV) What Paul seems to be saying is that we need to be very careful that we communicate to those we disciple that Christianity and our take of Christianity are not one and the same. Why is this important? For the sole reason that, in my opinion, what the vast majority of deconverts are rejecting is not Christ, but a version of "Christianity" that they have been told simply *is* Christianity itself. Naturally, when they come to find things about "Christianity" they find false, distasteful, or even immoral, they have no choice but to reject it. Thinking they have given Jesus and his religion the old college try, they leave with clear consciences. In reality, they have not rejected the way of Jesus, but more than likely some interpretation of it that was passed off as

Christianity without remainder, but was only a poor imitation. Over and over again one encounters this tragedy in deconversion narratives. Equating Christianity with an American style of evangelicalism, Republican political sensitivities, a sense of moral superiority, and a theological construction that requires affirming among other doctrines, a literal Hell, literal six-day creation, and inerrancy of the Bible, it is no wonder that so many feel if "that" is Christianity they have to reject it. Humility must force us to realize that our "Christianity" is greatly influenced by when we were born, where we live, and the assumptions about the Bible that we bring to the text. We must, as we occupy a particular and historically contingent Christian tradition, recognize that there are acceptable ways of being Christian otherwise. By this I mean there is nothing wrong with affirming that the tradition we stand in—whether evangelical, reformed, orthodox, Roman Catholic, or any other within the broad ecumenical creeds of the church—is, as far as we can tell, the one that is most closely aligned with the teachings of the Bible. But we also must be humble enough to admit that there are other traditions within the church universal that, as far as they teach the essential truths of the message of salvation and affirm the ecumenical creeds, are Christian as well.[7] Doing so offers struggling believers other alternatives to the ultimatum that says, "Either be a Christian or Don't," where Christian just means "my group's interpretation of Christianity."

If we want to be careful not to place the stumbling block of the *Tyranny of the Necessary* in the way of believers we are responsible for socializing into a robust faith, what is the alternative? The *Tranquility of the Sufficient* would lead us to identify those beliefs that are minimally sufficient to adopt to be considered a Christian and then emphasize those. I think there are two sets of beliefs that meet that requirement: The salvation message and the ecumenical creeds of the church. The first is sufficient for salvation; the second for orthodox belief.

Sirs, What Must I Do to be Saved?

As mentioned above, salvation, as far as correct belief is concerned, has to do with possessing a fond appreciation that the work of Christ on the cross and his subsequent resurrection are the means by which an individual has

7. The phrase "the essential truths of the message of salvation" is somewhat question-begging, since not all Christian denominations affirm the same set of essentials. I am speaking of what Christians throughout history have consistently affirmed, that one must believe that Jesus's death on the cross is the means by which we can have our sins forgiven and have a relationship with God. Belief in this sense is comprised of both intellectual assent and personal trust.

their sins forgiven and are reconciled to God. Fond appreciation, in this sense, includes believing what the Bible claims about Christ's substitutionary death and trusting him as the savior.[8] One does not need to comprehend the nature of the Trinity or even Christ's divinity to be saved. Christ promised the thief on the cross that he would be with him in paradise that very day, and I know of no theologian who thinks that the thief believed Jesus was the God-man. At most, he recognized him as Israel's long-awaited Messiah. Having said that, I want to acknowledge an issue that is lurking around in the background of this discussion, and that has to do with the difference between being ignorant of important truths and denying them. The thief on the cross was saved because he placed his faith in the person of Jesus, whom he recognized as the Messiah even though he did not identify him as God. I think that there are many people today who, like the thief on the cross, have saving faith without a complete understanding of who Jesus is. But what they do believe is accurate enough. Their faith maps onto the real Jesus. But what of those individuals who do not believe in the deity of Christ, not because they are ignorant of it, but because they deny it? Theirs is a different situation. If Jesus is divine and an individual denies that, it seems they have placed their faith in another Jesus because they are rejecting an essential property of who he is. The divinity of Jesus is not an accidental property, an inconsequential add-on, it is essential to who he is. An individual can be ignorant of it and still be saved, but it is highly questionable if an individual can deny it and still be saved. Salvation is not merely a matter of having faith. What matters just as much is the object one places their faith in. Denying an essential property of Jesus such as his divine nature would entail that an individual has placed their faith in an object that cannot save them. We see Paul making this argument in the book of 2 Corinthians, where he worried that if someone proclaimed another Jesus to the Corinthians they might trust in him. He says:

> For if someone comes to you and preaches a Jesus other than the Jesus we preached, or if you receive a different spirit from the Spirit you received, or a different gospel from the one you accepted, you put up with it easily enough. (2 Cor 11:4 NIV)

Admittedly, this raises a number of questions. Can an individual be ignorant of the divine nature of Jesus when they place their faith in him, become saved, and then lose that salvation if they subsequently become aware of the doctrine of the deity of Christ and reject it? Will all genuinely converted people come to affirm the doctrine of the deity of Christ when they are

8. One may affirm Christ's substitutionary work on the cross without affirming any particular substitutionary theory such as penal or as a payment to Satan.

presented with it? If so, does that mean that those who profess faith in Christ but reject that he is also divine mean they were never saved in the first place? These are challenging questions that warrant more attention than I am able or willing to give them at present. Suffice it to say, that when it comes to what is required for a person to affirm to be a Christian, soteriologically speaking, the number of beliefs are few.

There is more to being a Christian, however, than just being saved. There is also the matter of what the Christian community has identified as the boundary markers for correct belief. Soteriologically speaking, an individual may be a Christian, that is they are saved, but in the broader theological sense they may not be very Christian at all. A person can be born-again and hold to all kinds of aberrant and unorthodox theology.

In Paul's day, as we see in the concern expressed above, there were already other Jesus's, other gospels, and other spirits that were being preached. As time went on, it became clear to the Christian community, which did not have the canon of the New Testament, the importance of clearly delineating the doctrines that Christians ought to believe, not so much for salvation but to be theologically orthodox or to hold correct beliefs.

What Ought I Believe?

These attempts are best seen in the ecumenical creeds of the church, the Apostles' Creed 200 CE, the Nicene Creed 325 CE, and the Chalcedonian Creed 451 CE. These three creeds identify the minimal set of beliefs that a person ought to affirm to be orthodox in belief. Yet even that is probably too strong of a statement. A person does not have to affirm all of the beliefs in the ecumenical creeds to be considered theologically orthodox. Like the thief on the cross, one can be ignorant of what the creeds teach. One cannot be considered orthodox in terms of what Christians believe and deny the major tenets of the creeds. Ultimately the Bible, not the creeds, is the standard for orthodox belief. But the creeds do a good job of distilling the really important teachings of the Bible that nearly all Christians at all times have affirmed.[9] Theologian Michael Bird says, "In sum, the purpose of the creeds was to mark out the boundaries of the faith. The creeds were warnings to the effect that 'all who proceed beyond this point do so at the

9. Of the three major creeds, the Eastern Orthodox Church affirms the original wording of the Nicene Creed and the Chalcedonian creed. It does not reject the Apostles' Creed in content but, because it was not the product of an official church council, it does not recognize it as binding. The western Churches— Roman Catholic and Protestant—affirm all three creeds.

peril of their own souls.'"[10] These are the beliefs that the *Tranquility of the Sufficient* requires of a person who claims to be a Christian. That does not mean that these are the only important beliefs that a Christian should have a positive attitude toward. It just means that these are the essential beliefs we ought to require of those we are responsible to disciple. The reader may note a similarity between what I am calling the *Tranquility of the Sufficient* in terms of required beliefs and what C.S. Lewis famously referred to as *Mere Christianity.* Lewis compared "mere" or common Christianity with "a large hall out of which doors open into several rooms. If I can bring anyone into that hall I shall have done what I attempted."[11] Likewise, if the approach to Christian socialization I am suggesting in this book, particularly as it relates to the *Tranquility of the Sufficient,* helps in the retention of faith, then I shall have done what I attempted.

Socializing believers into the Christian faith by emphasizing what is sufficient to being a Christian soteriologically and, more broadly speaking, orthodox, does an end-run on the *Tyranny of the Necessary.* Where the *Tyranny of the Necessary* results in a house of cards faith that is fragile, inflexible, and dogmatic due to the sheer number of beliefs that must be affirmed to be biblically Christian, the *Tranquility of the Sufficient* gives the believer a faith that is sturdy and built upon a foundation of beliefs that have stood the test of time. It is also a faith that is flexible, allowing for the reinterpretation of nonessential beliefs when needed. Finally, it is a faith that avoids the dogmatism that projects an "our way or the highway" mentality. The *Tranquility of the Sufficient* is humble and aware that there are ways of being Christian-otherwise that are worthy of the name Christian, even if they are different from the community we stand in. Therefore, if a believer rejects our "take" of Christianity, they are not forced to reject Christianity altogether.

Spiritual Cultural Shock vs. Appropriately Acclimated

The second method of inadequate socialization we looked at was being under-prepared. Under-prepared believers suffer from *Spiritual Culture Shock.* Cultural shock is the feeling of being uncomfortable and out of place as a result of being in a different cultural setting. Anyone who has traveled to a foreign country that is significantly different from one's home country has experienced a kind of culture shock. Under-prepared Christians frequently experience something akin to culture shock not from traveling to

10. Bird, *What Christians Ought to Believe,* 24.

11. Lewis, *Mere Christianity,* xv.

another culture but in their home culture. Affirming the truths of orthodox Christianity in the disenchanted modern world can make a Christian feel self-conscious about how the church's social imaginary stands in relation to the social imaginary of the broader culture. Doing so can lead to feelings of doubt and skepticism about one's beliefs. This is especially acute for believers who have been socialized into a Sunday school kind of faith that never develops into an adult understanding of the narrative of the Bible.

One way to avoid culture shock is to be *Appropriately Acclimated* to a new culture. When traveling overseas, it can be helpful beforehand to learn as much as possible about the culture that you are visiting. Eating traditional dishes and learning the language of the new country before traveling there can also be helpful. Visiting local communities comprised of individuals from the country one is going to can help as well. None of these will completely inoculate you against the culture shock you will experience by going to a foreign country, but it can lessen it. One of the reasons we experience culture shock is that we are unaware that we too inhabit a culture. Our culture is, for the most part, invisible to us and, as a result, we assume that the "world" we indwell is just the world as it is. In reality, it is a cultural construct that we are as much ignorant of as a fish is of the water it swims in. Not being aware of this tends to produce in us a sense of cultural superiority when we visit other cultures because we may feel that the way they do things is wrong. In reality, what we think is wrong is likely just different. In fact, when it comes to food, customs, music, and a vast number of other things, there is no right or wrong, there are just different cultural constructs. When we understand this, we are on our way to mitigating the uncomfortable experience of culture shock. Recognizing that much of culture is a construct of people who share the same set of assumptions and lenses, is not just the first step in fighting culture shock in terms of going to a new country but also in being a Christian in the twenty-first century.

As I outlined in chapter 5, I am persuaded that being an educated, culturally sensitive, reflective believer in the West is becoming more challenging. Whereas bare theism retains a certain amount of intellectual respect, biblical theism no longer does. A modern, college-educated pagan looking at the universe in all its grandeur and precision, or at the complexity of and information in the cell, may be able to intellectually countenance the possibility that the existence of *a* god offers a rational explanation, but not the God of the Bible. Why is that? Because the God of the Bible is seen as an angry ancient tribal deity who prohibits his people from wearing clothes made from two fabrics, boiling a kid in its mother's milk, or keeping their foreskins! That god sounds like a product of the imaginations of a primitive people who inhabited an enchanted world and didn't know any better. Surely, if the god of quantum mechanics, transfinite induction, reverse mathematics, and electron superposition exists, he isn't concerned with whether people eat bacon, doesn't require animal sacrifices, doesn't command fornicators to be executed, and wouldn't send angels into the world as his representatives. Within our disenchanted world, there is no room for such a god. If this is a fair representation of the way that many in our increasingly secular culture think about the God of the Bible, it is no wonder that affirming a biblical, not just a theistic, worldview is difficult for some Christians.

Power Play

One of the first things we need to do in order to help believers avoid *Spiritual Culture Shock* is to aid them in recognizing the power that our constructed, contingent social imaginary has over what we take to be reasonable. Our languages, customs, dress, food, music, and so on are human creations. All of these elements create a "world" for us, a way of being that feels normal and natural. When we step outside of these "worlds" we feel a certain level of discomfort. For example, a Scotsman wearing a kilt in Edinburgh will feel quite at home. The same Scotsman wearing a kilt in the heart of South-Central Los Angeles will likely feel not only self-conscious, but profoundly out of place and possibly embarrassed. But that's only because of his setting, and not because of anything inherently embarrassing about his clothing. Just as what we *feel* is normal in terms of what we wear is influenced by our culture and social imaginary, so too is what we *feel* is reasonable to believe. If we indwell a cultural milieu or social imaginary where the concept of the biblical God is viewed as unsophisticated and primitive, we will likely feel embarrassed and out of place for holding to belief in the biblical God. Of course, not everyone living in the modern West lives in settings that are as secular and faith-challenging as I am making things out to be. There are enclaves in the United States that are less secular and where believing in the biblical God comes easy. But for well-educated believers in secular environments who are sensitive to how they are perceived by their cultured peers, affirming belief in the biblical God can be very difficult.

This is why the church needs to help believers realize that what they feel has little to do with what is true and is largely a product of their cultural setting and social imaginary. Truth is a matter of whether our beliefs correspond with reality, not how we feel. What we feel may or may not reflect the nature of reality. Helping believers become aware of the incredible power that culture and social imaginaries have to form both beliefs and feelings can help them recognize that what may be driving their doubts is not rational suspicion, but the formative power of culture. As they swim upstream in an increasingly post-Christian culture, we need them to become sensitive to the strong undercurrents of the modern social imaginary that remains largely hidden but threatens to drown their faith. That is why educating believers not only in worldview (which is cognitive in nature) but in the more subtle and dangerous power of social imaginaries is so important. Social imaginaries act as the gatekeepers for what cognitive claims will be *felt* or will seem reasonable or plausible. Being aware of the role social imaginaries play in our belief formation is the first step in being able to evaluate whether a doubt or objection to the faith is a legitimate concern or just a product of the dominant social imaginary of our modern secular culture.

It's All Been Done Before

Second, once we expose the power culture has to influence what we believe through social imaginaries, the next step is to help believers realize that the secular culture they inhabit and the modern social imaginary that influences how they feel about the world are as much a contingent construct as any primitive culture ever was. The secular is not simply the inevitable result of human progress. Nor is it the inescapable outcome of the rational maturation of humanity. It is not even the unavoidable consequence of the scientific revolution. Put another way, the secular is not a remainder or what is left over after we have shed the superstitions of the enchanted world. It is not the inevitable outcome of leaving behind superstitions and becoming more enlightened as a species. Rather, it is a construction, no different from any other way of inhabiting the world. It is an accomplishment, an achievement, not a subtraction story.[12] The modern secular world is the result of a series of changes taking place in the noetic structure of the West during the late Medieval Period. Charles Taylor identifies five specific reforms that ultimately created the modern secular social imaginary that we inhabit. Without these five changes in understanding, there would be no modern secular society.[13] To spend time unpacking what those are would take us far afield from the focus of this chapter. It is enough to note that he is clear that the modern secular imaginary was not inevitable; it could have been otherwise, had any of the five reforms in thinking not been adopted. It is, therefore, a contingent, cultural construct that offers its inhabitants a take on the world, no different in structure and function than all previous cultures. The difference comes only in the content of what the modern social imaginary deems

12. Smith, *How Not to Be Secular,*

13. Taylor, *A Secular Age*, 23–212.

reasonable to believe. Knowing this can help believers struggling with *Spiritual Culture Shock* as they discover that the emperor has no clothes. The social imaginary that infiltrates the lives of many of us in the secular West only has power over us when we are ignorant of its existence or take for granted that it is the inevitable product of human enlightenment and is bringing us increasingly in line with reality. When we realize that it is a contingent construct and one that does not necessarily accurately reflect the nature of reality, it will lose its power over us. We may still feel awkward and out of place on a university campus, in a corporate boardroom, or science laboratory, admitting that we identify with the biblical story, but we will no longer mistake those feelings for an indicator that our beliefs are wrong. Exposing the power of culture and social imaginaries over belief formation along with revealing the contingent, constructed nature of the modern secular social imaginary are the first two steps in helping believers avoid *Spiritual Culture Shock* and become *Appropriately Acclimated* to the world of the modern West at the beginning of the twenty-first century.

Ecclesiological Counterculture

Third, we need to help believers understand the importance of the church in their spiritual formation. Far from making them feel they have to go to church to be a good Christian, we need to help them see the church as a means of grace by which God actively brings about our flourishing by conforming us into his image. We inhabit multiple cultures all the time. There are school cultures, business cultures, sports cultures, etc. But all of those are part of the larger culture of the modern West, which means that we can never escape the influence it has on us. At best, we can counteract its influence by immersing ourselves in another culture, one that shapes and forms us in accordance with the word of God. If the culture that we inhabit shapes us and provides us with a social imaginary that informs how we view the world, we need to encourage believers to commit themselves to the resource God has given us to offset the formative power of the world, whether it be the world of the twenty-first century or that of the first, and that is the church. If, as I have argued, *Spiritual Culture Shock* is not primarily a matter of what we believe with our heads but what we feel in our gut; and what our guts feel is influenced by a subtle and powerful social imaginary, and the dominant social imaginary has little room for the biblical God, then it is imperative for believers to be committed to be part of a counter cultural culture, one that embodies and operates according to the biblical imaginary and acts as a plausibility structure for their Christians beliefs. Doing so can recalibrate our feelings about the biblical narrative. Through communal worship, remembrance of the Lord, prayer and teaching we are not only cognitively reformed but affectively reformed, as well. We leave meeting with God's people and hearing from God's word not only believing that it is true, but *feeling* "yes, this story makes sense." Regularly being around others who make sense of reality by seeing it through the biblical narrative and order their lives around the risen Christ can be an empowering experience, counteracting the narrative of the world.

A Return to Form-ation

Fourth, if being committed to the church is an important part of avoiding *Spiritual Culture Shock* and being *Appropriately Acclimated* to the surrounding culture, the church needs to actively engage in formation that counteracts the formation of the world. Healthy formation will be holistic, attending to the head, the heart, and the gut. For too long, fundamentalists and evangelical churches have held to an anthropology that viewed people as primarily thinking things, rational animals, brains on a stick. That assumption naturally leads to placing an emphasis on propositional Bible teaching. Of course, there is nothing wrong with Bible teaching, in fact it is not only good, but also essential for spiritual formation. It can, however, be overemphasized. This occurs when we fail to recognize that we are not primarily thinking things but worshiping, loving things. Real spiritual transformation happens in our lives not merely by gaining more information about the Bible through expository preaching. Real change comes when we engage in habits and bodily practices that instill those truths in us so that we become different people. Learning more information about the Bible is a good making practice, but it will not transform our lives, something more is required. It requires adhering to spiritual disciplines. Dallas Willard comments:

> I must learn and accept the responsibility of moving with God in the transformation of my own personality. Intelligent and steady implementation of plans for change are required if I am to lose the incoherence of the broken soul and take on the easy obedience and fulfillment of the person who lives ever more fully within the kingdom of God and the friendship of Jesus.[14]

Evangelical churches need to take seriously the practice of spiritual formation via means other than just hearing the Bible. We must take a holistic approach to discipleship that addresses the head, to be sure, but also the

14. Willard, "Spiritual Disciplines," 106.

heart. By training believers in the spiritual disciplines of prayer, biblical meditation, solitude, fasting, worship, service, and confession we attend to the heart, not just the mind. We also give believers tools by which they can see real spiritual transformation take place in their lives. Through practice and repetition of the spiritual disciplines, we indwell the counter-social imaginary of the kingdom. Doing so causes us to feel more at home within it and, in turn, we see it as "just the way things are."

Strangely Enough . . .

Finally, when we do communicate the Scriptures, we need to do so in ways that go beyond simplistic Sunday school understandings. We need to bridge the ancient world of the text to the modern world we live in. This does not mean that we demythologize all of the miraculous elements of the Bible so that it is more palatable with modern scientific sensibilities. That would be to betray our allegiance to the Bible as the word of God. What it does mean is that we receive the text as it presents itself to us, as a story, and seek to discover what role it is calling us to play. We treat the text seriously by listening carefully to what it is calling us to do and who it is calling us to be. Using all of our best resources available, we seek to discover what the Spirit intended to communicate when he moved the original authors to write the text and what it means for us in our day. This will often mean acknowledging the strangeness of the Bible. Author and apologist Natasha Crain points out that the Bible is filled with what seem to us as strange and wonderful stories that can stretch credulity. She perceptively points out that this includes cultural strangeness, supernatural strangeness, and theological strangeness. In terms of cultural strangeness, she notes:

> There are a lot of things in the Bible, particularly in the Old Testament, that are strange because they recount historical events tied to an ancient culture far different than our own. For example, in Genesis 15:9–21, God reiterates the covenant he had with Abraham by having him cut a bunch of animals in half and leave a path in the middle for God to pass through (as a smoking fire pot and flaming torch) . . . It was meaningful to Abraham based on his cultural context, but is a completely foreign concept to us.[15]

When presented with culturally strange practices such as the one described above, it is incumbent upon those teaching the text to discover and

15. Crain, "Parents, Please Don't Forget," lines 86–91; 96–97.

communicate the significance of the culturally strange practices. The cultural elements of stories that seem strange to us made perfect sense to those in the story. It is only time and our different cultural setting that cause us to see them as strange. By providing believers with the background and setting, it can not only take away some of the strangeness of some of the things we read in the Bible, it can also make them come alive in new ways. One effective way to do this is by pointing out that much of the cultural strangeness that we see God commanding in the Bible is not because in God's mind these strange practices have any inherent value. Rather, he is willing to accommodate his commands to the cultural setting of the people he is communicating with at the time. He does this to communicate timeless truths and principles in ways that time-bound humans can grasp. In the case of Abraham, God entered into a covenantal agreement with him by enacting a practice that was as normal in Abraham's day as signing a contract is in ours. I imagine God looks at cutting two animals in half and walking through them to signify a binding agreement to be as strange as we do today. There is nothing inherently valuable to God in that action other than the message it conveyed to Abraham. By helping believers understand the cultural and historical settings that produced the Bible and God's willingness to meet them where they are at, it can help reduce the suspicion that the God of the Old Testament reflects a tribal deity who places way too much emphasis on the superstitious practices of a Bronze Age Middle Eastern tribe.

Concerning supernatural strangeness, Crain notes that we should acknowledge that the miracles recorded in the Bible are strange events. There is no getting around the fact that miracles, by definition, are events that defy a natural explanation and which are extremely rare. Therefore, when we read about them in the Bible we should readily acknowledge that we find them to be strange in relation to our everyday experience. But we should also point out that:

> A lot of skeptics have the idea that the Bible reads like a fairy tale—page after page of events that defy common experience. Given the lack of a continual stream of similar events today, they say the Bible lacks credibility (why believe God used to endlessly play in the world during biblical times, but not today?). However, if you read the Bible carefully, you'll notice that throughout thousands of years of history, there were actually just three relatively brief but prominent periods of miracles: the time of Moses and the Exodus, the time of the prophets Elijah and Elisha, and the time of Jesus and the early church. Biblical miracles primarily occurred when God would have needed to authenticate his messengers and their message at key times in history. When

> considered in this context, there's good reason for believing that if God exists and he wanted to reveal himself to mankind, he would have used miracles in exactly the way we see.[16]

Theological strangeness, according to Crain, is exemplified in those times when God does things that confound us. Another way of saying it is that God, throughout the Bible, can seem very un-Godlike to us. Crain puts it this way:

> Some things in the Bible are strange to us because, if we're being honest, we just wouldn't have expected God to act in certain ways or say certain things. This is a very subjective strangeness, but an important one. Skeptics are often quick to point out that they don't believe in God because they don't believe God would (fill in the blank with any number of claims from the Bible).[17]

Her advice in dealing with theological strangeness is refreshing. She argues that it is okay to acknowledge that we find God's ways strange and perhaps even perplexing at times. Yet, she goes on to say that we also need to remember that God hasn't told everything we would like, and so we have to get use to not having all the answers to what we perceive as theological strangeness. But, in the person of Christ, God has given us good reason to trust that, despite what looks strange to us, he is wise, good, and in control.

By placing passages in their historical and cultural context, recognizing God's act of accommodation in his dealings with culturally and historically bound people and recognizing the strangeness of the Bible can help offset the cultivation of a Sunday school faith. When appropriate, it is also beneficial to engage in conversation with other knowledge traditions such as the disciplines of history, science, and critical studies to help us better understand the text and bridge the socio-cultural gap that exists between the time when the Bible was written and our day. In these ways, we can assist believers in advancing beyond Sunday school understandings of the Bible and provide them with a faith that is fit for the modern secular world they live in.

Conclusion

The *Tyranny of the Necessary* and *Spiritual Culture Shock* are two of the ways that believers are poorly prepared. The former results in being over-prepared, the latter in being under-prepared. By thinking well about the

16. Crain, "Parents, Please Don't Forget," lines 114–28.
17. Crain, "Parents, Please Don't Forget," lines 130–35.

nature of the Bible, the purpose of God in giving us the Bible, and reducing the number of beliefs that one needs to affirm to be a "biblical" Christian we can hopefully avoid confusing believers that our particular "take" on Christianity is identical to Christianity itself. In doing so, we will open up space for them to find faithful ways of being Christian-otherwise rather than not being Christian at all. Similarly, by exposing the power of culture and the social imaginaries they generate, demonstrating the contingent and constructed nature of all culture including the secular culture we find ourselves within, training believers to see the church as God's instrument for their betterment, and training believers in spiritual disciplines we can help them avoid *Spiritual Culture Shock* as they engage with a progressively post-Christian culture where the claims of the Christian faith sound increasingly strange and outdated.

Chapter 10

A Recipe for Success Part 2

Cooking well does not mean cooking fancy.

Julia Child

Half-Baked vs. Well Done

In the previous chapter we looked at two ways that former believers were poorly prepared and suggestions at how we can avoid making those mistakes going forward. We also looked at alternative methods that I am convinced are better approaches to socializing believers into the Christian faith. In this chapter we will look at the final two methods of poor preparation, and I will suggest two alternative approaches. The third way churches can poorly prepare believers is by instilling in them inadequate conceptions of God and the Bible that result in expectations concerning what the Bible is and what God will do. When the Bible does not meet their expectations, and when God doesn't behave the way they expect him to, a crisis of faith results. I referred to this as a problem of being *Half-Baked*. Believers are *Half-Baked* when the conceptions they have about God and the Bible are only partially accurate to what they represent. In this case, believers are ill-prepared for dealing with the disconnect between their conceptions and reality. To combat the problem of producing *Half-Baked* believers I offer the following suggestions, so instead they may be *Well Done*. By which I mean that they will be well or thoroughly prepared in how they conceive of important concepts that frequently shipwreck faith.

Standing on the Promises

As previously mentioned, a major stumbling block for former believers was the Bible itself. More specifically, they had a conception of the Bible that did not match what they eventually came to see it as. The culprit, in almost every case of disillusionment with the Bible, was the doctrine of inerrancy. Former believers had a conception of the Bible that allowed for no errors in it. When they discovered what they were convinced was an error in the Bible a crisis of faith ensued. How can we respond? In my opinion, there are two options for dealing with the issue of apparent problems with Scripture if we want to avoid setting up believers for a crisis of faith. First, if one is committed to the doctrine of inerrancy, they must articulate it accurately. It is not enough to say, "The Bible is the word of God and therefore contains no errors." The doctrine of inerrancy must be defined and explained in a detailed manner. Nothing less will do. It is a disservice to those we teach to proclaim that the Bible is inerrant without offering them a thorough explanation of what is meant by inerrant. Doing so will alleviate many of the apparent errors in the text. But doing so will take time and require doing some theological homework. In 1978, the International Council on Biblical Inerrancy produced the Chicago Statement on Biblical Inerrancy. The document is eight pages in length and contains nineteen articles, each addressing what inerrancy does and does not mean, what the statement applies to (the originals only), and what constitutes an error. Of particular importance is article 13, which states:

> We affirm the propriety of using inerrancy as a theological term with reference to the complete truthfulness of Scripture.
>
> We deny that it is proper to evaluate Scripture according to standards of truth and error that are alien to its usage or purpose. We further deny that inerrancy is negated by biblical phenomena such as a lack of modern technical precision, irregularities of grammar or spelling, observational descriptions of nature, the reporting of falsehoods, the use of hyperbole and round numbers, the topical arrangement of material, variant selections of material in parallel accounts, or the use of free citations.[1]

The exceptions cited in the "We Deny" section of the article are important for believers who are taught the doctrine of inerrancy to know and understand. Many of the supposed "contradictions" that former believers point to as reasons why they can no longer accept the Bible as God's word are

1. Council on Biblical Inerrancy, *The Chicago Statement*, 4.

mitigated by what is written therein. Without understanding what inerrancy in the above sense means, believers are left to assume their own definition of what constitutes an error, and usually it is a simplistic, common-sense assumption that is unwarranted in evaluating an ancient book from a different culture. In short then, the first approach in providing believers with a more accurate conception of the Bible is to provide them with an accurate understanding of inerrancy.

The second approach is to refrain from using the term inerrancy altogether. This isn't as radical as it may sound. It certainly does not mean that one has to give up the idea of inerrancy. It simply means that we speak about the result of inspiration in a more constructive manner. For example, instead of saying what the Bible isn't (inerrant), we should say what the Bible is, trustworthy and reliable in everything that God requires us to believe in terms of life and godliness. Which means even if there are errors in the copies (or the originals, for that matter), that doesn't mean that it is immediately disqualified from being the word of God. Errors in the originals might be a problem for a certain view of inspiration, but not for a view that takes the emphasis off what the Bible isn't and places it on what the Bible is. On the latter view, it simply does not follow that if the originals had a geographical or historical error that we have no reason to trust the Bible's grand narrative that culminates in Jesus's resurrection. If we found an error in a copy of *USA Today,* we wouldn't say, "Well, I guess I can't believe anything in here anymore," nor should we with the Bible. Admittedly, *USA Today* doesn't claim to be inspired by God, and that is a big difference between the Bible and a newspaper. But, unless one requires that inspiration entails inerrancy, the analogy holds. The analogy only fails if one assumes that inspiration entails inerrancy, but that begs the very question under discussion. Therefore, even if one were to find an error in the text, it shouldn't lead them to deny their faith. Indeed, the text can still be reliable even if it contains an error. Only if one is unflinchingly committed to the Single Error Argument should it lead to a denial of the faith. But isn't a more reasonable course of action to question the assumptions underlying the Single Error Argument—such as what inspiration entails—than to renounce one's commitment to Christ? Hear the words of renowned evangelical theologian, philosopher, and apologist William Lane Craig on this issue:

> I'm saying suppose somebody actually *did* demonstrate an error in Scripture that really is wrong—it is a mistake. Does that invalidate the Christian faith? And I am saying no. It would mean you would have to adjust your doctrine of inspiration; you would have to give up inerrancy of the Scripture. But it wouldn't

mean, as I say, that Christ didn't rise from the dead. It wouldn't even mean that you don't have good grounds for believing that Christ rose from the dead.[2]

Craig goes on to make a further point—crises of faith due to apparent errors in Scripture result from assuming the doctrine of inerrancy is essential to the Christian faith, when it is not:

> What we need to understand is that the doctrine of biblical inerrancy is a corollary of the doctrine of inspiration. As such, it is an important doctrine, but it is not a central doctrine to the Christian faith. You can be a Christian and not affirm it. If one does give it up, it will have some reverberations in your theological web of beliefs, but it won't be destructive to that fundamental web of Christian beliefs because it stands somewhere near the periphery.[3]

It is also worthwhile to point out that the assumption that the Bible must be inerrant is an a priori belief. A priori beliefs are those that are derived from what are taken to be self-evident truths of reason. A posteriori beliefs are those that are arrived at by way of investigation. According to the doctrine of inerrancy, the Bible must be without error because God inspired it and God cannot commit error. On the surface, this argument makes sense. But the proof is in the pudding. If, upon investigation, the Bible does contain errors, then the a priori argument is falsified. The question is, should the doctrine of inerrancy be based on a priori assumptions about what inspiration requires or an a posteriori investigation? Typically, evangelicals have affirmed the former over the latter. But what if we are wrong and coming to the Bible with expectations that it was never intended to bear? The answer is that it will not meet our expectations and we will be forced to decide which assumption we are going to give up; that the Bible is the word of God or the a priori assumption that it cannot have any errors in it. I am not arguing for an errant Bible, nor am I denying inerrancy. Rather, I am suggesting that it would be healthy to think through the assumptions we are instilling in those whom we disciple because they have real consequences. One of those assumptions that deconverts consistently point to is that the Bible will be without error of *any* kind (scribal, copyist, etc.). Another is that the Bible must conform to our a priori understanding of what inspiration has to entail. Having those expectations unmet by the Bible can be devastating. However,

2. Craig, "What is Inerrancy?" lines 102–06.

3. Craig, "What is Inerrancy?" lines 190–94.

instead of throwing away our confidence in the Bible as the word of God, we should rethink our expectations of it.

Many individuals who lose their faith attribute it to the fact that the Bible had errors in it. If so, it could not be the word of God. That being the case, they either had to ignore what they discovered about the Bible and try to keep believing despite the fact that the Bible did not live up to their expectations or stop believing in the Bible. Believing something you don't find to be the truth is difficult. Perhaps if they had a more robust view of what inerrancy means rather than the Single Error Argument they could have authentically continued to believe. Or, if they had been willing to question their assumptions of what inspiration entailed, they could have done so, rather than taking the drastic step of committing apostasy.

Besides addressing the issue of inerrancy, it is also vital to expose believers to the history of the Bible. The Bible, like Jesus, is divine and human, and like him it has a history. That history is important for believers to know in order to avoid being blindsided when they hear it for the first time. The Bible is a collection of books written by authors who lived in times and places that are radically different from our own. The original manuscripts of those books are lost to history, but we have many copies of varying quality. It is true that the copies themselves differ from one another so much that there are more differences between the manuscripts than the total number of words in the New Testament. But this is unproblematic because the sheer numbers of manuscript copies we possess allow us to determine the original reading. In fact, we have so many copies that we are confident we have accurately reconstructed the originals to a very high degree. At some point, the books to be included in the canon of Scripture were recognized by people. In the case of the Old Testament, it is difficult to pin down when the Old Testament canon was closed, but by 200 BCE there was near-universal agreement on the thirty-nine books of the Old Testament. In the case of the New Testament, the canon was officially recognized by the Council of Hippo in 393 CE and the Council of Carthage in 397 CE. Discussion and debate surrounded which books would be included and which would be excluded. While most of the books had broad recognition as bearing the marks of divine inspiration, there were a few that were debated and were not so clear. In the end, the church recognized the twenty-seven books of the New Testament as Scripture. Acknowledging this process does not make the New Testament any less authoritative or divine, or cause us to doubt it, it merely recognizes the way that God chose to give his word to us. He inspired the books, Christians preserved the books by copying them and, over time, the church recognized the books that were inspired by God and collected them into a single book we call the New Testament. Christians need to hear that story and they need to hear it from other Christians, not from internet skeptics who frame the story in ways intended to cast doubt on the Bible.

My God, My God . . . Have You Forsaken Me?

The second conceptual problem deconverts have is with God, specifically that he did not act in ways that they expected him to. The reason for their disenchantment with God is due in large measure to their unbalanced conception of God and what they expected from him. A common characteristic of deconversion narratives that point to disappointment with God as a catalyst for the loss of faith is that deconverts conceived of God almost exclusively as good, kind, and loving. Therefore, when difficulties came into their life and God did not intervene, they felt betrayed, and a crisis of faith followed. I am not saying that had former believers been given a better understanding of God and what they could expect from him, they would not have fallen away during times of suffering. I am saying that if former believers had a more biblical conception of God, they wouldn't have been caught so off guard when God did not meet their expectations. The reason why is because they would have known to expect suffering and hardship as a normal part of being human and a Christian. The Bible not only doesn't promise us a life free of hardship; on the contrary, it tells us to expect it.

My good friend David has gone through one of the most difficult experiences that I can imagine. David and his wife Debbie were committed Christians at the church I attended for a number of years. David occasionally preached on Sunday mornings, and he and Debbie volunteered to lead the youth group for a time. They loved the Lord and each other and had a growing family of five girls. Tragically, however, Debbie was diagnosed with an aggressive form of breast cancer when she was seven-months pregnant with their sixth child. She carried the baby to term and delivered a healthy baby boy. They now had six children ranging in age from fourteen to a newborn. Debbie went through rounds of chemo that took a toll on her and the family. David continued to work full-time as an electrician to pay the bills. Debbie's condition eventually got worse, and David had to take on more of the responsibilities around the house. He was the sole breadwinner, and as Debbie's condition deteriorated, he became the primary caregiver for his six children as well. About two years after she was diagnosed, Debbie passed away, leaving David to care for all six children by himself. The Christian community stepped up throughout their entire ordeal, assisting him with everything from the mundane chores around the house to providing him with financial gifts. But, naturally, the burden for the care of his children (including making sure they had lunches for school, getting them ready in the morning to catch the bus, taking the youngest to the babysitter before he went to work, picking them up again at the end of his day, and then going home to make supper, clean the house, and put the kids to bed) and making a living fell on him. This routine went on for a number of years. I don't know how he did it. I asked him how he managed to retain his faith in God after the hand he was dealt. He thoughtfully replied, "I believe as Christians we have a lot of preconceived, adopted, or just plain misled ideas of who we are, who God is, and just what our relationship is supposed to look like." He identified those preconceived notions as seeing God as "our buddy," someone who "protects us from all problems," or as "a big 'easy button' in the sky that we get to hit when we're in trouble."[4] Pointing out the problems with such views, he asked, "What happens when bad things happen? Does God cease to exist anymore? Does he become the enemy?" Unfortunately, all too often, former believers do conclude that he doesn't exist or that he isn't good. In David's opinion, when that happens it may indicate a fundamental problem of faith that "our view of God during and after major crises in our lives depends on whether our faith in him and his son Jesus beforehand is real faith." For David, the concept of God that we place our faith in makes all the difference when trials come or when God does not act in the way we expect him to. He explained this by pointing to his belief in the Sun as an analogy: "I believe that the Sun in the sky is the source of warmth for our planet. I know this to be true because I have felt it. When the temperature drops to forty below zero in the dead of winter, do I suddenly abandon my belief in the Sun? If I did, I would say that my original belief in the Sun was not authentic to begin with." So, too, with belief in God in the midst of suffering. "I believe God is good. So, that being said, what is my response when tragedy strikes my life? Does the Sun suddenly cease being the Earth's source of heat just because it's cold out? That would be silly," he argued. When Debbie got sick and her health continually deteriorated, David was able to retain his faith in God in part because he had a biblical perspective on God. He believed in the goodness of God but also that God is sovereign. He believed God loved him and his family, but he also believed that they were part of a larger story that God is writing. Being part of that story may mean not having all the answers. Perhaps, most importantly, David turned to Jesus as the primary reason to trust in God. "I believe in a holy, triune God that loved us so much that he allowed his Son to become a sacrifice for our sin." In Jesus, David found two things. First, he found an example of not just a faithful servant of God suffering, but the only truly righteous person who ever lived suffering.

good

4. David in discussion with the author, May 2018.

Jesus and his experience should forever disabuse all Christians of the idea that God's people are immune to suffering. Second, he found an example of a horrendous evil having a redeemable purpose. That gave him hope that Debbie's suffering and the strain and hardship on his family likewise had a purpose and would be redeemed. Because of that, David could affirm, "I still believe that God is good. I've seen it. Felt it. Lived it. I love him. Trust him. Believe in him." And yet, in a moment of admirable honesty, he adds, "But I am not happy with him . . . our relationship may not be what it once was . . . but maybe, just maybe, it was predicated on an assumption that was errant." Even though his conception of God was healthy and balanced enough for him to be able reconcile his difficult experience with the goodness of God, he recognized that his displeasure with God is an indicator that his understanding of God still needs some fine-tuning. "Maybe I know him a little better than I did before. Maybe now it's up to me to get to know him all over again," he said.[5]

To help believers avoid being *Half-Baked* in terms of their conception of God we need to do a better job of helping them form realistic expectations about who God is and what they can expect from him. Yes, God is good, kind, and loving, but he never promised believers a life devoid of pain, suffering, and heartache. Nor has he promised to respond to our prayers in the way we want. Nor does he work on the reciprocity principle; that if we live our lives in sacrificial service for him, we should expect him to return the favor and bless us by giving us the things that we really want. In fact, the Bible is abundantly clear—if only we have eyes to see it—that in this world we should expect pain, suffering, and heartache for two reasons. The first is that the cosmos is a fundamentally broken place, and the second is that the world is hostile to God. Living in this environment will inevitably impact us negatively. And God has told us this repeatedly throughout the Bible. Time and space prohibit me from cataloguing the verses and narratives that should tell us that God's people are not immune from hardship and suffering. Jesus himself warned the disciples, "if the world hates you, keep in mind that it hated me first. If you belonged to the world, it would love you as its own. As it is, you do not belong to the world, but I have chosen you out of the world. That is why the world hates you." (John 15:18–19 NIV) And then, to put a finer point on his message, he tells them why he is warning them. "All this I have told you so you will not fall away." (John 16:1 NIV) Jesus is deeply concerned that persecution will cause them to doubt their faith, resulting in their apostasy. What is important to note here is that God will allow the world to mistreat them. He will not intervene

5. David in discussion with the author, May 2018.

and protect them from the world's hostility. He will not recompense them in this life for their faithful service. Instead, they will be abused and even killed. Not long after he said these things to the disciples, Jesus, the most faithful member of the covenant community that ever lived, was unjustly condemned, beaten, and publicly murdered—a man seemingly accursed by God. If God allowed that to happen to his Son, why do we find it so difficult to rationalize why bad things happen in our lives? It's not only suffering that comes at the hands of other people that we can expect but the suffering and evil that comes from living in a fallen world. For example, Paul not only suffered at the hands of people hostile to the gospel, but he also suffered from natural evils, such as being shipwrecked three times, and once being adrift in the sea for a day and a night before being rescued. He had sleepless nights, went hungry, he was thirsty, often without food, and stranded in the cold without shelter.[6] God allowed Paul to endure all of these hardships. He could have prevented them, but he chose not to. If he allowed Paul to go through such difficult circumstances, we should not be surprised when we find ourselves going through difficulties. As C.S. Lewis said about Aslan, 'Course he isn't safe. But he's good. He's the King I tell you."[7] God has been upfront with us when he invited us to join him in reconciling the world to himself. He has not promised us that it would be a safe journey, in fact he has told us it will not be. But he has promised that he is good, and in the person of Christ and his self-sacrificial death on our behalf, we have reasons to trust him. One, because there is no greater demonstration of love and goodness than to lay one's life down for another; two, because he has demonstrated that in the death of Christ, he has the ability to take the greatest injustice ever perpetrated and suffering ever experienced and turn it into an eternal good beyond what we could have ever imagined had we been at Calvary on Good Friday.

It needs to be recognized that possessing a more balanced and biblical view of God and what we can expect from him will not completely solve the problem of being disillusioned with God entirely. There is a good reason why believers frequently have a lopsided conception of God, one that focuses on his goodness, kindness, and love to the exclusion of what the Bible says about suffering; and that is because the Bible tells us that God is good, kind, and loving. Moreover, it tells us that if we live a certain way we should expect positive results. And not only that, it tells us that God hears and answers prayer. All of which are true. God is wholly good, kind, and loving, but that doesn't always look like we think it should. It is conceivable

6. 2 Cor 11:25–29.

7. Lewis, *The Lion, the Witch and the Wardrobe*, 146.

that God allows suffering in our lives precisely because he is good, kind, and loving. Furthermore, the Bible does teach the general truth that living according to the will of God does bring with it blessings and benefits. But the Bible also contains within itself exceptions to these general truths. The book of Job is an extended critique of the idea that God has to operate according to the reciprocity principle that says if we are faithful, he has to bless us in ways we expect. Likewise, Jesus's parable about the landowner who hired groups of workers to work for varying periods of time but paid them all the same amount shows that God is not bound by our conception of what is fair. When Peter asked Jesus what he would receive for leaving his family to follow him and preach the kingdom, Jesus responded by telling him he would get far more in return than what he sacrificed.

> "Truly I tell you," Jesus replied, "no one who has left home or brothers or sisters or mother or father or children or fields for me and the gospel will fail to receive a hundred times as much in this present age: homes, brothers, sisters, mothers, children, and fields." (Mark 10:29–30a NIV)

Peter expected something from following Jesus, and what Jesus promised him for his sacrifice was both more and less than what he expected. Jesus promised to give him more houses, brothers, sisters, mothers, children, and fields than Peter had given up. This speaks to the fact that Jesus isn't just fair, but he repays his followers abundantly. Yet, Peter never received any of these things in a literal way. I am, for various reasons, strongly inclined to think that Peter took Jesus's words literally. If so, then Peter would go on to receive less than what he expected from Jesus because he did not receive such things. He didn't have more children or houses or fields. But he did receive something of greater value, which he was unable to comprehend at the time Jesus spoke those words to him. He received the familial blessing that being a member of the family of God brought with it, which would include deep, abiding relationships with others who would, in the future, place their trust in Christ. In that way, Peter would receive spiritual brothers, sisters, mothers, and children. So, while it may be generally true that if we live according to the word of God we can expect to be blessed, what those blessings look like may not meet our expectations. And, even though God is unqualifiedly good and loving, he is not bound by our understanding of those concepts. He reserves the right to act in ways that do not always look good or loving. When he does so, he has given us good reason to trust him, and that reason is Jesus. Having a conception of God that takes the above into consideration will not guarantee that believers will be able to weather the storm when God looks like he has failed them. But it will give them a fighting chance against emotions and feelings that will otherwise overwhelm them.

Friendly Fire vs. the Faithful Wounds of a Friend

As we have seen, being hurt by church leadership and other believers appears frequently in deconversion narratives. When that happens, it can result in a feeling of betrayal and a crisis of faith. Being hurt by fellow believers can open up space for them to consider suppressed doubts about important Christian beliefs. In the case of Devyn and others, the way they were treated by church leadership and fellow believers demonstrates the power of authoritative communities and the role they play in our lives. Clearly, how we treat each other matters. That does not mean we ought to ignore sinful behavior in the lives of other Christians. We have seen, in the case of James, that when done well it can have positive results. The difference between Devyn's story and James's is the difference between *Friendly Fire* and what the Bible calls the *Wounds of a Friend*.

The author of Proverbs tells us that "Wounds from a friend can be trusted," (Prov 27:6a NIV) which means that a friend is willing to speak the truth even if it means it will hurt us, if it will result in our good. True friends have our welfare in mind when they point out our failings. They operate out of a concern not so much for righteousness's sake but for our welfare. The wounds of a friend are faithful because they are motivated by grace rather than judgment. So, what's a church leader to do? I respond, practice *Grace-Based Leadership* and let the chips fall where they may.

Grace-Based Leadership takes seriously the charge to "speak the truth in love" by courageously holding fast to the truth of God's word in a way that is characterized by patience, kindness, hopefulness, and long-suffering, while at the same time is not easily angered, does not keep a record of wrongs, nor dishonors others. (1 Cor 13) The responsibility of leadership is to shepherd the people of God and that includes instructing, exhorting, and at times correcting believers, in and with the truth. Yet the truth is not an end in itself. Instructing, exhorting, and correcting are only the means to accomplish an end, which is being conformed to Christ. If the way leadership goes about standing for the truth short circuits that process, something is wrong. Leadership's primary purpose is not to speak the truth for the sake of truth, but for flourishing of the flock. What does *Grace-Based Leadership* look like, practically speaking? It begins by following Jesus's instructions to treat others the way we would want to be treated. It is marked by humility and recognition of our own shortfallings. It seeks to cover a multitude of sins, not call out every wrong to be accounted for. Of course, there are sins that need to be called on the carpet, but not every sin. Being addicted to coffee is sin, so is eating too much, and habitual exaggeration, but I suspect that most would agree that pointing these and other similar sins out in the lives of those in the church is probably counterproductive to their spiritual growth; there are bigger fish to fry. All Christians, not just leadership, are called to exercise discretion in regard to what sins and offenses we "uncover" and confront believers with. Finally, *Grace-Based Leadership* is not overbearing, forcing others into obedience, but leads by example and serves those in the church. (1 Pet 5:2–3; Matt 20: 25–26) However, it is not only leadership that needs to base their interactions with those they serve on grace. Those of us not in leadership need to do so as well. What do *Grace-Based Relationships* between the rank and file believers in the church look like?

Grace, Grace, God's Grace . . .

In the book *Grace-Based Parenting*, author Tim Kimmel makes the point that how parents relate to their children is a reflection of how they view God and how they think he views them. Naturally then, if parents have a flawed view of God it will impact how they interact with their children. It can "set up children to miss the joy of God, the heart of God, and the power of God in their personal lives.[8] The same is true in how we relate to other believers. If we have a flawed view of God, then it can negatively impact how we interact or lead fellow believers. Kimmel identifies a toxic attitude that is characteristic of defective parenting styles, and I might add, characteristic of incidents of *Friendly Fire*; that attitude is legalism. Legalism focuses on keeping rules and regulations as the means by which one either earns favor with God or grows spiritually. Legalists often are ignorant as to the intention of the rules and regulations in the first place. They see them as ends in themselves. Legalists will often set up extra "boundary" laws to ensure we do not violate a genuine prohibition. For example, I have heard it argued that drinking alcohol is wrong because it could lead to becoming drunk and being drunk is a sin; or, that dancing is wrong because it could lead to premarital sex! Despite the fact that there is nothing inherently wrong with either drinking alcohol or dancing, in the mind of the legalist they should be avoided because of what they might lead to. Legalism frequently rears its ugly head in relation to the Bible's instruction to not "conform to the pattern of world, but be transformed by the renewing of your mind." (Rom

8. Kimmel, *Grace-Based Parenting*.

12:2 NIV) "Worldliness," as it is sometimes referred to, is the sin of being too much like the world. But just what is the "world" that we are not to be conformed to? Theologian David McLeod defines it as "the value system or 'worldview' [that] impregnates the world, impels it, molds it, and degrades it. It affects our culture and our institutions. It is the mold that threatens, twists, malforms the thinking of all who belong to it."[9] The world, then, is the manifestation of ethical and ideological systems that are antithetical to the beliefs and values of the kingdom of Heaven. The ethical and ideological systems of the world take on different forms in each age. As such, believers are to be always on guard against unwittingly adopting them and being squeezed into the world's mold. Legalists take the command to not be conformed to the world as an opportunity to identify specific actions and practices that they take to be expressions of worldliness and then require others to conform to their interpretation. It needs to be said that there is nothing wrong with identifying expressions of worldliness and avoiding them in our own lives. In fact, Christians should be trying to identify and avoid them. The problem is that identifying expressions of worldliness is not an exact science. On the contrary, it is always a subjective judgment call. This means that we cannot require other believers to live according to our interpretation. For example, if a believer thinks that tattoos are a contemporary expression of rebellion toward God and therefore believe that it would be wrong for them to get a tattoo, that is not legalism. Legalism occurs when they go further and say that it is wrong for a Christian to get a tattoo. If the Bible prohibited tattoos for Christians or identified tattoos as expressions of worldliness, then it would not be legalism to affirm that tattoos are sin. But since it doesn't, Christians have no right to say that getting tattoos is wrong. That would be legalism.

Legalists tend to understand the rules and regulations to be what God ultimately cares about. The truth is that in most cases the rules and regulations only perform the role of pointing us to Christ and revealing to us the state of our heart. This was clearly the intent of the Mosaic Law in the Old Testament. It was to be our "guardian" and bring us to an awareness of our need for Christ. (Gal 3:24 NIV) And Christ is anything but a legalist, rather he is full of "grace and truth." (John 1:14 NIV) When John describes Jesus as being full of grace, he is saying that Jesus shows kindness and favor to those who are unworthy of it. When John describes Jesus as being full of truth, he is saying that Jesus is the genuine article. He communicates the truth of God in his attitude, actions, and words. Saying that we need to relate to other believers in a manner that shows them kindness, even when

9. McLeod, "The Consecrated Christian," 111.

they are in the wrong, is not to say that we are to avoid all confrontations and difficult conversations. At times doing so is required, and when it is Paul instructs us to "speak the truth in love" (Eph 4:15 NIV) from a heart of compassion, remembering that we all far short at times. It's easy to forget that, and when we do we border on the kind of self-righteousness that leads to pharisaical legalism and mistakenly think that God desires judgment instead of mercy. Which is why it can be helpful to take a second look at who God is and what is his heart toward people. Doing so can help avoid hitting other believers with *Friendly Fire.*

A Second Look

Grace is at the heart of how we ought to relate to others in the family of God because it is at the heart of how God relates to us. It is easy to forget this at times. As an individual reads through the Old Testament, they cannot help but conclude that God is a God of holiness and justice. Nowhere is this seen more clearly than the in Law of Moses. The Mosaic Law was all-encompassing and regulated all aspects of Jewish life. It also meted out harsh penalties for violations. Although grace can be found woven throughout the law, the purpose of the law wasn't primarily to demonstrate grace. Rather, the primary purpose of the Mosaic Law was to communicate to the people of Israel and the surrounding nations the holiness of God and their own sinfulness. That is why at times the Old Testament looks so harsh. As far back as Genesis chapter 12, God sought a people for himself. He chose Abraham and promised him that his descendants would become his own chosen people. But the descendants of Abraham had become slaves in Egypt, and although they were certainly aware of the promises made by Yahweh to Abraham, they would have known little about him and his nature. God used Moses to lead the people out of Egypt and give them the law. There were a number of purposes behind doing so, not the least of which is that it established them as a nation and acted as the covenant between the people and God. But one of the primary purposes of the law was to teach the people who Yahweh was. The Israelites needed to recognize that the God of Abraham, who delivered them and made them his special possession, is, above all else, holy. They also needed to recognize that they were not. They were guilty before him and could not keep all of his statutes despite their protestations to the contrary. (Exod 24:7) Because of his great love for his people, God gave them a sacrificial system that would temporarily cover their sins through the offering of animals, but these sacrifices did not take away sin for good. The sacrificial system allowed God's justice to be stayed, but it did not satisfy it. The fact that justice demands that sin be paid for—and that penalty is death—combined with the great love God had for his people presents a challenge. On the one hand, how can God be holy and righteous and ignore the sin of his people? On the other hand, how can God destroy those whom he loves? We know, living on the other side of Calvary, that the dilemma was resolved by God himself becoming an Israelite and paying the price on behalf of his people and the Gentiles. In Christ's death, God's righteousness was satisfied, and God expressed his love for sinful people. On the cross, Christ became our substitute by bearing our sins and experiencing the judgment of God. The atoning work of Christ propitiated God's wrath and reconciled us to God. God's undeserved favor in sending his son to die on behalf of those who were his enemies is the greatest example of grace conceivable.

The result of God's graciousness is that even though we still fall short of his righteous standard we are no longer in danger of his judgment. Because Christ has borne the responsibility for our sin, all that is left for us is to experience the abundant love of God. No doubt, God is still a God of justice and truth, but in giving his son as an atoning sacrifice on our behalf he demonstrates that he is also abounding in grace. When we were his enemies, God gave us Christ, not just as a counselor, friend, or religious teacher, but as our atoning sacrifice. Grace is so central to the Christian faith that it could be argued that it is the main way that God relates to humans this side of the cross. C.S. Lewis claimed that grace is *the* distinguishing aspect of the Christian faith and what sets Christianity apart from all other religions. Because of Christ, God does not have to treat us according to our sins. He can, as it were, cut us some slack, because his righteous standard has been met and his wrath satisfied. God does not approve of our shortcomings and sinful actions, and because he loves us, he will discipline us when we continually walk in sin, but because of Christ, he does not count our sin against us. God, in his great wisdom, solved the problem of what appeared to be his irreconcilable attributes of holiness and love, and he did so with grace; he gave us something we didn't deserve, his son. His justice was satisfied, and for those who are in Christ, there is now not only no condemnation, but nothing can separate us from the love of God. (Rom 8:35–39) Paul, quoting David, puts it this way, "Blessed are those whose transgressions are forgiven, whose sins are covered. Blessed is the one whose sin the Lord will never count against them." (Rom 4:7–8 NIV)

If God can now deal with us in love, not counting our sins against us, then that is how we should deal with fellow believers. That is why Peter tells his readers, "Above all, love each other deeply, because love covers over a multitude of sins." (1 Pet 4:8 NIV) Pointing out the faults, sins, and shortcomings of other believers, leading them with a heavy hand, or lording it over them has no place in how we relate to one another given the way God relates to us. God's grace gave us what we didn't deserve, kindness and favor. When we think that other believers are in the wrong (being too worldly according to our standards) or have actually sinned, we are to love them and show them kindness and favor even though they may not deserve it. That doesn't mean we don't address issues or that we never engage in discipline. Doing so can actually be expressions of grace. What it does mean is that we, like God, treat others better than they deserve to be treated because that's what God did for us in giving us Christ. It also means we treat each other like family.

Family Ties

Maintaining that Christians should treat one another like family can, unfortunately, be more harmful than helpful. That's because many individuals have only dysfunctional families as models. Regardless, I think the metaphor for the church as family is still a good one because all of us, despite our experience, have a deep intuition about what families are supposed to look like and how family members are supposed to relate to each other. This deep intuition that we all share is what Paul was counting on when he repeatedly encouraged believers in the first century to consider each other as brothers and sisters, members of the family of God. For Paul, the church was to be a loving family. Paul used a number of metaphors to refer to the church but refers to the church as a family so often that "the comparison of the Christian community with a 'family' must be regarded as the most significant metaphorical use of all."[10] Christians, according to Paul, were to see themselves as members of a divine family with God as their Father. Through Jesus and their identification with him, God has adopted them as his children. As children of God, Paul encourages them: "Therefore, as we have opportunity, let us do good to all people, especially to those who belong to the family of believers." (Gal 6:10 NIV) To the church at Ephesus, he wrote, "you are no longer foreigners and strangers, but fellow citizens with God's people and also members of his household." (Eph 2:19 NIV) If seeing the church as a family wasn't enough, Paul makes it explicit how believers should relate to one another within the family. Repeatedly, Paul instructs the churches he corresponds with that love should be the central virtue that characterizes them. He desired that "the Lord make your love increase and overflow for each other and for everyone else, just as ours does for you." (1 Thess 3:12 NIV) He reminded the church at Rome that they should "Be

10. Banks, *Paul's Idea*, 49.

devoted to one another in love. Honor one another above yourselves." (Rom 12:10 NIV) To the Corinthians he penned his most moving and articulate description of what love looked like, and reminded them that without it all of their spiritual activity was worthless:

> Love is patient, love is kind. It does not envy, it does not boast, it is not proud. It does not dishonor others, it is not self-seeking, it is not easily angered, it keeps no record of wrongs. Love does not delight in evil but rejoices with the truth. It always protects, always trusts, always hopes, always perseveres. Love never fails. (1 Cor 13:4–8a NIV)

To the Philippians he wrote, "Do nothing out of selfish ambition or vain conceit. Rather, in humility value others above yourselves, not looking to your own interests but each of you to the interests of the others." (Phil 2:3–4 NIV) The Colossians were to clothe themselves with "compassion, kindness, humility, gentleness, and patience. Bear with each other and forgive one another if any of you has a grievance against someone. Forgive as the Lord forgave you. And over all these virtues put on love, which binds them all together in perfect unity. (Col 3:12–14 NIV) Love is so central to Paul's Christian communities that he goes so far as to tell the Galatians that, at the end of the day, "the only thing that counts is faith expressing itself through love." (Gal 5:6 NIV)

For Paul, the church was a family that was to be characterized, above all else, by love for one another. The way in which the brothers and sisters in the family of God were to relate to one another was with patience, kindness, compassion, and humility. They were to think first of others and their needs. They were to avoid holding grudges, keeping records of offenses, or valuing themselves above others. What does that look like in practice?

Practically Speaking

Loving brothers and sisters as members in the family of God is not always easy. Just as not all of our biological siblings are easy to get along with, not all of our brothers and sisters in the faith will be easy to get along with. Furthermore, sometimes love requires that we do need to engage with members of the family. How do we go about that in the context of pursuing *Grace-Based Relationships*? I suggest the following four points:

1. Romans 15:7 reminds us to "accept one another then just as Christ accepted you in order to bring praise to God." (NIV) Jesus accepted us as we were, warts and all. He came not to condemn the world but to save

it. (John 3:17) It's not that Jesus wasn't aware of our sins, shortcomings, and failures, but in his first coming he came to redeem us, not judge us. Likewise, as ambassadors for Christ, we should accept other believers, warts and all. Our job is not to judge them. Having said that, it doesn't mean we never speak into the lives of fellow believers. But, in my opinion, before we do, the following conditions are meet.

a. We have the authority to address the issue. Some issues are the responsibility of church leadership, not ours.
b. We have the kind of relationship that gives us the right to speak into another person's life.
c. We have the right motive. Not merely to point out error, but to assist a fellow believer in their walk with Christ.
d. We have dealt with our own sins by taking the log out of our own eye before helping others take the speck out of another's.

2. Ask yourself if the issue you are going to raise is worth the interpersonal problems it may create. If it probably isn't, then don't raise it. God values love and unity among believers above nearly all else. (John 13:34; 17:20) If raising the issue is going to cause problems, make sure it is an issue that is important.
3. Ask yourself if the need to raise an issue with a fellow believer has more to do with your own bitterness and the need to point out wrongs than a genuine concern for the other believer. If it is just for the sake of pointing out their failures, or self-righteously passing judgment, don't do it.
4. Remember that loving someone doesn't mean condoning their actions. In the case of Tammy, she felt shunned because she was going through a divorce, and believers from her church abandoned her. I think it's safe to assume that they did so because they thought she was sinning and being friendly to her would imply they condoned her choice to get divorced. But it's okay to love people who you might think are sinning, it doesn't mean you condone their behavior. I realize there are times when love must be tough; Paul was quite clear about that. Some sins require meaningful church discipline, but that's a leadership issue, not an individual one.

Practicing *Grace-Based Relationships* has the potential to radically impact our relationships with one another in our local Christian communities for the better. There will be times when we need to confront, encourage, and exhort each other, but as we do let us remember that the wounds of a friend need to be seasoned with grace. Otherwise they will amount to little more than incidents of *Friendly Fire.*

Chapter 11

Conclusion

A conclusion is the place where
you get tired of thinking.

Arthur Bloch

In the previous chapters, I have argued that in trying to understand deconversion we ought to think about it in terms of a recipe of sorts. Just as a recipe has three elements: the ingredients, the preparation, and the cooking, so do deconversions. The first element, the ingredients, correspond to the personality and psychological traits of individuals. It is clear that there are a number of traits that contribute to the likelihood that an individual will deconvert. The third element, the cooking, occurs in what is becoming an increasingly secular and post-Christian culture. Because the cultures we are immersed in exert such a powerful influence on what we are likely to believe, our culture is an important contributing factor in the loss of faith. It seems to me that, as Christian parents and leaders, we have little control over these two components of the "deconversion recipe." Individual personality traits and the shape of culture are largely beyond our ability to do much about. Which leaves the second element of the recipe, the preparation. How believers are prepared, by which I mean how they are socialized into the Christian faith, or discipled is critically important, especially for those individuals who possess the personality traits commonly associated with deconverts. Of the three elements that comprise the "deconversion recipe," the preparation stage is unique because it is entirely determined by the church. How the church goes about preparing believers can result in a recipe for disaster or a recipe for success. Tragically, the church has not always done a good job in preparing believers to thrive. In many cases, they have set them up for a crisis of faith. They have done so by over-preparing them (by inflicting them with the *Tyranny of the Necessary*), under-preparing them (resulting in the experience of *Spiritual Culture Shock*), ill-preparing them (leaving them theologically *Half-Baked*), and painfully preparing them (wounding them with *Friendly Fire*). The combination of these inadequate methods of preparation, an individual who possess the traits associated with deconversion, and our disenchanted, increasingly post-Christian pressure cooker of a culture results in *A Recipe for Disaster*. In response, I have offered four methods of preparation that I believe contribute to a recipe for success. It is my prayer that, in light of what I have shown in this book, churches will re-evaluate how they are preparing believers and adopt these suggestions. In doing so, they may not only avert *A Recipe for Disaster*, but discover *A Recipe for Success*.

Appendix

The Role of the Internet

On the Internet, Christianity is losing by a long shot.

HEMANT MEHTA

Internet, Out of Faith

A SIGNIFICANT NUMBER OF deconverts mention the works of the New Atheists as being meaningful in their journeys to atheism. The New Atheists are a cadre of authors from different backgrounds who are united in their disbelief in the existence of God and in their conviction that religion is a force for evil that should be abandoned for the good of all. Their scathing critiques of arguments for the existence of God and withering criticisms of religion have earned them a wide hearing in a post-September-11th world. The most influential of the New Atheists are sometimes known as the Four Horsemen: Richard Dawkins, Daniel Dennett, Christopher Hitchens, and Sam Harris.

As previously mentioned, statistics show that unbelief in America is growing. Not all unbelievers are atheists, however; a growing number of Americans identify as simply nonreligious. The New Atheists are surely part the reason for that increase. What may be having an even greater impact on the rise of unbelief than the books and movies of prominent atheists like Dawkins is the access millions of people now have to the Internet. The Internet is the great equalizer when it comes to providing atheists with a platform to communicate their message.

Christianity in the West, especially in North America, has had the benefit of a deeply entrenched social and cultural infrastructure by which it has effectively communicated the message of the gospel. Think about it for a minute; churches in the United States and Canada are ubiquitous. Christian bookstores that provide apologetics and evangelistic literature are only slightly less ubiquitous. Christian radio and television stations fill the airways with evangelistic and apologetic preaching, evangelical publishing houses churn out books on apologetics, and a large number of high-profile apologetic ministries provide believers and unbelievers reasons to believe Christianity is true.

Contrast that with the atheist infrastructure. Atheists tend to be isolated individuals who do not belong to anything resembling a church community. Until recently, there were few atheist social groups and even fewer atheist activist groups. There were no atheist bookstores to speak of, an insignificant number of atheist radio programs, and fewer still atheist radio stations or networks. As far as I know, there is only one atheist television station. Up until recently, the number of secular publishing houses could be counted on one hand.

All of this has made the progress of atheism rather pedestrian. If one never encounters arguments against the existence of God, then perhaps one never experiences serious doubts and remains a believer. Likewise, if a believer never experiences atheist counter-apologetics that attempt to refute and undercut the arguments of Christian apologetics, their confidence in the Christian faith will likely remain high. For the last fifty years, Christians had a bevy of apologetic resources at their fingertips and almost zero access to any counterarguments. This produced a certain amount of false confidence in the case for Christianity. It is amazing to discover how many former believers identified as former apologists for the faith before deconverting. What caused them to lose their faith? They finally encountered objections from intelligent atheists who challenged many of the apologetic arguments they had so much confidence in.

They didn't encounter atheist counterarguments by stumbling into an atheist social group meeting in the basement of the local library, or by finding an atheist bookstore, or even by hearing an atheist radio program. They encountered the arguments on the Internet. The Internet has changed everything for atheism. It provides not only a platform for atheists to advance their worldview but to also form virtual communities. Dan Gilgoff, religion editor at CNN.com, says that, "the Internet has become the de facto global church for atheists, agnostics, and other doubters of God, who of course don't have bricks-and-mortar churches in which to congregate."[1] Hemant Mehta, known online as the Friendly Atheist, agrees: "Until the Internet came along, we didn't have our version of [church]. Now that we have a

1. Gilgoff, "Where was God," lines 1–3.

space where we can talk about our (lack of) religious beliefs, it's that much easier to communicate our views."[2]

And atheists are effectively doing just that. There are literally hundreds, if not thousands, of atheist websites. Many are dedicated to refuting Christian apologetics. Some focus on problems with the Bible, others with philosophical objections, still others the negative impact of Christianity. Many are the product of former believers seeking to deconvert Christians. Some websites are unsophisticated attacks on Christianity. Others are highly sophisticated counterattacks made by well-informed, highly educated skeptics.

Mitch, a former believer who shared his story with me, offered the following observations about the importance and influence of the Internet on his deconversion: "I think Dan Dennett is the one [who] thinks the Internet will completely change the future. I feel . . . that the Internet has opened and raised my consciousness to a point that I have very different priorities on what's important, as opposed to what I did before I had this information. The Internet started opening my eyes that the atheist movement had been out there."[3]

Brandon Peach at *RELEVANT* magazine noted that on Mehta's website a question in the forums asked if former believers would have left their faith if the Internet didn't exist.[4] A significant number said they would not have. This is supported by the April, 2014 MIT Technological Review entitled "How the Internet is Taking Away America's Religion: Using the Internet Can Destroy Your Faith."[5] The article highlighted the findings of Olin College of Engineering professor Allen Downey, who correlated the sharp decline in religious affiliation with the rise of Internet use. Allen argued that between 1990–2010, the number of Americans with no religious affiliation went up from 8 percent to 18 percent. That corresponds to about 25 million people who no longer consider themselves religious. The article points out "in the 1980s, Internet use was essentially zero, but in 2010, 53 percent of the population spent two hours per week online and 25 percent surfed for more than seven hours. This increase closely matches the decrease in religious affiliation."[6]

Social websites like Facebook make it possible to communicate and form meet-up groups that never could have existed prior to the World Wide

2. Mehta, "On the Internet," lines 46–49.
3. Mitch in discussion with the author, February 2014.
4. Peach, "Will the Internet Kill."
5. MIT Technological Review, "How the Internet is Taking Away."
6. MIT Technological Review, "How the Internet is Taking Away," 43–49.

Web. The reason why is that it provides an opportunity for atheists—who are relatively small in number compared with the general population—to find each other and form communities for support and encouragement. "A lot of millennials who are coming of age have found that the Internet is a fantastic place to talk about their doubt,"[7] says Jesse Galef, communications director for the Secular Student Alliance. "Before the Internet, there was no place for young people to do that. The only place to go was really church, and that wasn't always a welcoming place."[8]

Some of these communities are live in-person meet-ups with local atheists who have met online. Others remain virtual, but no less significant for those who find in them a measure of solidarity that otherwise was absent in their life. In fact, Brandon Peach reports that:

> The web's largest atheist forum is a subcommunity of the social media site Reddit, launched in 2005. Its Alexa traffic ranking puts it in the top fifty sites in the United States with 2 million unique visitors per month, many of those to its "Atheist" sub-community of 154,000. The Christian "subreddit," a devoted group comprised largely of recovering evangelicals with a zeitgeist-oriented view of Scripture, enjoys less than a tenth of the atheists' readership.[9]

Prior to the Internet, if one wanted to find counterarguments to the Christian faith they had to look hard to find them. Today, those arguments are as close at hand as the laptop on your desk, the tablet in your living room, and the phone in your pocket. The case for atheism is only a click away. Josh McDowell is correct when he laments that, "the Internet has given atheists, agnostics, skeptics, the people who like to destroy everything that you and I believe, the almost equal access to your kids as your youth pastor and you have . . . whether you like it or not."[10]

As more and more believers are exposed through the Internet to the counter-apologetics of atheists and the case they make against the existence of God, there will inevitably be a rise in rate of deconversion from Christianity. What are Christians to do with the influence of atheism on the Internet? An initial response may be that we should discourage Christians from looking at websites that are threatening. But hiding from the challenge of atheism does not produce a robust faith. In fact, what it tends to do is set people up for future disaster. Sheltering believers from challenges is

7. Gilgoff, "Where was God," lines 16–20.

8. Gilgoff, "Where was God," lines 16–20.

9. Peach, "Will the Internet," lines 34–43.

10. Kumar, "Apologist Josh McDowell," lines 7–9.

unhealthy. On the other hand, feasting on atheist apologetics is equally unhealthy, in fact it's probably worse. There needs to be wise guides shepherding Christian young people as they encounter Internet atheism. Otherwise, for some, it can be the beginning of the end.

There is a common theme that runs through the stories of former believers for whom confidence in the truthfulness of Christianity rests heavily on apologetic arguments. They tend to experience a crisis of faith when they encounter online atheist apologetic counterarguments. Multiple deconverts have shared with me that they considered themselves amateur apologists prior to their deconversion. Then they came across counterarguments online. They were deeply troubled by what they read and found the atheist objections compelling. They eventually went on to lose their faith and now they are amateur apologists for atheism.

What can we do to stem that tide? Here are three practical suggestions to remind believers of as they encounter online atheist apologetics. First, although there are lots of websites offering counterarguments and attacking the case for Christianity, there is no need to panic. I remember when I first encountered a website that appeared to me to level a very damaging charge against the reliability of the New Testament. To say the least, I was very troubled. It caused me a lot of anxiety, and I wondered, "What if it's true?" I had never come across the information before, and I was unaware of any responses to it. Looking back, I realize that I overreacted. There were responses; I just needed to find them. There are many good apologetic websites online that are responding to the charges raised by atheist challengers.

Second, it is helpful to acknowledge that online atheist apologists may appear to have powerful arguments against Christianity. They do offer a different and challenging perspective on the data. They argue against Christianity by raising objections and counterarguments that many apologetically-minded believers have never encountered before. This can be mind-blowing for believers who have never experienced any doubts about their faith. However, what needs to be said is that atheist apologetics look impressive largely due to the fact that Christian apologetics has never had to play defense in the way the Internet is forcing it to do today, and it has been caught flat-footed. As mentioned above, for years Christian publishing houses have churned out apologetic books making the case for Christianity. Rarely were any of those books or the arguments contained in them challenged in a way that was accessible to the average Christian. The lack of atheist infrastructure (publishing houses, bookstores, radio stations, etc.), made it nearly impossible for the atheist counterarguments to get any exposure among the general public, let alone Christians. Therefore, Christian apologetics didn't need to respond because there was pretty much nothing to respond to. Apologetics was easy.

In a courtroom, after the prosecution presents its case, the defense has the opportunity to pick it apart. They meticulously analyze all of the prosecution's arguments looking for alternate explanations, logical fallacies, and counterevidence. Good defense attorneys will call expert witnesses to support their case, seeking to either rebut the prosecution's case or undermine it entirely. In the end, it is up to the jury to decide who presents the better case. For the better part of the last forty years, Christian apologists have played the role of the prosecutor making the case that Christianity is guilty of being true. They have presented compelling arguments on behalf of their belief that Christianity is true, and many have found them persuasive enough to convert. The problem is, that in all that time there has not been a defense attorney in the courtroom to challenge the case made by the prosecution.

Times, however, have changed. The Internet has allowed 1,000 defense attorneys to bloom! And the problem is, as every good debater knows, whoever speaks last has the advantage in the debate. Such is the case with online atheist apologetics. Every unanswered atheist objection gives the impression that the atheist challenge has carried the day. Typically, apologetics has largely made a positive case for Christianity. Atheist counter-apologetics has now responded to our best arguments online and offered what may seem to some as good counterarguments. Unless they are rebutted, it can give the impression that they have defeated the Christian claims. A number of Christian apologetics ministries are beginning to respond. Directing troubled believers to these websites can be helpful but requires that parents and church leaders have an awareness of which online apologetics ministries are sound.

Third, it needs to be pointed out that some of the atheist apologetic material online is uninformed rhetoric, not reasoned argument. The same can be said of some of the Christian apologetic material online as well. There are atheist websites that are informed and good sources of challenging objections to Christianity, but they are almost always measured in their appraisal of the evidence and rarely engage in name-calling and insults. A sure sign of an unbalanced and uninformed web page is when it contains statements like the following: "There are no good reasons to believe in Christianity," "All arguments for the existence of God have been defeated," "No rational person can look at the evidence and remain a believer." Such statements reveal more about the personality of the person(s) responsible for the web page than they do the state of the evidence. The same can be said for Christian websites that give the impression that all atheists are idiots. The fact is, the evidence is not conclusive one way or the other. It may be conclusive in the minds of some folks, but that's just a subjective evaluation, not an accurate description of an objective state of affairs. Otherwise, there would be nothing to debate, we would all agree.

A final word needs to be said. Despite the best efforts of Christian apologists, not everyone will find their arguments persuasive. Some believers will find the arguments and objections raised by online atheists to be better than the Christian responses and lose their faith. Some will not find the objections impressive at all, and their faith will remain strong. In the end, it is difficult to say why one person finds an argument persuasive and another doesn't. I suspect it has more to do with a host of factors that we are largely unaware of more than it does pure reason or intelligence. In my opinion, atheists do raise some difficult objections to the existence of God and also make challenging counterarguments intended to rebut the arguments of Christian apologists. I don't find them ultimately persuasive, but I can see how others might. Christians have responded and are responding to the Wild West of Internet atheist apologetics. Whether they do a good job is always going to be a judgment that is person-relative. Not all believers will find those responses are sufficient and, as a result, will walk away from their faith. In their mind, the atheist has made the better case, and in the name of intellectual integrity they can no longer believe in something they have come to see as false. Let us do our best to ensure that does not happen by being ready with answers and resources that make the best case possible for the good news of the gospel of Jesus Christ.

Bibliography

Alexander, T. Desmond, and David W. Baker. *Dictionary of the Old Testament*. Downers Grove, IL: InterVarsity, 2003.

Altemeyer, Bob, and Bruce Hunsberger. *Amazing Conversions: Why Some Turn to Faith & Others Abandon Religion*. Amherst, NY: Prometheus, 1997.

Andrews, Seth. *Deconverted: A Journey from Religion to Reason*. Denver: Outskirts, 2013.

Astin, Alexander, W. Helen S. Astin. "Spirituality in Higher Education." https://www.heri.ucla.edu/monographs/TheAmericanFreshman2014.pdf&p=DevEx.LB.1,5487.1.

Attaway, Chris. "Deconversion After Religious Abuse - Camels With Hammers." Faith on the Couch. http://www.patheos.com/blogs/camelswithhammers?s=deconversion after religious abuse.

Banks, Robert. *Paul's Idea of Community: The Early House Churches in Their Cultural Setting*. Peabody, MA: Hendrickson, 1994.

Barker, Dan. "I Just Lost Faith In Faith." https://ffrf.org/legacy/books/lfif/?t=lostfaith.

Bates, Daniel. "Atheists Have Higher IQs: Their Intelligence Makes Them More Likely to Dismiss Religion as Irrational and Unscientific." http://www.dailymail.co.uk/news/article-2395972/Atheists-higher-IQs-Their-intelligence-makes-likely-dismiss-religion-irrational-unscientific.html.

Baumeister, Roy F. *Meanings of Life*. New York: Guilford, 1991.

Baumeister, Roy F., et al. "Ego Depletion: Is the Active Self a Limited Resource?" *Journal of Personality and Social Psychology* 74 (1998) 1252-65. doi:10.1037/0022-3514.74.5.1252.

Berger, Peter L. *A Far Glory: The Quest for Faith in an Age of Credulity*. New York: Anchor, 1993.

———. *The Sacred Canopy: Elements of a Sociological Theory of Religion*. New York: Anchor, 1990.

Bird, Michael F. *What Christians Ought to Believe: An Introduction to Christian Doctrine Through the Apostles Creed*. Grand Rapids: Zondervan, 2016.

Bourget, David, and David J. Chalmers. "What Do Philosophers Believe?" *Philosophical Studies* 170 (2013) 465-500. doi:10.1007/s11098-013-0259-7.

Boyd, Gregory A. *Benefit of the Doubt - Breaking the Idol of Certainty*. Grand Rapids: Baker, 2013.

Brewster, Melanie E. *Atheists in America*. New York: Columbia University Press, 2016.

Brooke, Chris. "'I've Lost My Faith But I'm Happy': Jonathan Edwards Reveals That He No Longer Believes in God." *Daily Mail Online* (March 01, 2014). http://www.dailymail.co.uk/news/article-2570747/Ive-lost-faith-Im-happy-Jonathan-Edwards-reveals-no-longer-believes-God.html.

Center for Inquiry. "About Center for Inquiry." https://www.centerforinquiry.net/about.

Challies, Tim. "God Hates Hypocrisy." https://www.challies.com/articles/god-hates-hypocrisy/.

Chester, Tim, and Steve Timmis. *Total Church: A Radical Reshaping Around Gospel and Community*. Wheaton, IL: Crossway, 2008.

Clark, Fred. "The All-or-nothing Lie of Fundamentalist Christianity (part 1)." Faith on the Couch. http://www.patheos.com/blogs/slacktivist/2012/12/03/the-all-or-nothing-lie-of-fundamentalist-christianity-part-1/.

Cooper, Sheldon. My Secret Atheist Blog. October 13, 2012. Accessed May 28, 2018. http://www.mysecretatheistblog.com/search?q=sheldon cooper.

Cotter, John. "Investigation into E. Coli Outbreak Linked to Flour Closed." *Global News* (June 27, 2017). https://globalnews.ca/news/3559653/e–coli–flour–investigation–closed/.

Coulter, Dale M. "Wrestling with Charles Taylor." *First Things* (February 27, 2015). https://www.firstthings.com/blogs/firstthoughts/2014/03/on-secularity-and-social-imaginaries.

Craig, William, L. "What Is Inerrancy?" https://www.reasonablefaith.org/media/reasonable-faith-podcast/what-is-inerrancy/.

Crain, Natasha. "Parents, Please Don't Forget How Strange the Bible Is." http://christianmomthoughts.com/parents-please-dont-forget-how-strange-the-bible-is/.

Daniels, Kenneth W. *Why I Believed: Reflections of a Former Missionary*. Duncanville, TX: K. Daniels, 2009.

Davenport, David. "Elites and Courts Push America Into a Post-Christian Era." *Forbes* (July 29, 2015). https://www.forbes.com/sites/daviddavenport/2015/07/29/elites-and-courts-push-america-into-a-post-christian-era/#15e955993c50.

Delms, Mike. "What Made You Become an Atheist?" https://www.quora.com/search?q=mike delms, atheism.

Devine, Devyn. *Born Again, to Porn Again*. Toronto: Salacious, 2009.

Dobson, James. *When God Doesn't Make Sense*. Chicago: Tyndale House, 1997.

Drosera. "Reasons to Deconvert from Christianity." YouTube (December 26, 2013). https://www.youtube.com/watch?v=VpWmSHRKeY8 delms, atheism.

Dyck, Drew. *Generation Ex-Christian: Why Young Adults Are Leaving the Faith . . . and How to Bring Them Back*. Chicago: Moody, 2010.

Ediger, Edwin Aaron. *Faith in Jesus: What Does It Mean to Believe in Him?* Bloomington, IN: West Bow, 2012.

Ehrman, Bart D. *Forged: Writing in the Name of God - Why the Bible's Authors Are Not Who We Think They Are*. New York: HarperCollins, 2012.

Ehrman, Bart. "The Daily Show with Jon Stewart" (video clip). Comedy Central. http://www.cc.com/video-clips/ujoodz/the-daily-show-with-jon-stewart-bart-ehrman.

———. *God's Problem: How the Bible Fails to Answer Our Most Important Question—Why We Suffer*. New York: Harper One, 2009.

———. "Leaving the Faith." https://ehrmanblog.org/leaving-the-faith/.

———. *Misquoting Jesus: The Story Behind Who Changed the Bible and Why*. New York: Harper One, 2007.

Endō, Shūsaku. *Silence*. New York: Picador, 2017.

Enns, Peter. *The Sin of Certainty*. New York: HarperCollins, 2017.

Fee, Gordon D., and Douglas K. Stuart. *How to Read the Bible Book by Book: A Guided Tour*. Grand Rapids: Zondervan, 2014.

Fincke, Daniel. "Faith on the Couch." http://www.patheos.com/blogs/camelswithhammers?s=since my deconversion.

Folley, Malcolm. *A Time to Jump*. New York: HarperCollins, 2001.

Fowler, James W. *Stages of Faith: The Psychology of Human Development and Quest for Meaning*. London: Harper & Row, 1995.

Frady, Marshall. *Billy Graham: A Parable of American Righteousness*. New York: Simon & Schuster, 2006.

Fuller Youth Institute. "Sticky College Campuses." https://fulleryouthinstitute.org/articles/sticky-college-campuses#fn-1-a.

———. "The Sticky Faith Research." https://fulleryouthinstitute.org/stickyfaith/research.

Galen, Luke. "Profiles of the Godless: Results From a Survey of the Nonreligious." *Free Inquiry* 29. (2009) 41–45. http://www.centerforinquiry.net/uploads/attachments/Profiles_of_the_Godless_FI_AugSept_Vol_29_No_5_pps_41-45.pdf.

Gallup, Inc. "Most Americans Still Believe in God." http://news.gallup.com/poll/193271/americans–believe–god.aspx.

Geisler, Norman L., and Thomas A. Howe. *When Critics Ask: A Popular Handbook on Bible Difficulties*. Grand Rapids: Baker, 1992.

Gilgoff, Dan. "'Where Was God in Aurora?' Comments Show Internet as Church for Atheists." CNN. http://religion.blogs.cnn.com/2012/08/01/where-was-god-in-aurora-comments-show-internet-as-church-for-atheists/.

Gladwell, Malcolm. *Outliers*. Harmondsworth, UK: Penguin, 2009.

Hesse, Monica. "Camp Quest is Atheists'Answer to Bible School." *The Washington Post,* July 26, 2011. https://www.washingtonpost.com/lifestyle/style/camp-quest-is-atheists-answer-to-bible-school/2011/07/19/gIQAe1hRbI_story.html?utm_term=.9826f55e8f68.

Hewitt, Hugh. *The Embarrassed Believer: Reviving Christian Witness in Age of Unbelief*. Dallas: Word, 1998.

Holahan, Carole K., and Robert R. Sears. *The Gifted Group in Later Maturity*. Stanford: Stanford University Press, 1995.

Hood, Ralph W., et al. *The Psychology of Religious Fundamentalism*. New York: Guilford, 2005.

Hui, Harry C., et al. "Psychological Changes During Faith Exit: A Three-Year Prospective Study." *Psychology of Religion and Spirituality* 10 (2018) 103–18.

Hunter, James Davison. *To Change the World: The Irony, Tragedy, and Possibility of Christianity in the Late Modern World*. Oxford: Oxford University Press, 2010.

Jeskin, Alan. *Outgrowing God: Moving Beyond Religion*. Scotts Valley, CA: Create Space, 2010.

Keillor, G. *Lake Wobegon Days*. London: Faber and Faber, 1985.

Kimmel, Tim. *Grace-based Parenting*. Nashville: Thomas Nelson, 2006.

Kingsriter, Dayton, A. "Is the Lower Cost Worth the Higher Price?" *General Council Assemblies of God*, 2007. http://agchurches.org/Sitefiles/Default/RSS/AG%20 Colleges

Kinnaman, David, and Gabe Lyons. *Unchristian: What a New Generation Really Thinks About Christianity—and Why it Matters.* Grand Rapids: Baker, 2012.

Kline, Kathleen Kovner. *Authoritative Communities: The Scientific Case for Nurturing the Whole Child.* New York: Springer Science, 2008.

———. *Hardwired to Connect: The New Scientific Case for Authoritative Communities.* New York: Institute for American Values, 2003.

Krueger, Julie A. "The Road to Disbelief: A Study of the Atheist De-conversion Process." University of Wisconsin La Crosse Journal of Undergraduate Research XVI, 2013.

Kumar, Anugrah. "Apologist Josh McDowell: Internet the Greatest Threat to Christians." *The Christian Post* (July 16, 2011). https://www.christianpost.com/news/apologist-josh-mcdowell-internet-the-greatest-threat-to-christians-52382/.

Lewis, C. S. *A Grief Observed.* London: Faber and Faber, 1966.

———. *The Lion, the Witch and the Wardrobe (The Chronicles of Narnia).* New York: HarperCollins, 2001.

———. *Mere Christianity.* Nashville: Broadman & Holman, 2017.

LifeWay Research. "Reasons 18-to 22-Year-Olds Drop Out of Church." https://lifewayresearch.com/2007/08/07/reasons-18-to-22-year-olds-drop-out-of-church/.

Livermore, David A. *Cultural Intelligence: Improving Your CQ to Engage Our Multicultural World.* Grand Rapids: Baker Academic, 2009.

Lobdell, William. "He Had Faith in His Job." *Los Angeles Times,* July 21, 2007. http://articles.latimes.com/print/2007/jul/21/local/me-lostfaith21.

Loftus, John W. *The Christian Delusion: Why Faith Fails.* Amherst, NY: Prometheus, 2010.

MacArthur, John. *2 Timothy.* Chicago: Moody, 1995.

Marriott, Robert John. "The Cost of Freedom: A Grounded Theory Study on the Impact of Deconversion from Christianity to Atheism." PhD diss., Biola University, 2015.

Mars Hill Church. "The Resurgence Report." http://marshill.se/marshill/2014/12/02/the-resurgence-report.

McCray, William, G. "The Divorce is Final!" http://www.bing.com/cr?IG=EEDD85F950D14025AF854917E535137A&CID=15C25F0283996F0929FC54FC82646E47&rd=1&h=YPLJAj6EXks9wKhGDsv7nh7fnKoZrRCT4NzSNk_4zJA&v=1&r=http://obnoxioustv3.rssing.com/chan-7355908/all_p25.html&p=DevEx.LB.1,5455.1.

McCullough, Michael E., et al. "The Varieties of Religious Development in Adulthood: A Longitudinal Investigation of Religion and Rational Choice." *Journal of Personality and Social Psychology* 89 (2005) 78–89. doi:10.1037/0022-3514.89.1.78.

McKnight, Scot. *The Blue Parakeet: Rethinking How You Read the Bible.* Grand Rapids: Zondervan, 2016.

McLeod, David J. "The Consecrated Christian and Conformity to the World." *The Emmaus Journal* 4 (1995) 99–124.

Mehta, Hemant. "On the Internet, Christianity is Losing By a Long Shot." http://www.patheos.com/blogs/friendlyatheist/2011/08/25/on-the-internet-christianity-is-losing-by-a-long-shot/.

Merriam-Webster. https://www.merriam-webster.com/dictionary/culture shock.

MIT Technology Review. "How the Internet Is Taking Away America's Religion." https://www.technologyreview.com/s/526111/how-the-internet-is-taking-away-americas-religion/.

Mohler, Albert. "Transforming Culture: Christian Truth Confronts Post-Christian America." https://albertmohler.com/2004/07/15/transforming-culture-christian-truth-confronts-post-christian-america/.

Muehlhauser, Luke. "Live Blogging My Deconversion." http://commonsenseatheism.com/?p=11292.

Murray, Rheana. "How Eating Raw Cookie Dough Led to One Mom's Death, Son Recalls." *ABC News* (November 13, 2014). https://abcnews.go.com/US/eating-raw-cookie-dough-led-moms-death-son/story?id=26896037.

Mykytiuk, Lawrence. "53 People in the Bible Confirmed Archeologically." https://www.biblicalarchaeology.org/daily/people-cultures-in-the-bible/people-in-the-bible/50-people-in-the-bible-confirmed-archaeologically/.

Nerlich, Brigette. "Imagining Imaginaries - Making Science Public." http://blogs.nottingham.ac.uk/makingsciencepublic/2015/04/23/imagining-imaginaries/.

Orr, James. *Revelation and Inspiration*. Miami: Hard, 2013.

Packer, James I. *"Fundamentalism" and the Word of God: Some Evangelical Principles*. Leicester, UK: InterVarsity, 1958.

Parrot, Leslie. *Saving Your Marriage Before it Starts: Seven Questions to Ask Before—and After—You Marry*. Grand Rapids: Zondervan, 2015.

Peach, Brandon. "Will the Internet Kill Christianity?" *RELEVANT Magazine*, August 22, 2011, https://relevantmagazine.com/culture/tech/features/26539-will-the-internet-kill-christianity.

Pinckney, T. C. "We Are Losing Our Children." http://www.schoolandstate.org/SBC/Pinckney-WeAreLosingOurChildren.htm.

Placher, William Carl. *Unapologetic Theology a Christian Voice in a Pluralistic Conversation*. Louisville: Westminster John Knox, 1995.

Public Religion Research Institute. "America's Changing Religious Identity." https://www.prri.org/research/american-religious-landscape-christian-religiously-unaffiliated/.

Redford. "1.5 Deconversion: The Bible (A)." YouTube. October 20, 2009. Accessed May 28, 2018. https://www.youtube.com/watch?v=70SYwkoH_yc&t=292s.

Resnick, Brian. "How Many American Atheists Are There Really?" *Vox*, April 13, 2017, https://www.vox.com/science-and-health/2017/4/13/15258496/american-atheists-how-many.

Rose, Galen. "The Bible: Primitive Nonsense." http://articles.exchristian.net/2008/11/bible-primitive-nonsense.html.

Ross, Karen Heather. *Losing Faith in Fundamentalist Christianity: An Interpretative Phenomenological Analysis*. Master's thesis, University of Toronto, 2009.

Sagioglou, Christina, and Matthias Forstmann. "Activating Christian Religious Concepts Increases Intolerance of Ambiguity and Judgment Certainty." *Journal of Experimental Social Psychology* 49 (2013) 933–39. doi:10.1016/j.jesp.2013.05.003.

Saroglou, Vassilis, et al. "Values and Religiosity: A Meta-analysis of Studies Using Schwartz's Model." *Personality and Individual Differences* 37 (2004) 721–34. doi:10.1016/j.paid.2003.10.005.

Schaeffer, Francis A. *The Great Evangelical Disaster*. Westchester, IL: Crossway, 1986.

Schulz, J. W. "Hypocrisy as a Challenge to Christian Belief." *Religious Studies* 54 (2017) 247–64. doi:10.1017/s0034412517000105.

Shenhav, Amitai, et al. "Divine Intuition: Cognitive Style Influences Belief in God." *Journal of Experimental Psychology: General* 141 (2012) 423–28. doi:10.1037/a0025391.

Smith, Christian Stephen. *The Bible Made Impossible: Why Biblicism is Not a Truly Evangelical Reading of Scripture*. Grand Rapids: Brazos, 2012.

Smith, Christian, and Melinda Lundquist Denton. *Soul Searching: The Religious and Spiritual Lives of American Teenagers*. Oxford: Oxford University Press, 2011.

Smith, James K. A. *How (Not) to be Secular: Reading Charles Taylor*. Grand Rapids: Eerdmans, 2015.

Sommers, Joseph C. "Some Reasons Why Humanists Reject The Bible." https://americanhumanist.org/what-is-humanism/reasons-humanists-reject-bible/.

Spielvogel, Jackson J. *Western Civilization: A Brief History*. Boston: Wadsworth/Cengage Learning, 2011.

Stearns, Denis. "FDA: Raw Dough's a Raw Deal and Could Make You Sick." *Food Poison Journal* (July 02, 2016). http://www.foodpoisonjournal.com/food-poisoning-information/fda-raw-doughs-a-raw-deal-and-could-make-you-sick/.

Stephens, Randall J., and Karl Giberson. *The Anointed Evangelical Truth in a Secular Age*. Cambridge: Belknap Press, 2011.

Stetzer, Ed, and Kerilee Van Schooten. "Churches in America—Part 1." https://www.christianitytoday.com/edstetzer/2016/july/state-of-american-church-part-1.html.

———. "The State of the Church in America: When Numbers Point to a New Reality, Part 1." https://www.christianitytoday.com/edstetzer/2016/september/state-of-american-church-when-numbers-point-to-new-reality.html.

Streib, Heinz. *Deconversion: Qualitative and Quantitative Results from Cross-cultural Research in Germany and the United States of America*. Göttingen, DE: Vandenhoeck & Ruprecht, 2009.

Subotnik, Renara, et al. *Genius Revisited: High IQ Children Grown Up*. Norwood, NJ: Ablex, 1994.

Swatos, William H. *Encyclopedia of Religion and Society*. Walnut Creek, CA: Alta Mira, 1998.

Swindoll, Charles, R. "Keeping Your Balance." http://www.insight.org/resources/daily-devotional/individual/keeping-your-balance.

Syed, Matthew. "'I Have Never Been Happier' Says the Man Who Won Gold but Lost God." *The Times*, June 27, 2007. https://www.thetimes.co.uk/article/i-have-never-been-happier-says-the-man-who-won-gold-but-lost-god-jmslbj385c7.

Tarico, Valerie. *Trusting Doubt: A Former Evangelical Looks at Old Beliefs in a New Light (2nd Ed.)*. Independence, VA: Oracle Institute, 2017.

Taylor, Charles. *A Secular Age*. Cambridge: Belknap Press, 2007.

Taylor, Daniel. *The Skeptical Believer: Telling Stories to Your Inner Atheist*. Saint Paul, MN: Bog Walk, 2013.

Templeton, Charles Bradley. *Charles Templeton: An Anecdotal Memoir*. C1983. https://www.templetons.com/charles/memoir/

———. *Farewell to God: My Reasons for Rejecting the Christian Faith*. Toronto: McClelland & Stewart, 1999.

Terman, Lewis M. *Genetic Studies of Genius*. Stanford: Stanford University Press, 1926.

The Barna Group. "Most Twentysomethings Put Christianity on the Shelf Following Spiritually Active Teen Years." https://www.barna.com/research/most-twentysomethings-put-christianity-on-the-shelf-following-spiritually-active-teen-years/.

———. "The State of the Church 2016." https://www.barna.com/research/state-church-2016/.

The Chicago Statement on Biblical Inerrancy. Oakland: Council, 1978.

Tozer, A. W. *The Knowledge of the Holy: The Attributes of God: Their Meaning in the Christian Life*. New York: HarperOne, 1992.

UCLA Graduate School of Education and Information Systems. "The College Student Survey." http://www.gseis.ucla.edu/heri/css_po.html.

/FAQ/Is%20the%20Lower %20Cost%20Worth%20the%20High%20Price_.pdf

Vanhoozer, Kevin J. *Is There a Meaning in This Text?: The Bible, the Reader, and the Morality of Literary Knowledge*. Grand Rapids: Zondervan, 2009.

Vanhoozer, Kevin J., et al. *Everyday Theology: How to Read Cultural Texts and Interpret Trends*. Grand Rapids: Baker Academic, 2007.

Walker, John. "Family Life Council Says it's Time to Bring Family Back to Life." http://www.sbcannualmeeting.net/sbc02/newsroom/newspage.asp?ID=261.

Weise, Elizabeth. "General Mills Recalls 10 Million Pounds of Flour." *USA Today*, May 31, 2016. https://www.usatoday.com/story/news/2016/05/31/general-mills-issues-rare-flour-recall/85203618/.

Westphal, Merold. *Whose Community? Which Interpretation? Philosophical Hermeneutics for the Church*. Grand Rapids: Baker Academic, 2009.

White, James Emery. *Mind for God*. Place of publication not identified: Intervarsity Press, 2013.

Wiesel, Elie, and Marion Wiesel. *Night*. New York: Hill and Wang, 2017.

Willard, Dallas. "Spiritual Disciplines, Spiritual Formation, and the Restoration of the Soul." *Journal of Psychology and Theology* 26 (1998) 101-9.

Wilson, Rodney. *Killing God: Christian Fundamentalism and the Rise of Atheism*. Place of publication not identified: Createspace, 2015.

Wink, Paul, et al. "Religiousness, Spiritual Seeking, and Personality: Findings from a Longitudinal Study." *Journal of Personality* 75 (2007) 1051–70. doi:10.1111/j.1467-6494.2007.00466.x.

Wormald, Benjamin. "America's Changing Religious Landscape." *Pew Research Center's Religion & Public Life Project*, May 12, 2015. http://www.pewforum.org/2015/05/12/americas-changing-religious-landscape/.

Wright, Bradley R., et al. "Explaining Deconversion from Christianity." *The Journal of Religion and Society* 13 (2011) 1–17.

Wright, Bradley. "Why Do Christians Leave the Faith? Breaking Up with a God Who Failed Them." http://www.patheos.com/blogs/blackwhiteandgray/2011/11/why-do-christians-leave-the-faith-breaking-up-with-a-god-who-failed-them/.

Wuthnow, Robert. *The God Problem: Expressing Faith and Being Reasonable*. Berkeley: University of California Press, 2012.

Zuckerman, Phil. *Faith No More: Why People Reject Religion*. Oxford: Oxford University Press, 2015.